P9-DTJ-048

SHIFTING CIRCLES
OF SUPPORT

Map indicating regions and countries of case-studies

SHIFTING CIRCLES OF SUPPORT

Contextualising Gender and Kinship in South Asia and Sub-Saharan Africa

Edited by
Rajni Palriwala and Carla Risseeuw

PRESS

A Division of Sage Publications, Inc.
WALNUT CREEK • LONDON • NEW DELHI

Copyright © 1996 by AltaMira Press, A Division of Sage Publications, Inc.

A Division of Sage Publications
1630 North Main Street, Suite 367
Walnut Creek, CA 94596

SAGE Publications Ltd.
6 Bonhill Street
London EC2A 4PU
United Kingdom

SAGE Publications India Pvt. Ltd.
M-32 Market
Greater Kailash I
New Delhi 110 048 India

Printed in New Delhi, India

Library of Congress Cataloging-in-Publication data

Shifting circles of support: contextualising gender and kinship in South Asia and
    Sub-Saharan Africa / edited by Rajni Palriwala and Carla Risseeuw.
        p.   cm.
    Includes bibliographical references and index.
    ISBN   0–8039–9275–0
    1. Kinship—Africa, Sub-Sahara—Case studies.   2. Kinship—South Asia—
Case studies.   3. Sex role—Africa, Sub-Sahara—Case studies.   4. Sex role—
South Asia—Case studies.   5. Women—Africa, Sub-Sahara—Social conditions—
Case studies.   6. Women—South Asia—Social conditions—Case studies.
I. Palriwala, Rajni, 1955–   II. Risseeuw, Carla.
    GN651.S55   1996   306.83′0954—dc20   95–30053

95 96 97 98 99 10 9 8 7 6 5 4 3 2 1

Interior Design and Production by Pagewell Photosetters, Pondicherry
Cover Design by Bharati Mirchandani

For Rosie

For Rosie

Contents

Foreword

It was a delightful privilege for the University of Nairobi and, in particular, for the Department of Sociology, College of Social Sciences and Humanities, to have been requested to host the conference on 'Changing Gender and Kinship in Sub-Saharan Africa and South Asia'. The Nairobi Conference co-organisers are deeply indebted to the University of Leiden, in particular VENA (Women and Autonomy Centre), and to the Government of the Netherlands (Ministry of Development Cooperation), for not only funding the conference, but helping towards the publication of this volume.

This book is the outcome of hard and dedicated work on the part of the organisers, editors and authors. It is not only an intellectual challenge to the developing world, but a living testimony that the theme 'gender and kinship in a changing context' is an important and crucial issue in relation to the development of both families and societies. The book is, more importantly, a dynamic expression of the new, emergent South-South and South-North relationship, where scholars from South Asia, Sub-Saharan Africa and Europe sat together, as equal partners, and shared academic and real life experiences in the areas of social change and state formation, and their impact on family, kinship, and gender.

Marriage, family and kinship as concepts and institutions have experienced tremendous changes in the geographical areas covered

10

Shifting Circles of Support

by the conference. I am extremely delighted that the articles by Francien van Driel, Carla Risseeuw, Dzodzi Tsikata and K. Saradamoni have, each in their own way, delved into this topic in the first part of the book. They are a convincing affirmation of the concern of the conference with changing family and kin relationships. The background of social change, political processes, state formation—particularly in relation to traditional, customary and modern law—and economic developments, which are expressed in the division of labour, formal education, marriage, structural adjustments programmes (SAPS) and changing aspirations and perceptions, were central to not only the conference, but also to this book. Papers by Leela Dube, Rajni Palriwala and Parveen Walji Moloo persuasively show the fundamental role played by institutions of kinship, marriage and the family, and how social, economic and political developments have had an impact, both partial and whole, on these institutions. The third part of the volume, with contributions by lawyers K. Kibwana, Athaliah Molokomme and Savitri Goonesekere, elaborates on the complexity of issues outlined in the historical and anthropological studies in the first two sections of the volume, highlighting the urgency of reform in the area of our concern.

The Department of Sociology, and I in particular, are extremely pleased that this book is a reality. It is a contribution to the analysis of macrosocial change as human experience. Voices from the North, East and South are blending to make a claim for 'change'—change in family rights, change in laws related to child maintenance, change in laws and public policy pertaining to family relations. It is the hope of the South (Asia and Africa) that the readers will be fulfilled, nay, be open to the winds of change, as they read the contributions to this volume.

Judith Mbula Bahemuka
Professor
Department of Sociology
University of Nairobi

Acknowledgements

The articles in this book include 10 of the 25 papers originally presented at the conference on 'State and Market Influences on Gender, Family and Kinship Relations in Sub-Saharan Africa and South Asia', held in Nairobi in early 1993. Historians, lawyers, anthropologists and sociologists came together to discuss the conference theme. The focus was on change and continuity in the intimate life arrangements centred on kinship, family and gender relations and the degrees of support and security they offer, in view of the influence of macroeconomic and political processes.

The conference was an outcome of cooperation at various levels. It was held at the University of Nairobi, where the Department of Sociology kindly hosted the 31 participants from South Asia, Sub-Saharan Africa, and the Netherlands. The flexible and well-organised manner in which this was done allowed in-depth discussions and even extra sessions at the participants' request, making it possible to learn from each others' experiences. It is a pleasure to thank the Nairobi organisers—Maurice Yambo, Judith Mbula Bahemuka, Parveen Walji Moloo, Enos Njeru, Ken Ouko, Frida Maua Mutinda and Bonafas Wambua—for the successful arrangements and the ease with which they created a relaxed atmosphere, conducive to further dialogue and cooperation at the conference itself as well as afterwards.

We sincerely thank Leela Dube in New Delhi, at that time Chairperson of the Commission on Women, International Union of Anthropological and Ethnological Sciences, for her initial backing to the idea of the conference. Further, not only did she give a valuable key-note address at the conference, but we continued to receive her assistance also in bringing this publication to fruition.

At Leiden University, we thank Peter Geschiere and Jose van Santen for their support in the preparations towards the conference. At the Department of Anthropology, the Centre for Women and Autonomy undertook the preliminary organisation. Our thanks go particularly to Joke van Benten and Nellie Verschuur for the efficiency with which they facilitated the smooth running of the conference and for their input in realising the first report in mid–1993, *Gender between Family and State*, written by Kamala Ganesh, Department of Sociology, University of Bombay, and Carla Risseeuw.

The conference and much of the preparation of this volume was made possible by a grant from the Ministry of Development Co-operation, the Netherlands. We express our deep appreciation of their support.

As editors we wish to extend our sincere thanks to the writers of the articles included in this book. Our acknowledgement is not only for the quality of their contributions, but also the enthusiasm and perseverance with which they dealt with comments on earlier drafts—and at such long distance. They gave priority to their contributions in relation to their already manifold commitments at work and at home. The input to each article has been substantial and extremely valuable. We also thank all the other participants at the conference, whose input at Nairobi and after, has in various ways fed into this volume. We would further like to acknowledge the students who participated in our course (Gender and Kinship) in Spring 1994, at the Department of Social and Cultural Studies, Leiden University. Their discussions and questions formed a valuable reference point for us.

In preparing the book for publication, we gratefully thank Rosie Risseeuw for her swift and perceptive text corrections, and Hannie van der Plas in the Netherlands and Nandan in New Delhi for the typing involved. To Herman de Tollenaere our appreciation for coming to our aid in preparing the map. Our gratitude to the Foreign Bureau, University of Leiden, for its extended administrative support. Our thanks to the University of Delhi for giving Rajni Palriwala study leave, enabling us to work together on the book. And finally we must thank each other for seeing this volume through all the ups and downs of writing, illness and displacement, and for the continuous support and intellectual stimulation which made it possible and pleasurable.

This volume has emphasised issues in the field of history and colonialism in relation to current processes in the area of daily living arrangement as well as the law. A second volume is planned, focusing on the same themes in relation to urban society, education, structural adjustment and displacement due to (civil) war.

Rajni Palriwala
Carla Risseeuw

1 Introduction: Shifting Circles of Support

Carla Risseeuw and Rajni Palriwala

The contributions to this volume, and the conference from which it emerged, address three apparently separate themes, which in the framework of this book are seen as inextricably intertwined. First is the dialectical relationship between macroeconomic and political processes and structures on the one hand and the relationships of gender, family and kinship on the other. Second is the mutual implication of kinship and gender relations themselves. These relationships have by and large been ignored by mainstream economics, political studies and kinship studies. Third is a historical perspective on these issues. The individual cases discussed in the chapters broadly argue that not only do the first two themes entail each other, they also necessitate a specific orientation on kinship and gender relations. These must be viewed as dynamic and shifting structures, rather than as unchanging principles moving at the most from one fixed set of rules to another.

The dynamics of kinship do not form a closed system, nor can kinship and gender relations be viewed as one integrated, self-contained whole. Placed in their wider context, subtle shifts emerge in apparent cultural continuities. The separation of the studies of gender relations, kinship, economics and politics was linked to a static view of culture, community and the meaning of family. This was also related to the division between the personal and the social, and to implicit universalising and/or naturalistic assumptions. The various contributions to this volume focus on different dimensions of changing kinship and gender relations, how people view them, make them, live in them, choose or do not choose for them, and in the process are made by and deal with their wider economic and political environment. Notions of personhood, community and relationship, responsibilities and rights are implicated, negotiated and transformed.

The case-studies cover countries in Sub-Saharan Africa and South Asia, which in their commonalities and differences highlight the foregoing themes. The comparisons within and across regions ensure the surfacing of insights which could otherwise be overlooked. Social change is a continuous and often subtle process, not solely a result of wider economic and political dynamics, but particular periods of history and specific events have been marked by acute social change. This was true of the colonial experience of countries in Sub-Saharan Africa and South Asia.

Various macroeconomic and political processes enter the discussions. They include dimensions of colonialism and colonial rule, the more or less successful establishment of an overarching and/or centralised state, legislation—both state-initiated and those following demands made by sections of people—the penetration of a money-based and capitalist economy, new economic opportunities and mobility, the emergence of a world economy and large-scale migratory patterns and, most recently, the shift from state-directed development to market-oriented economic policies. These macroeconomic and political changes have influenced the position of women in various ways. However, they have never affected women in isolation. Women operated from within networks of marriage, family and kinship, and it was (the position of women within) these relationships that were subject to reinforcement or change.

This volume argues for a framework incorporating the dynamic interrelationships between domains, the historical processes of change and the negotiated quality of relationships. In the process it points to the duality of kinship and family networks as systems of support and systems of sanction, and the increasing imbalance between support and power, between controlled care-givers and resource controllers. The homeless, the kinless, the resourceless and the unsupported are an increasing reality worldwide. Yet systems of care and responsibility have been largely undervalued and ignored, whether in the designing of development programmes for the 'Third World', the establishing of working conditions in the 'First', or in the analysis of women's and men's relationships to kinship and the economy. The necessity for historical and comparative research on changing systems of care, responsibility and social security/support, whether kinship-based or state-based, emerges as a central conclusion of this volume.

The Academic Separation of Domains of Enquiry

Streams of feminist and Marxist studies over the last two decades have been arguing for aspects of the framework as advocated here, integrating the above mentioned themes of study. This is evident from recent reviews and discussions of anthropology and sociology (cf. Moore 1988; Yanagisako and Collier 1987). Not only did kinship/family studies fall to the lot of these disciplines, but for a substantial period kinship studies were the hallmark of anthropology. In evaluating kinship studies, the early push of women's studies to develop interdisciplinary research was taken further to question analytically distinct domains within anthropology (Yanagisako and Collier 1987).

The very division of society into distinct domains, and a perspective which saw kinship dynamics as lying internal to itself, reinforced a static view of kinship and family in much of anthropological scholarship. Gender relations were sidetracked. The structuralist elimination of agency and the subject was undoubtedly another factor. Even when anthropologists explicitly eschewed the study of kinship as a static 'thing-in-itself', highlighting for example the relationship between kinship, marriage and property relations, and even aspects of women's social position, women were not the doers, the actors or the players in any of their studies (Leach 1961; Obeyesekere 1967; Tambiah 1958). In a general environment of gender-blind scholarship, kinship studies was the one area in which there was some information, some discussion of women and gender. However, women entered into these descriptions and analyses only in the 'domestic' arena of kinship. Women's extra-household relationships, kinship and otherwise, were ignored (Flax 1982; Moore 1988). In the process there was an equation of the family, the domestic, procreation, sexuality and women, naturalising both kinship and gender relations, mainly emphasising women as 'reproducers' (Collier et al. 1982; Harris 1980; Palriwala 1990; Stolcke 1981; Yanagisako and Collier 1987). This may be related to the dominant theoretical frameworks in these disciplines and their underlying 'folk models' (Yanagisako and Collier 1987).

Two common threads running through functionalist, structural-functionalist, and structuralist anthropology are pertinent here. One was the idea that kinship was an objectively defined system (Dumont 1961), complete in itself. This was reflected in views on the place of kinship in various societies. On the one hand a division of the subject matter of study and 'modern society' into analytically and empirically distinct domains was largely unquestioned. On the other hand, it was accepted that in stateless and 'pre-modern' societies kinship relations were the organising principles of social, economic, political and religious life. The apparent contradiction between these views was resolved through a second thread—the implicit, underlying notion that 'change' occurred only in 'complex', industrialised societies. History and change in 'timeless' pre-industrial societies began with 'modernisation' brought by the 'West'. In either view, kinship was a 'thing-in-itself', the essential structure of which could be laid bare without referral to the historical, political or economic context.

Critiques of early evolutionary and diffusionist anthropology had led to an explicit closure of questions on change and the historical in anthropology, and particularly in studies of family and kinship. However, uncritical evolutionary assumptions remained, particularly in sociology and 'modernisation' studies. Societies were taken as moving from multiplex to unifunctional social relationships, establishing distinct domains of economics, politics and the family. The impact of industrialisation, urbanisation and 'modernisation' was to move all societies towards the pattern now presumed to be dominant in the 'West'; a pattern which was taken to represent an essential, irreducible, and functionally necessary and sufficient structure of the family—the conjugal, nuclear family of a housewife-mother and breadwinner-father and their young, unmarried children (Caldwell 1982; Parsons and Bales 1957). The continuum between intra-household, extra-household and wider community relations was ignored (see following section). This reproduced in its sharpest form the ideological division between the private/domestic/female and the public/political/male spheres of society.

Simultaneously, the premise that kinship provided the organising principles in some societies was at times analysed within a theoretical framework in which change and history were not reduced to 'modernisation', as in some of the works of French Marxist anthropologists (cf. Godelier 1977).[1] By and large stimulating and innovative studies of the family in economic and social history (Ariès 1962; Flandrin 1976; Goody et al. 1976; Stone 1977) influenced only a few individual anthropologists (cf. Goody 1983) or penetrated the discipline in an extremely simplified form as arguments for and against the link between 'modernisation' and the emergence of the nuclear family. Rejection of the ethnocentric assumptions underlying modernisation theories did not lead to concrete historical studies of the emergence and interaction of analytically separated domains, of the impact of context-specific economic and political processes and trends on kinship networks, extended families and gender relations. Rather, they again led to a closure of historical questions in the discipline.

Another theme running through functional and structural-functional studies of kinship and family was the idea that altruism was the characteristic value of the domestic sphere and reciprocity that of wider kinship relations, as against self-interest which was the driving force of economics. The family, in particular the nuclear family, was the sphere of harmony, pooling and sharing. Various academic disciplines underplayed the conflict and power dynamics in family life. In much of the psychology and (popular) socialisation literature published after the 1950s, the potential of conflict between parents and children was underestimated and certain questions were never posed (Elshtain 1982). As the critique of the ideological premises of functionalism gained new strength in the 1960s, the notion of the harmonious family was confronted (Lasch 1979; Zaretsky 1976; 1982). Feminists, through their own life experiences and scholarship, brought out the recurring inegalitarianism and oppression in this 'sharing and pooling', especially in maintaining a sphere of apparent harmony despite persistent and potential conflicts (Barrett and McIntosh 1982; Rapp et al. 1979; Thorne and Yalom 1982; Young et al. 1981).

In contrast to anthropologists, economists and political scientists, with their orientation to wider political and economic processes, ignored the phenomenon of the family altogether. This stemmed from the earlier mentioned notion of a deep division between the private and the public. This was true of most studies of macro-economic and political changes, including those of colonialism, the development of capitalism, agrarian structures, social mobility and differentiation, large-scale migratory processes, revolutionary movements and the emergence of nation-states. Even where the idiom of kinship was identified as a feature of social relationships, the dynamics of kinship and of gender relationships were not seen as part of the problematique. This was also true of Marxist political economy, despite the explicit linkage made between economic and political formations, family and kinship, and women's position in classical Marxism (Engels 1986). For political scientists family became an issue only when it became a problem, in the sense that it no longer provided for systems of maintenance, consensus and stability (Elshtain 1982a).

It is in this background that there was an early elaboration in feminist anthropology of the private/public dichotomy as an explanatory framework for gender inequalities and power differentials (Rosaldo 1974). Subsequently, the explanatory value and philosophical roots of this dichotomy were questioned—on grounds of its ahistorical and universalising nature; its reassertion of the dominant valuations of the public; and its analytical isolation of the 'private' (Harris 1981; Pateman 1989; Rapp 1982).

Though the radical feminist critique played an important role in 'revaluing' the private, it took the demarcation between private and public as enabling a critique of the family independent of extra-family processes (Fox-Genovese 1982). It tended to obscure the historically and culturally specific creation of marriage and family, and disconnected women from class, race, ethnicity and religious belief. Women were abstract individuals, except for their sex. In a different way, much of the autonomy literature, in focusing on individual empowerment, also reinforced the tendency not to view women as operating within and being formed by economic, political and kinship relationships. At the same time some feminist scholars were asserting that 'family' reflected and shaped the material forces which embedded people in gender and class relations (Rapp et al. 1979). However, even with the shift of problematique from women's position to gender relations, the critique of family seemed to equate these relations with conjugal and/or heterosexual relations (del Valle 1993). Kinship and the range of relationships such as siblingship and friendship expressed as fictive kin, which in various cultures, contexts and times were seen as family, were written out.

Feminist insights had deconstructed the picture of the sharing, harmonious family, and joined anthropologists in emphasising the gap between people's family ideologies and on-the-ground living together and householding arrangements (Harris 1981; Rapp et al. 1979). However, in declaring the family-household as not just a domain of oppression, but as *the* domain of oppression, much feminist scholarship and politics not only drew attention away from the interlocking of class, race and gender oppressions, but did not address the issue of kinship and family as a shifting network of support and care (Finch 1989; Flax 1982; Humphries 1982). This was reflected in the 1980s in reactions of Third World women and women of colour in Europe and North America to the feminist movements there (Amadiume 1987; Davis 1981; *Feminist Review* 1984; Joseph and Lewis 1981). In consequence, when these approaches were applied in South Asia and Sub-Saharan Africa, the manner in which responsibilities and reciprocities, controls and support were shifting and being transformed under the impact of so-called 'developmental' forces—intensifying vulnerabilities and resuscitating oppressions—were seen one-dimensionally and/or as continuities. Women tended to remain abstract, homogeneous and passive, embedded in structures against their best self-interests.

As the foregoing discussion indicates, past scholarship, particularly trends in feminist and Marxist studies, has offered a wealth of theoretical and empirical insights upon which further analyses can be built. However, a perspective on change within kinship, family and gender relations tended to be eclipsed or viewed in isolation. In bringing together these various insights, along with a critique of them, this book hopes to make a contribution to a holistic and dynamic view.

The Absence of History: Ideological and Policy Constructs of the Family

A consequence of the tendency to look at kinship and gender relations ahistorically, and in isolation from wider economic and political change, was to make room for common sense and ideological constructions of the family in much of developmental and state policy (cf. Kabeer 1994). Two contradictory, but often coexistent, constructs of the family unaffected by wider processes can be pointed out. On the one hand there is the assumption of the nuclear family, such that the wider kinship and community relations and responsibilities of players in the developmental process are assumed to be of no significance. On the other hand there is the premise of unchanging and well-functioning family and kinship networks, which facilitate the writing out of state welfare measures from policy agendas. The consequences of these policy assumptions for the manner in which women and men are constrained in their relations and responsibilities are discussed in this volume.

Interpretations of the family in state policy can become norms with which to discredit and ignore not only variations in living arrangements and differences in power and responsibility within the family, but also changes taking place in the domain of marriage, family and kinship. A powerful state can, through economic and legal measures, superimpose its norms, to the detriment of those in non-recognised living arrangements (cf. Donzelot 1979). The absence of legal support acts against weaker family members (Finch 1989). Various examples may be given. Goonesekere elaborates on the effects in Sri Lanka of the combination of the withdrawal of welfare measures and the non-recognition of children born outside marriage (non-marital children), both resting on the dominant notion of a legal family with a male breadwinner. Molokomme describes how, in Botswana, procedural rules do not account for women's embeddedness in kinship, thus disabling women from taking advantage of legal measures apparently introduced in their favour. A number of the chapters discuss the absence of women's legal rights in marital property as a result of the social and official non-recognition of the contribution of women's non-monetised labour to family survival.

In Kenya, wider kinship arrangements that are morally condoned within their own cultural spheres tend not to be reflected in legislation. Persons who are not part of the 'nuclear' core thus find it difficult to ensure their rights within the family (Kibwana). As upward and downward mobility and the range of economic opportunities expand, a growing series of conflicts within the wider kinship sphere can be expected, even as family support is assumed (Palriwala). Economically successful members of a kinship network can base their withdrawal from kinship obligations on state policy measures and a legal system which is blind to such withdrawal, wherein the position of the individual is central rather than the relationships in which his/her position is embedded (Risseeuw, Tsikata). Several chapters emphasise that men's withdrawal from networks of responsibility is occurring on an expanding scale. This is reflected in the growth of women-headed households in Botswana (van Driel), which now account for nearly 50 per cent of all existing households. One can speak of the emergence of a new form of family arrangement, for which infrastructural and legal provisions are still absent or inadequate (Molokomme).

It is interesting to note in this context that the critique of ethnocentrism with regard to the dominant notion of the nuclear family does not go far enough. This notion is inappropriate to describe the historical development of 'family' even in Euro-American societies, or their currently existing variations. This is illustrated by the work of a range of family historians, and anthropologists and sociologists who worked with a historical perspective over the last three decades (cf. Ariès 1962; Coontz 1992; Donzelot 1979; Goody 1983; Medick and Sabean 1984; Stone 1977). Many of these studies, in describing changing marriage and family patterns, have related them to transformed material conditions. The relative lack of recognition of their findings beyond their own scholarly circles is comparable to the experience of many feminist writers who attempted to unmask the so-called 'naturalness' of the relations between the sexes.

While the extended family, as it is known in parts of Africa and Asia, may never have existed in much of Europe, neither was the nuclear family as it is conceived today. Ariès (1962) and Coontz (1992) trace the relatively recent and 'modern project of the nuclear family' in France and in the United States respectively. Both relate the dominance of nuclear family thinking to a devaluation of the claims of extended kinship networks, homosociability and friendship. In his study covering the last eight centuries of history in France, Ariès argues that 'The family was a moral and social, rather than a sentimental reality' (1962: 368). For a long time the bonds with the larger community simply did not allow a withdrawal into the family. Slowly a new code of manners evolved which elaborated childhood and emphasised the respect for a 'private life' of families consisting of parents and children. Both he and Coontz show how modifications in family life cannot be analysed within themselves, but have to be understood through the changing relationship between family and community.

Coontz, in her study (1992) covering the last two centuries in the United States, describes a comparable process of the invention of a 'traditional' family in which the all-encompassing ideal of marital, lifelong, romantic companionship is connected to the creation of the 'family-home'. She points to the undeniable gains of democratisation of family relations, with the more recent expansion of women's options outside the family and men's responsibilities within it. Warning against a nostalgia for 'the way we were', Coontz argues that families have always been in flux if not crisis. At the same time new and disturbing developments in terms of violence, alienation, and the situation of children are very much in evidence. It is in this context of severe problems coupled with definite gains, that Coontz argues for the need to insert knowledge instead of ideology on how families have and have not worked in the past.

Both writers show that the historically changing character of the family and of the relationships an individual maintained within the community at large have been obscured due to the all-powerful ideal of the nuclear family form which gained persistent ideological dominance as natural and timeless. In this context, what must also be noted are the particular (re-)presentations of the emergence of capitalism in Europe and North America (and of developmental processes in the South). These are implicated as neutral, if not positive, processes of industrialisation, urbanisation, productivity growth and modernisation. They changed the pace of life and introduced a progressive competitiveness. Further, though the processes of differentiation and the struggle for resources, the simultaneous growth of poverty and wealth, dispossession, and unequal opportunities on the ground may not have been erased everywhere, nor were they the fruits of capitalism or 'development'. Rather, they were the outcomes of differential individual initiative and ability. In this context, the family came to be described as a haven from the travails and aggression of the world beyond, rather than being in dynamic relation to the wider structural inequalities.

The sway of such constructs can be seen in two popular views held in the South on family and marital relations in the North. On the one hand 'modernisation' and the nuclear family are assumed to lead to a democratisation of public life as well as family and gender relations, which obscures continuing inequalities. On the other hand the prominence of individualism, marital breakdown and single-parenthood are related to a 'Western' materialistic outlook on life and implicitly taken as unchanging, cultural phenomena of Euro-American societies rather than situations grown out of historical, economic and political processes. The latter stereotypical view is often coupled with the tendency to idealise family-systems 'at home', to assert that they are still intact and uncontaminated or to deny the possibilities or need for change.

These contradictory stereotypes are reflected in policy in the South. Thus the premise of most family planning programmes is that women can act independently in this sphere. However, as Walji's study of Nairobi Asians indicated, it was as members of families whose reproductive strategies changed with their changed life conditions, including a recognition that adult children and aged parents may not live together, that women chose for fewer children. Opposite examples are the denial of the need for old age pensions on the grounds of the continuing extended family and traditional morality. Women, it is assumed, are supported by the men of the family and do not need equal employment or pay. Yet in Botswana and Sri Lanka the family of support increasingly consisted of economically marginalised women, while in Rajasthan (India), the extended family was narrowing its circle of support. The complexities of the current changing familial and kinship relations, the variations between communities and classes and the historical transformations are all denied in these stereotypes.

Summarising, within scholarship and within developmental thinking there exists a form of 'common sense' in relation to supposed 'family relations', which has proved extremely difficult to dislodge. This is the assumption of the male-breadwinner within an unchanging family and its isolated existence ('the last refuge') from community as well as macroeconomic and political processes of change. Domains are not only analytically distinguished, but conceived as empirically separate. Thus, questions are erased before they can be posed. In the process, the view that development processes and the state should not 'interfere' with familial relations are given sustenance. This idea is likewise kept alive by local (middle class) re-inventions of family life and the idea that it can be guarded from the assumed processes of disintegration of family life in the West.

Changing Kinship Relations and Re-inventing Tradition

Feminists have pointed out, that

> It is through their commitment to the concept of family . . .
> [people] enter into relations of production, reproduction, and
> consumption with one another—they marry, beget children,
> work to support dependents, transmit and inherit cultural and
> material resources . . . . the concept of family . . . glosses over
> the variety of experiences that social categories of persons have
> within households (Rapp et al. 1979: 177).

Family and marriage arrangements are taken as the concrete ways
in which persons can be located in time and space, with other
persons—living, dead and not yet born—and with the cosmos.
Kinship norms and values often cast these arrangements as not
only 'our way', as what has been done for generations, but also as
common sense and 'natural'. These 'ways of being' are related to a
morality and tied to ideas of community membership, religious
beliefs or spiritual values. This family ideology is part of householding and kinship relations.

The embeddedness of family, kinship, and marriage arrangements in cultural norms and values often makes the translation of
the language of kinship of one culture into the cultural terms of
another problematic. The naming of one type of (kinship) relation
can easily be misunderstood if translated without its context and
without the wide web of (shifting) networks from within which it
obtains its meaning. This is seen in anthropological and colonial
discussions on whether specific forms of unions in colonised cultures
could be called marriage or were merely cohabitation. Complexity
due to cultural diversity, in many cases present within one nation-
state, is another reason why in the domain of (state) policy fictional,
common sense notions of a given, unchanging family can creep in.
This makes the need to contextualise relations of gender, family
and kinship all the more crucial. There is a need to distinguish
between the norms/ideals of family and family relationships and
the practices through which people are giving shape to these ideals
in their living together arrangements, within various sub-cultures
of class, upward and downward mobility, ethnicity and religion.

It should be noted here that there is no neat correlation between
a religious and a kinship system. Dube's contribution on the

Muslims of Lakshadweep (India) elaborates on the contrast between kinship and gender relations in that society with stereotypes of Muslim communities in the subcontinent. She emphasises that it was the combination of Islam and matriliny, and the upholding of both sets of values as one whole, which gave the system its flexibility and security to both women and men. Historically and currently in Sub-Saharan Africa and South Asia, changes have often followed or been justified by religious conversion, by orthodoxy, 'true' religion or tradition, or reinterpretation of 'accepted' values. Saradamoni indicates how demands for change in matrilineal gender and family relations in Kerala were justified by protagonists in terms of Brahmanical Hinduism as the 'true' basis for morality. Similarly, the permissibility of change may be denied on grounds of religious belief and traditional values. In South Asia fundamentalist movements from within both Hinduism and Islam are reasserting patrilineal values as central to 'culture' and identity. In Sub-Saharan Africa, the Christian influence on marriage legislation is visible, while evangelical sects in West Africa are asserting their views of family and gender relations, often in contradiction to existing and customary practice.

The problematic character of 'tradition', of the nostalgia for the 'way we were', is highlighted when noting the tremendous and changing variation in living arrangements and gender relations over the last century or longer, demonstrated by the discussions in this volume, particularly in the first section. In Botswana, consequent on colonialism, Christianisation, economic changes and the pressure to migrate, 'families' have lost their productive roles and kinship networks no longer act as arenas of social sanction and support. Unmarried motherhood has become widespread, as children retain a value, even if marriage cannot be ensured. A new matrilinear household of three generations of unmarried mothers and daughters has emerged (van Driel). In Sri Lanka, over the last two centuries, the patrilineal bias in its bilateral system has been strengthened. Monogamous, lifelong unions, the social and economic dependency of women, and a category of 'bastards' emerged, along with limited and/or diminishing employment and wage opportunities for women (Risseeuw). In Ghana (Tsikata) and in Kerala, India (Saradamoni), the conjugal family gained in importance, as economic and political innovations made the internal differentiation of lineages and the possibilities of individual (especially male) incomes real. In both Kerala (India) and Sri Lanka women lost the security of their natal 'families', without retaining (Sri Lanka) or gaining (Kerala, Ghana) rights as widows.

The embeddedness of family in 'unchanging cultural' norms and values can gloss over varied, changing experiences and possibilities. Family ideology then becomes a powerful base for the re-invention and reclaiming of traditions which never were or never had the dominance now claimed, both in academics and popular perceptions (Chanock 1982; cf. articles in Sangari and Vaid 1989). This was discussed earlier in relation to Europe and North America. In Sri Lanka, whereas in the past marriage tended to be viewed as a contract, the sacramental element has gained influence under the impact of colonial, Christian, Victorian and Hindu values. Goonesekere describes how in middle-class Sri Lanka 'divorce' is currently experienced as an alien phenomenon to be rejected as one of the dangerous developments of modernisation. This is ironical, for divorce procedures in precolonial Sri Lanka were relatively simple, marriage being linked to property systems which guarded the interests of the individual (including the woman) to a higher extent than the so-called 'civilized' arrangements of today (see also Risseeuw). Studies undertaken in the mid-20th century assumed that the male manager of the matrilineal extended family in Kerala, traditionally held the immense authority he was seen to exercise at the end of the nineteenth century (Saradamoni). Dowry is taken as being a traditional custom among castes and communities in South Asia who had not practised this form of marriage prestation earlier. These groups had taken to this practice in changed economic and political conditions as part of their claims to higher status, formulated within the social and ritual frameworks of an earlier elite.

In Kenya the moral superiority of a monogamous marriage is growing under the influence of Christian norms, although parliamentary action to prohibit polygamy has been rejected several times. Simultaneously, in the name of culture, claims are made to keep a polygamous tradition intact, even as contemporary trends of commercial land-ownership do not guarantee the husband, let alone his wives, a steady and permanent access to this major resource. As such, the marital and kinship relations within polygamy are transformed. Women find themselves in situations of growing insecurity, where a position as co-wife entails not only an extremely uncertain position on widowhood, but also jeopardises the rights of inheritance of her (male) children. Men's claims to their polygamous traditions entail a greatly reduced responsibility towards their wives and offspring in comparison to former generations.

With the constant re-invention of tradition and the equation between cultural identity and particular kinship and gender relations, there is an oft-expressed view that the state and state-directed developmental processes should not intervene in familial relations.[2] This would be an unwanted meddling with local 'cultural' norms and the cultural rights of people. This has become a highly charged area in South Asia, particularly in the context of cultural plurality and the decontextualising character of law (discussed later in this chapter), insecure minorities, and religious and ethnic movements where self-appointed representatives of a community or a 'nation' seek to impose their own systems. Thus cultural rights and tradition are advanced as grounds to deny reforms in particular laws and the gender-biased notions contained therein. This argument arises even where plurality is not the issue. In Ghana (Tsikata), inheritance practices which exclude both spouse and children are being reasserted as custom and simultaneously recast to exclude wives and widows, but not children. A question raised by women's movements and proponents of legal reform in the countries under discussion (Agnihotri and Palriwala, forthcoming) is whose designation of cultural norms and of plurality is to be accepted? Whose interests are being served by existing practices? Too often 'cultural rights' become justifications of practices that are discriminatory towards women and the vulnerable.

Negotiating Networks of Responsibility and Support

Analyses of historical processes of change, some over periods of a hundred years or more, ensure a perspective of change, which anthropology has often lacked. However, change need not only have the character of dramatic shifts, but can take place as a series of unnoticed adjustments. People make 'choices', manoeuvre, and renegotiate their relationships and living arrangements in their day-to-day interactions, even as they argue that they are upholding age-old practice and norm. In many contexts, only the exceptional cases of conflict surface in the courts. It is in these very operations that apparently disconnected macroeconomic and political processes are met and influence the most intimate and unquestioned relations within the family and among kin. Seemingly incidental variations can amount to a subtle pattern of change or remake existing structures.

The nature of these processes and trends emerges through detailed analytical description of people's daily lives, which one expects would be the strength of anthropologists. However, the dominance of functionalist and structuralist frameworks and the absence of the idea of agency, such that people were seen to simply enact rules (cf. Bourdieu 1977), especially in the sphere of kinship, helped to 'fix' tradition. Change and the fact that it is people who 'make their own history [but] . . . in circumstances given and transmitted from the past' (Marx 1969: 398) was obscured.

While all the chapters touch on these processes to a greater or lesser extent, the chapters in the second part on 'Negotiating (in)security', focus on them most directly. Among some groups of Nairobi Asians (Walji), individual and community roles of women received a new emphasis, replacing activities in the domestic sphere and extended kinship network, while among others this shift had not taken place. This variation and shift may be related to changes in support networks, the value of children, and practices of rearing and socialisation, and to strategies which built on geographically dispersed families. Decisions were taken to have fewer children in order to be able to educate them into 'quality-children', and thereby promote their social and economic flexibility so as to cope with the imminent possibility of migration. Walji shows that the shifts were the greatest in the Ismaeli community, which was better equipped to handle (inter)national mobility and the narrowing of kin-based security. Women had taken to regularly visiting the mosque in a manner not common to Muslim communities in South Asia, and participated in the growing importance of the community in the lives of their families.

Among the matrilineal dwellers of the Laccadive Islands (India), women's natal homes were a source of security unparalleled in most parts of patrilineal South Asia. Their marital situations never left them helpless destitutes on divorce or at widowhood. Recent attempts to change the property system failed to garner the support of many men. Dube relates this to the flexibility of the prevailing system and the security it provided men along with minimum responsibility. Multiple sources of authority in the society balanced the powers of men and women, such that the former could not appropriate the labour, resources or children of the latter. Over their life-cycle men had to negotiate their relationships with their wives and children, as for example through donating gifts and property, in order to ensure care in old age.

In Rajasthan, increasing economic uncertainties and dependence on individual, non-agricultural employment, intensification of the struggle for land and pressures to migrate have led to elusive changes in human relations and the operation of patriliny (Palriwala). The last was being manipulated to exclude the extended kin group and women from property while maintaining the extended group as a source of social support and sanction. Overlapping networks of kinship, caste and clientage appeared to be reinforced, even as the creation of a base for individual rights, particularly for men, was evident. Paradoxically, women's rights as residual heirs had been strengthened, but along with dowry becoming more pervasive, they had been devalued as workers and as maintainers of social networks, and were increasingly dependent on individual male kin and/or their husbands.

The gendered shifts within the household outlined here can be easily missed, especially where idealisations of the family assume that the value of altruism leads individuals to sacrifice themselves for the interests of a (presumed to be) non-differentiated group. They emerge through a focus on the dynamics and negotiatory nature of relationships, and also through, for example, the conflicts between sons and fathers, between brothers, and between inmarried women. While some trends were discerned in Palriwala's study, such as the earlier division of households, no simple models of change, of advantages and disadvantages for the various categories of women sufficed.

Family-kinship systems differ in the degrees of variation they will accommodate, the extent of support they provide, and the type of sanctions they exercise in relation to breach of cultural/ familial norms, and hence in the nature and extent of negotiation they sustain. Some systems embody greater opportunities to create 'fictive' kin and/or incorporate friendship than others, providing participants a matter-of-fact morality to re-establish relationships. The threat of total rejection from the kinship circle, a real possibility in some societies, is conceptually impossible in others. Sanctions are gendered in that the consequences for absconding from one's responsibilities are often disparate for women and men. More generally sanctions differ for more or less powerful members of the family or kinship network. Agency and resistance are differentially circumscribed. Within a process of change, some kin become more powerful than others and (kin) relationships are revalued and reshaped. This may lead to a transformation of living arrangements as participants renegotiate areas of conflicting interests. The outcomes of this process are various, involving a greater or lesser breakdown of former arrangements as well as a creation of new forms and networks of cooperation and support (see Baerends 1994; Palriwala 1994).

Colonial Processes, Law and the State: Kin Affiliation and Citizenship

The four chapters in the first section (van Driel, Risseeuw, Tsikata, Saradamoni) and the last in the volume (Goonesekere) variously examine the impact of colonialism on kinship and gender relations in colonised societies. This is the implicit context for the other contributions also. One reason for focusing this volume on South Asia and Africa below the Sahara was the similar, though distinct, experiences of colonialism in the countries in these regions. As Goonesekere points out, this is not just a historical question, but an issue of continuing consequences. The effects of colonialism did not end with the political independence of the former colonies, as should be clear from the above discussion on the re-invention of traditions. At the same time, Leacock's (1981) caution (see Risseeuw) that in these countries history did not begin with colonialism has to be kept in mind. Rather, the nature of the colonial enterprise meant that it was a period of acute social change, but at times a new stagnation and rigidity also, for the then colonies. Further, as argued by some of the participants in the conference from which this volume emerged (Ganesh and Risseeuw 1993), the move towards structural adjustment and free market economic policies being pushed internationally and their social effects in these countries exhibit many of the characteristics of colonialism.

The influence of various colonial institutions, interests and participants are outlined in the contributions. Three intertwined aspects, central to the colonial enterprise, are analysed to different degrees. These are the economic interests and policies of the colonisers; the nature of the colonial state in terms of governance through law and administration; and the social and moral values and norms, particularly in the arena of marriage and family which the colonisers brought with them. While the first and second aspects have been much studied, the implications for family and gender relations have rarely been explored.[3]

The primary driving force of colonialism was linked to a particular emergent economic system—developing capitalism. Local systems of production were reoriented to international trade and became vulnerable to the vagaries of this market. The control of resources, particularly land, was reorganised in ways which the colonisers thought would be better suited to individual initiative, free movement of labour and production adaptable to the market, give their own members new property bases, and help them retain their political hold. Migration (van Driel), new economic opportunities and mobility, increased differentiation and a competitive struggle for resources (Tsikata, Risseeuw, Saradamoni), widening poverty and narrowing social responsibility (Risseeuw) were among the direct effects.

As the chapters bring out, the success of colonialism, particularly in influencing kinship and gendered values, lay in part in its ability to ensure the support of sections of the local people, particularly the elite. This was a result of assorted factors in the various case-studies. These included pre-existing hierarchies and a desire to maintain or acquire social and economic positions (Risseeuw); the compatibility between precolonial gendered biases and the patriarchal values of colonial personnel (Risseeuw); religious conversion and the influence of Christianity (van Driel); the acceptance of a link between economic wealth, 'progress', 'civilisation', and the values of the colonisers (Saradamoni); and dual administration and division of responsibilities between British (all the case-studies in this volume are of British colonies) officers and local chiefs and headmen (Tsikata).

The last aspect brings us to the process most often the focus in these case-studies: colonial governance through law and the establishment of centralised states. For all the societies discussed, the appropriation by a centralised authority of the right to establish and adjudicate norms on marriage and family was revolutionary, more so in those African societies where there had been no state organisation. The impact of a centralised state was mediated and differentiated through layers of administration and social groups.

Colonial codifiers established customary laws through selected informants and the filters of their own values. In the process, differences and flexibility within groups were ironed out, and divisions instituted where they had not existed. Chanock (1982) demonstrated for central Africa how interpretations/practices regarding divorce of particular sections in specific situations were made valid for all in all situations. The contextuality of kinship was denied and tradition was made rigid.

Two main features of colonial legal systems emerge: characteristics which define the legal heritage pertaining to family and marriage in the societies described. One was the decontextualising basis of the legal system and the judicial process through the fixing of rules grounded in notions of the abstract individual, concepts alien to the pre-existing systems. The second feature was the creation of dual legal systems.

The law and state policies in post-colonial countries continue largely to be based on liberal political and legal theory which assumes the abstract individual as its unit. On the one hand, this notion asserts the ideals of democracy and the equality of citizens, where rights are not tied to one's rank, status, religion, lineage, occupation, sex or class. Rights and responsibilities are now said to be a derivative of citizenship, rather than family membership and kinship status. The processes of increasing individuation to which these ideals were tied have formed a substantial counter-force to oppressive kinship bonds. These ideas were and are extremely powerful and attractive concepts in the struggles of colonised peoples against indigenous or colonial rulers and oppressors. They have been used—with varying degrees of success—in feminist struggles in the South (Agnihotri and Palriwala, forthcoming; Molokomme 1991). They have been a base from which to critique the harsh situations of wives, widows or unmarried women within kin-systems by emphasising their theoretically equal position to male citizens. Equally, this perspective can enable legal or other intervention on the issue of abuse of children within kin-systems and living units.

However, it is important to recognise that these notions of democracy and citizenship come to operate in cultural traditions where diverse notions of personhood, of community, as well as of relationships exist, such that an individual is only in and through her relationships. Simultaneously, many 'traditional' kinship systems were characterised by high degrees of individuation within strong kinship groupings and network (Dube, Goonesekere). The flexibility of these systems protected the rights of individuals. Marriage could be dissolved relatively easily as property systems entailed combinations of group-based and individual ownership, while a second marriage was only one bond within the multiple other kinship bonds. The children's position then remained secure.

In contrast, the notion of the abstract individual is embedded in notions of the highly atomised person, individualised personhood, and of relationships turned into property and possession. Sevenhuijsen (1991) demonstrates, with cases in Holland, how the competing claims of divorced parents to a child are based on reasoning located within a discourse of individual property and possessive rights, reflecting the overall legal system. In the process, the child's interests are pushed to the background.[4]

This notion assumes on the part of governments that their citizens are disembodied, decontextualised, de-historicised persons, starting from a point of equality in their dealings with each other and with the state. The formal equality of the abstract individual and the citizen becomes a myth to obscure the real inequalities and differentials of power between classes, races and sexes (cf. Pateman 1989). It can become the ground on which to argue against special legal and policy measures for the more vulnerable in society. Law rooted in this philosophic idea does not take into account the concrete conditions of people's lives, in terms of reliefs given or legal procedures entailed. This emphasises the necessity for less decontextualised, narrow and individualistic principles on which to base the issue of rights and legal jurisdiction (Smart 1989).

The second characteristic of colonial legal systems—the dual legal systems—is a crucial issue in all the chapters on law (especially Kibwana, Molokomme, Goonesekere). These systems were/are administered through dual institutions (Botswana), or plural legal systems implemented by a single judiciary (South Asia). The establishment of plural systems and 'customary' law laid the grounds for current irresolvable problems in legal reform. The equation between cultural identity, religion or 'ethnicity', and laws pertaining to marriage and family is a particular legacy of the colonial state (Goonesekere). Law was central to the re-invention of traditions discussed earlier, and to the remaking of flexible practice as fixed rules. Culture was then made a justifier of discriminatory laws in the arena of the 'private'—marriage and family—areas which paradoxically were neither seen as private earlier, nor governed by centralised laws.

Contemporary opposition to legal reform is at times bolstered up by an argument that the plurality of laws, including the existence of general personal laws, allows for choice. Each of the various legal systems has a different range of influence and, as Molokomme (and Tsikata) bring out, is manipulated by people in giving shape to their living arrangements and relationships. However, Kibwana indicates that this is only an apparent choice. First, these laws are not equal in terms of the recognition of the rights of women in different phases of their lives, the rights of children and the rights of other kin. The various laws or systems are all biased against women (Molokomme) or any particular law allows for equality in one aspect and gender-bias in another. Goonesekere (1984) points out that a plurality of laws containing differential rights for women can lead to a devaluation of the laws asserting greater equality.

Second, the ability to move from one law to another is not equal (Kibwana) because of the way laws are framed, the exigencies of social life, differentials in resources and power (Molokomme), and the institutionalised link between particular laws and cultural identity. Looking at law based on the abstract individual along with the issue of pluralism, we see that women and men are assumed to be equal and abstract within their cultural or religious identities. A review of judicial decisions can be demanded not on the basis of life conditions, but by arguing conversion, etc. Not only can this favour the more gender-discriminatory law, it also allows for a manipulation of the law by the stronger contender. Molokomme argues for a plurality in law based not on the individual abstracted from all, but a fixed cultural identity. Rather, she suggests a plurality based on the exigencies of the real life conditions of people.

The chapters highlight the deep impact that colonial law had on people's living arrangements and continues to have. They discuss the various ways in which law enters, intervenes or is manipulated by people. In doing this, the volume belies an oft-heard argument as to the futility of legal reform due to the vast gap between law and social practice. Undoubtedly, if social practice is taken as a fixed set of rules, which if law cannot immediately change should be left alone, this view holds. However, this is too simplistic a conclusion for the processes described. Both Risseeuw and Goone-sekere delineate the transformation in kinship, marriage and gender relations, which the state realised through various legal measures. Saradamoni tells us of legal reform that led to even more far-reaching changes than its proponents had envisaged. Dube points to how people separate and integrate 'customary' practice and Islamic injunctions in different contexts. Molokomme describes how a 'failed' law, introduced to enforce maintenance from fathers of children born out of wedlock, had become a part of people's lives, though to varying degrees and in different ways from what may have been intended. The various writers argue the need for legal reform and in the process point to the reasons for past 'failures' in the post-colonial period and the apparent gap between law and society.

Dual messages, in and through contradictory laws, are a major factor in the failures as the lawyers Goonesekere and Kibwana elaborate. Contradictoriness is contained not only in legal clauses and concepts. It is present in procedural law and also the conflict-ing interpretations by the embodied—culturally and socially embedded—members of the judiciary. Hence the need is not for piece-meal reform, but a thorough overhaul of the legal system. The lack of dissemination and the will to implement on the part of state institutions and functionaries are critical, highlights Molo-komme. All these aspects point to the conflict of social interests which limit reform (Tsikata). The questions which need to be asked here are which interests dominate, which interests does the state act for and protect?

The centrality of this question is seen in noting that this duality and contradictoriness of messages and concepts is reinforced by the lack of support to vulnerable social categories from other state policy measures. This is demonstrated by an aspect taken by most of the chapters as central to a gender sensitive law for equitable relations in marriage and family: the need to ensure women's rights in marital property and assets, which become crucial on abandonment, divorce, or widowhood. The significance of such a right is related to the continuance of patrilineal inheritance, male bias in access to resources including government employment, and the devaluation of women's non-monetary earnings and non-waged employment in judicial decisions equating monetary contribu-tion to rights (Kibwana).[5] Economic reforms based on market principles and cuts in welfare expenditures (already minimal in many of the countries under discussion) adds to the vulnerabilities of women without male support (Goonesekere). Paradoxically, it is these very economic policies, which implicitly assume the continuance of extended and functional kinship and family units, that have intensified the fragility of kin support networks through increasing the inability and disinterest of members to provide for others. An obverse of this is again the re-invention of tradition, such that kinship, marriage and family, rather than being relationships which people make and sustain, become structures in which people must fit. They become ends in themselves, which those with greatest resources can use to their own best advantage.

At the conference from which this volume originated, the case was elaborated of Kenyan women, who found the support systems they attempted to construct jeopardised by changing 'tradition', 'economic development', as well as by usages of modern legislation. Mothers, with lesser resources, supported their children during their years of infancy and youth, while the fathers were absconding. However, bride price practices as well as Christian and legal marriage rules allowed the men, despite their stronger resource position and lesser responsibilities, to claim the children once they were grown. Women in these situations urged for legislation which recognised their parenthood and the long years of upbringing and support to the children. Discussions indicated the search for a legal basis to actual support networks, loosened from 'traditions' of marriage and family, and under increasing strain as a result of economic processes.

This brings us to the last point to be noted in this section. The case-studies also suggest the weakness of both liberal and post-modernist arguments against legal measures pertaining to the family. These arguments are couched in terms of cultural rights and/or the protection of individual rights and privacy from the hegemonic power of the state. They are based on notions of the equality of abstract individuals, the atomistic nature of personhood in modern society and hence their inability to confront a hegemonic state power over and above them, and on implicit notions of the possibility of isolating private spheres from macro processes. As discussed in the previous pages, these premises cannot hold, even as the necessity of concrete measures to ensure individual rights vis-à-vis the state are recognised. Furthermore, given the interaction between domains, it may be asserted that even where the state does not directly intervene, it does so indirectly through the economic and political processes it promotes. Inaction on the part of the state can be read as support for a status quo and the continuance of the present balance of power and rights; as an abdication on the part of the state to introduce policies which ensure equality and justice.

Shifting Circles of Support: Contextualising Gender and Kinship

Why have we chosen the title *Shifting circles of support* for this volume and pointed to the need to contextualise gender and kinship relations? The aim is not solely to critique the academic separation of domains of study or the absence of a dynamic concept of change in much of anthropology. Nor is the study of the impact of colonialism, or the analysis of the negotiation and remaking of relationships within kinship and gender, or the elaboration of the complexities of legal reform each an end in itself. The attempt is to arrive at a more holistic analysis, driven in part by the understanding that the concept of 'family' is of too generalising a nature to have meaning or heuristic relevance. The shifting relationships of care, responsibility and security embedded in these kinship systems, and the communities and state structures within which they operate remain muted as arenas of analysis.

Marriage, family and kinship are social domains characterised by a duality. They carry elements of security, support and care even as they entail elements of control—even oppression—limiting people's options to realise their own welfare and interests or of those for whom they take particular responsibility. The interests of the socially and economically most powerful members of a network as well as group interests can and do create forms of oppression from which the more vulnerable and dependent cannot extricate themselves easily, if at all. Yet these structures continue to be the main social arenas providing care in the regions covered here. Hence this volume makes a case for an integrated, historical and comparative analysis of the 'traditionally' separated academic fields of kinship, gender, political economy, and law, in order to focus on the shifting kin responsibilities and systems of security, care, and justice as specific areas for concern and study.

As discussed earlier, intensified negotiation of relations within kin networks changes the form and content of these relationships over time. New living arrangements and forms of support may be created. More often the latter have been reduced, even as the moralities in which they are embedded undergo change. Shifts in principles of reciprocity are noted and acted upon. Children experience the changing relations between their male and female providers—their parents, kin, neighbours and friends, the growing vulnerability of certain categories of elders and are exposed to different forms of socialisation. Specific relationships are not only shaped differently, but are experienced in new ways emotionally, entailing changed meanings and ethics for future generations. It is within this context that notions of responsibility and control are reshaped by forces both within and beyond the networks of kin.

The changing economic structures have been integrally tied to the formation of state systems and notions of citizenship initiated during the colonial era. They have emphasised individual ownership, new avenues of employment and social mobility, and generated further inequalities, class exploitation, gender oppression and a growing insecurity. Different classes and kinship groups have had unequal access to the new opportunities. The last have seldom been open to family and kinship networks as a whole, but rather to the socially better situated members within them—to those cast as superiors, elders, or the core. Within these processes the disparity between the ideals of security and continuity for members of a kinship network/family and the oppressive manner in which they may be ensured can become exacerbated. There has been a growing disjunction between the interests of those involved in avenues of social mobility and those involved in day-to-day care systems (cf. Fischer and Tronto 1990). Women, particularly of the elite, have not been completely excluded from the 'benefits', but by and large this process has been gendered, leaving women with less control over resources, further circumscribing their manoeuvrability, ease of resistance and 'agency'.[6]

These processes carry direct implications for the domains of kinship and citizenship. Political and economic developments had led to the establishment of varying forms of state security in advanced capitalist societies (de Swaan 1988; Zaretsky 1982). The welfare state was part of the social democratic project of giving social meaning to formal rights in a class-divided society (Pateman

1989); an acceptance of responsibilities of the state towards its citizens in an apparent response to the post-1917 'threat' of socialism (cf. Hobsbawm 1969). However, care and security systems tended to be awarded a position of secondary importance in economic policy vis-à-vis the centrally placed issue of economic growth (cf. Kabeer 1994). Thus, with economic recession social security systems have come under attack and are matters of intense political debate. Furthermore, as feminist critiques of the welfare state have highlighted, assumptions regarding the 'private' and the 'family' obscured gendered dimensions of support and care within living units in these systems (Fischer and Tronto 1990; Pateman 1989; Wilson 1977).

Care systems may be classified as operating at three levels: the domestic, the community and the state welfare/security system. In many countries in the South, state responsibility for social support has seldom appeared on national or international policy agendas. Nevertheless their necessity and feasibility have been analysed in various parts of the world (Hirtz 1994; Mundle 1994; von Benda-Beckmann et al. 1988). In countries such as Sri Lanka, state welfare systems, built up after Independence, have been dismantled under the aegis of World Bank—IMF structural adjustment programmes. This has had a serious impact on large sections of the population, stretching day-to-day living arrangements to the limit, leading to heightened social tensions. These and other experiences call for an urgent rethinking of the current models of development pushed by international agencies, which thrust economic growth without consideration of the dimensions of security, care and growing inequalities.

The focus on state welfare systems is connected with issues arising from the idea and phenomenon of citizenship. National and international agendas are purportedly based on claims of equal rights of all citizens to social betterment and the basic facilities the state is to provide. However, as discussed earlier, the formal equalities attributed to abstract individuals/citizens bypass structural inequalities, leaving the idea of democracy as an appealing but often ineffective construct. Coupled with increasingly unequal access to resources, in practice it creates a growing gap between promise, hope and reality.

Feminist critiques have questioned this notion of the citizen, with rights and duties vis-à-vis the state, but devoid of a network of relationships with others (Elshtain 1982; Kabeer 1994; Meehan and Sevenhuijsen 1991; Smart 1989). The mystification of 'the family' and its changing relation to the wider community as well as the disregard of gender relations are widespread both in the North and the South. This has facilitated the neglect of issues of care, responsibility and security in both legal systems and notions of 'development'. As several of the papers in this volume indicate, the notion of the disembodied citizen has deep repercussions not only on the notion of person or on the perception and expression of relationships between people, but also affects the differential and shifting responsibilities and social controls with which different categories of persons operate. Contextualising the processes of initiating and maintaining relationships of support and responsibility makes apparent the alarming impact of policy agendas dominated (implicitly and/or explicitly) by such constructs of the family and person.

A critique of liberal philosophy and the issue of rights does not, however, mean a simplistic negative evaluation of processes of individuation, or categorisation of them as unwanted 'Westernisation', to be avoided in societies where 'family' and 'kinship' are not only superior but 'intact'. A knowledgeable reassessment has to be made of changing relationships of kin support and sanction. It is on this basis that legislation and social support measures may be designed, such that the state assists the elements of care and responsibility within these relationships where they occur. The alternative is to simply abandon people to the formal equality of the individualising market or make them fit into existing legal arrangements, leaving many—such as widows, divorced women, the elderly and orphans—far too vulnerable.

The failure and the urgency for reform in the South is related to the repercussions of capitalist development and a political model of the state based on liberal philosophy in which a thinking on state responsibilities towards people's living conditions is absent. Currently, the growing disparities created by an economic system advantageous to certain countries, communities, classes, and members of gender, family and kinship systems reflect an increasing marginalisation of their counterparts on each level. The issues addressed in this volume become all the more urgent, emphasising the need to incorporate the so-called micro areas of growing insecurity within gender, family and kinship relations into political agendas. Attention must be directed to the expanding vacuum of support within day-to-day living arrangements, reinforced by state policy and the deletion of state welfare responsibilities from governmental agendas. Combined, the processes related to kinship and citizenship surface the increasing dangers of growing insecurity, especially for the more vulnerable, the resourceless and dependents.

Notes

1. These writings were, however, problematic in other ways, including the manner in which gender was (not) treated.
2. It is an interesting phenomenon that Western development planners and the most conservative elements in the 'donor' countries can often find many areas of agreement on such issues.
3. Except where there is a specific focus on women or gender relations. See Leacock and Etienne (1980); Sangari and Vaid (1989).
4. Esther Goody's comparison (1984) of fostering practices in West Africa and England is pertinent in this context. Whereas adoption was presumed to be permanent in England, West African systems envisaged long-term fostering in order to widen children's networks and skills, and a return of children to their natal families on maturity. The English legal system was unable to deal with this.
5. It may be noted in this context that societies with a matrilineal and bilateral past in South Asia tend to have better life indicators for women and children than adjoining patrilineal societies (Ganesh and Risseeuw 1993).
6. Abu-Lughod (1990) and Behar (1993) discuss the problem of overcompensating the view of women as passive victims by an assumption of women as constantly, if silently, resisting subjects, where agency and resistance seem to become synonymous. Such an assumption can deny the realities of structural constraints and inequalities.

References

Abu-Lughod, L., 1990, 'The romance of resistance: Tracing transformations of power through Bedouin women'. *American Ethnologist* 17: 41–55.
Agnihotri, I. and R. Palriwala (forthcoming), 'Tradition, the family and the state: Politics of the contemporary women's movement in India', in T.V. Sathyamurthy (ed.), *Terms of Political Discourse in India*. Delhi: Oxford University Press.
Amadiume, I., *Male Daughters, Female Husbands: Gender and sex in an African society*. London: Zed Press.
Ariès, P., 1962, *Centuries of Childhood: A social history of family life*. New York: Random House.
Barrett, M. and M. McIntosh, 1982, *The Anti-social Family*. London: Verso.

Baerends, E.A., 1994, *Changing Kinship, Family and Gender Relations in Sub-Sahara Africa*. Leiden: Women and Autonomy Centre, University of Leiden.

Behar, R., 1993, *Translated Woman: Crossing the border with Esperanza's story*. Boston: Beacon Press.

Bourdieu, P., 1977, *Outline of a Theory of Practice*. Cambridge: Cambridge University Press.

Caldwell, J., *Theory of Fertility Decline*. Sydney: Academic Press.

Chanock, M., 1982, 'Making customary law: men, women and courts in colonial northern Rhodesia, 1897', in M. Hay and M. Wright (eds.), *African Women and the Law: Historical perspectives*. Boston: Boston University Press.

Coontz, S., 1992, *The Way We Never Were: American families and the nostalgia trap*. New York: Basic Books.

Collier, J., M.Z. Rosaldo and S. Yanagisako, 1982, 'Is there a family? New anthropological views', in B. Thorne and M. Yalom (eds.), *Rethinking the Family: Some feminist questions*. New York: Longman Press.

Collier, J.F. and S.J. Yanagisako (eds.), 1987, *Gender and Kinship: Essays toward a unified analysis*. Stanford, California: Stanford University Press.

Davis, A., 1981, *Women, Race and Class*. New York: Random House.

de Swaan, A., 1988, *In Care of the State: Health care, education and welfare in Europe and the USA in the modern era*. Cambridge: Polity.

del Valle, T. (ed.), 1993, *Gendered Anthropology*. London: Routledge.

Donzelot, J., 1979, *The Policing of Families*. Translated by R. Hurley. London: Hutchinson.

Dumont, L., 1961, 'Marriage in India. The Present state of the question—I: Marriage alliance in south-east India and Ceylon'. *Contributions to Indian Sociology* 5: 75–95.

Elshtain, J.B. (ed.), 1982, *The Family and Political Thought*. Amherst: University of Massachusetts Press.

———, 1982a, 'Towards a theory of the family and politics', in J.B. Elshtain (ed.), *The Family and Political Thought*. Amherst: University of Massachusetts Press.

Engels, F. 1986, *The Origin of the Family, Private Property and the State: In the light of the researches of Lewis H. Morgan*. London: Penguin Books. First printed in 1884.

Feminist Review, 1984, 'Many Voices, One Chant: Black feminist perspectives'. No. 17. Autumn 1984.

Finch, J., 1989, *Family Obligations and Social Change*. Cambridge: Polity Press.

Fischer, B. and J. Tronto, 1990, 'Towards a feminist theory of caring', in E.K. Abel and M.K. Nelson (eds.), *Circles of Care: Work and identity in women's lives*. New York: New York Press.

Flandrin, J., 1976, *Families in Former Times: Kinship, household and sexuality*. Cambridge: Cambridge University Press.

Flax, J., 1982, 'The Family in contemporary feminist thought: A critical review', in J.B. Elshtain (ed.), *The Family in Political Thought*. Amherst: University of Massachusetts Press.

Fox-Genovese, 1982, 'Placing women's history in history'. *New Left Review* 133: 5–29.

Fox-Genovese, 1991, *Feminism Without Illusions: A critique of individualism*. Chapell Hill: The University of North Carolina Press.

Ganesh, K. and C. Risseeuw, 1993, 'Gender between family and state', Report and recommendations of the conference on state and market influences on gender, family and kinship relations in Sub-Saharan Africa and South Asia. Organised by Women and Autonomy Centre, University of Leiden, in cooperation with Department of Sociology, University of Nairobi and the Commission on Women (IUAES), New Delhi. Leiden: Women and Autonomy Centre. (mimeo)

Godelier, M., 1977, *Perspectives in Marxist Anthropology*. Cambridge: Cambridge University Press.

Goody, E., 1984, 'Parental strategies: calculation or sentiment? Fostering practices among west Africans', in H. Medick and D.W. Sabean (eds.), *Interest and Emotion: Essays on the study of family and kinship*. Cambridge: Cambridge University Press.

Goody, J., 1983, *The Development of the Family and Marriage in Europe*. Cambridge: Cambridge University Press.

Goody, J., J. Thirsk and E.P. Thompson (eds.), 1976, *Family and Inheritance: Rural society in western Europe 1200–1800*. Cambridge: Cambridge University Press.

Goonesekere, S., 1984, 'The application of personal laws in Sri Lanka: A reappraisal', in H. Claude (ed.) *Sansoni Felicitation Volume*. Colombo: Cave and Co.

Harris, O., 1981, 'Households as natural units', in K. Young, C. Wolkowitz and R. McCullagh (eds.), *Of Marriage and the Market: Women's subordination in international perspective*. London: CSE Books.

Hirtz, F., 'Issues and authors in the field of social security in the Third World: An introduction', in F. von Benda Beckman, K. von Benda Beckman and H. Marks (eds.), *Coping with Insecurity*. Focaal, Special issue 22/23: 231–37.

Hobsbawn, E.J., 1969, *Industry and Empire. The Pelican Economic History of Britain Vol. III: From 1750 to the present day*. Harmondsworth: Penguin Books.

Humphries, J., 1982, 'The working-class family: A Marxist perspective', in J.B. Elshtain (ed.), *The Family in Political Thought*. Amherst: University of Massachusetts Press.

Joseph, C. and J. Lewis, 1981, *Common Differences: Conflicts in Black and White Feminist Perspectives*. New York: Doubleday, Anchor Press.

Kabeer, N., 1994, *Reversed Realities: Gender hierarchies in development thought*. London: Verso.

Lasch, C., 1979, *Haven in a Heartless World: The family besieged*. New York: Basic Books.

Leach, E., 1961, *Pul Eliya, a Village in Ceylon: A study of land tenure and kinship*. Cambridge: Cambridge University Press.

Leacock, E., 1981, *Myths of Male Dominance: Collected articles on women cross-culturally*. New York: Monthly Review Press.

Leacock, E., and M. Etienne (eds.), 1980, *Women and Colonization: Anthropological perspectives*. New York: Praeger.

Marx, K., 1969, 'The eighteenth Brumaire of Louis Bonaparte', in K. Marx and F. Engels, *Selected Works*, Vol. I. Moscow: Progress. First printed in 1869.

Medick, H. and D.W. Sabean, 1984, 'Interest and emotion in family and kinship studies: A critique of social history and anthropology', in H. Medick and D.W. Sabean (eds.), *Interest and Emotion: Essays on the study of family and kinship*. Cambridge: University of Cambridge Press.

Meehan, E. and S. Sevenhuijsen (eds.), 1991, *Equality Politics and Gender*. London: Sage.

Molokomme, A.L., 1991, *Children of the Fence: The maintenance of extra-marital children under law and practice in Botswana*. African Studies Centre Research Report No. 46. Leiden: African Studies Centre, University of Leiden.

Moore, H.L., 1988, *Feminism and Anthropology*. London: Polity Press.

Mundle, S., 1994, 'Deprivation and public policy: Defining the developmental state', Wertheim Lecture 1994, Amsterdam: Centre for Asian Studies, University of Amsterdam.

Obeyesekere, G., 1967, *Land Tenure in Village Ceylon*. Cambridge: Cambridge University Press.

Palriwala, R., 1990, 'Introduction', in L. Dube and R. Palriwala (eds.), *Structures and Strategies: Women, work and family*. Women and the Household in Asia, Vol. 3. New Delhi: Sage.

———, 1994, *Changing Kinship, Family and Gender Relations in South Asia: Processes, trends, issues*. Leiden: Women and Autonomy Centre, University of Leiden.

Parsons, T. and R.F. Bales, 1957, *Family, Socialisation and Interaction Process*: London, Routledge and Kegan Paul.

Pateman, C., 1989, *The Disorder of Women: Democracy, feminism and political theory*. Cambridge: Polity Press.

Rosaldo, M.Z., 1974, 'Women, culture and society: A theoretical overview', in M.Z. Rosaldo and L. Lamphere (eds.), *Women, Culture and Society*. Stanford, California: Stanford University Press.

Rapp, R., 1982, 'Family and class in contemporary America: Notes toward an understanding of ideology', in B. Thorne and M. Yalom (eds.), *Rethinking the Family: Some feminist questions*. New York: Longman Press.

Rapp, R., E. Ross and R. Bridenthal, 1979, 'Examining family history'. *Feminist Studies* 5(1): 174–200.

Sangari, K. and S. Vaid (eds.), 1989, *Recasting Women: Essays in colonial history*. New Delhi: Kali.

Sevenhuijsen, S., 1991, 'Justice, moral reasoning and the politics of child custody', in E. Meehan and S. Sevenhuijsen (eds.), *Equality Politics and Gender*. London: Sage.

Smart, C., 1989, *Feminism and the Power of law*. London: Routledge.

Stolcke, V., 1981, 'Women's labours: The naturalisation of social inequality and women's subordination', in K. Young, C. Wolkowitz and R. McCullagh (eds.), *Of Marriage and the Market: Women's subordination in international perspective*. London: CSE Books.

Stone, L., 1977, *The Family, Sex and Marriage in England 1500–1800*. London: Penguin Books. Reprinted in 1984.

Tambiah, S.J., 1958, 'The structure of kinship and its relationship to land possession and residence in Pata Dumbara, central Ceylon'. *The Journal of the Royal Anthropological Institute of Great Britain and Ireland* 88 (1): 21–44.

Thorne, B. and M. Yalom (eds.), 1982, *Rethinking the Family: Some feminist questions*. New York: Longman.

Thorne, B., 1982, 'Feminist rethinking of the family: An overview', in B. Thorne and M. Yalom (eds.), *Rethinking the Family: Some feminist questions*. New York: Longman.

von Benda-Beckmann, F., K. von Benda-Beckmann, E. Casino, F. Hirtz, G.R. Woodman and H.F. Zacher (eds.), 1988, *Between Kinship and the State: Social security and the law in developing countries*. Dordrecht: Foris Publications.

Wilson, E., 1977, *Women and the Welfare State*. London: Tavistock.

Yanagisako, S.J. and J.F. Collier, 1987, 'Towards, a unified analysis of gender and kinship', in J.F. Collier and S.J. Yanagisako (eds.), *Gender and Kinship: Essays toward a unified analysis*. Stanford, California: Stanford University Press.

Young, K., C. Wolkowitz and R. McCullagh (eds.), 1981, *Of Marriage and the Market: Women's subordination in international perspective*. London: CSE Books.

Zaretsky, E., 1976, *Capitalism, the Family and Personal Life*. New York: Colophon Books.

———, 1982, 'The place of the family in the origins of the welfare state', in B. Thorne and M. Yalom (eds.), *Rethinking the Family: Some feminist questions*. New York: Longman.

I

Changing Marriage and Kinship
Relations Under Colonialism

2 Marriage—From Rule to Rarity? Changing Gender Relations in Botswana

Francien van Driel

The processes leading to the current high percentage of female-headed households and unmarried mothers in rural Botswana are explored. The impact of colonisation and Christianity on gender relations in general, and on marriage in particular, are considered so as to understand the growing acceptance of unmarried mother-hood, the diversification of household types and the emergence of matrilinear households. The political, economic and homestead systems of precolonial Bamangwato society (central Botswana) are described, in which the sexual division of labour, kinship, the regulation of sexuality and fertility through marriage and marriage prestations were central. The introduction of a money economy and trade—including in cattle—the possibilities and necessity for migration and the absence of men, the abolition of customary practices under the joint initiative of missionaries and the local leadership, and new norms and values drastically altered the place of kinship as a system of support and sanction, diminished the value of women's labour and marriage, and transformed reproduction strategies. Women remain the food providers, but with lesser and differentiated eco-nomic opportunities and little support from the fathers of their children. Female-headed households are characterised by poverty.

Introduction[1]

Currently about half the households in the rural areas of Botswana are headed or managed by unmarried, widowed, divorced or deserted women, while the figure is about 40 per cent in urban areas. About 57 per cent of all women with children are unmarried. The large number of female heads of households and unmarried mothers is in sharp contrast with the situation in former times, when headship of households was restricted to men, and unmarried motherhood was highly tabooed and heavily sanctioned.[2]

In the past, a rather elaborate system of rules and customs, especially in relation to marriage, regulated the social and economic organisation of the Bamangwato, a Tswana tribe in the Central District of Botswana.[3] The head of a household was a man and gendered spheres were clearly demarcated. Marriage was the destiny for both sexes; the household and subsistence agriculture being the woman's domain, while cattle raising and the political arena were the domain of men. Unmarried women either fell under the guardianship of their father or his male relatives, and married women under the guardianship of their husband or his male kin. Marriages were arranged and they established kinship bonds of reciprocal obligations of support and protection between the family groups involved. At present, most couples decide to marry independently of their mutual families.

In Paje, the Bamangwato village where I conducted my research, I was struck by the high number of households managed by women, especially households headed by women *de jure*, i.e., those which are run independently by women and where no adult male can claim to be head. The households with a male head temporarily absent due to migration or other reasons I call '*de facto* headed by women'. During my stay in Paje I found that 56 per cent of the households were headed by women.[4]

The high number of *de jure* versus *de facto* female heads of households in this village, 54 per cent and 2 per cent respectively, is outstanding in comparison with data from the National Migration Study of the late 70s. According to this study, an average of 11 per cent of the households in rural Botswana were *de facto* headed by women. This study also makes clear that widowhood was the most common cause of a woman becoming a permanent household head (Izzard 1985: 263). However, of the 56 per cent female heads of household in Paje, more than half of the women had never been married. This casts doubt on the assumption that widows represent the largest group of permanent household heads and suggests that unmarried mothers are also becoming household heads in increasing numbers.[5]

This chapter will consider the impact of Christianisation and colonisation on gender relations in general, and on marriage in particular, and pay special attention to the growing acceptance of unmarried motherhood and the diversification in household types. What effect did the introduction of Christian norms and values and the rise of wage labour, migration and commercialisation have on the organisation of kin in Botswana? Why is it that female–headship of households exists beside male–headship?

In the first two sections, I focus on the production and reproduction relations and the significance of marriage agreements and regulations for the social organisation of Tswana society before the advent of missionaries and colonists in the 19th century.[6] Here, conventional household composition, economic activities, sexual division of labour, socialisation, marriage customs, bride-price and the regulation of sexuality and fertility, as well as family linkages and support systems will be outlined.

In the third and fourth sections I deal extensively with the socioeconomic and cultural changes in colonial Bechuanaland, especially among the Bamangwato. Christianisation, trade, colonisation, migration and their consequences for the society at large will be discussed. Finally, I shall address the impact of these processes of change on household composition, support networks, sources of income and the increase in unmarried motherhood.

Customary Tswana Life

In Tswana tribal society life was organised along kinship lines. The household headed by a man was the basic socioeconomic unit of Tswana society. A collection of households under the leadership and authority of a hereditary headman formed a ward, the principal political unit. The ward mostly consisted of a patrilineally organised kinship group, sometimes complemented with non-related servant families. One or more wards formed a village, headed by the chief, the village headman. All villages were ruled and protected by the paramount chief of the Tswana tribe, who resided in the royal town. Small villages were comprised generally of inhabitants of the same ethnic community, whereas big towns like Serowe, the most recent headquarters of the Bamangwato, contained many foreigners.[7]

The varied origins and status of the population were expressed in specific ranks: the nobles, the descendants of local chiefs, commoners, the descendants of foreigners incorporated long ago, recent immigrants and serfs. Marriage was a means of establishing kinship bonds within a group's own ranks and with immigrants to ensure their loyalty. Wealthy people from the higher ranks placed *mafisa*—'loan cattle'—among the poor and newcomers to secure their obedience (Schapera 1984: 28, 36). Both exchange of women through marriage and the loan of cattle functioned as a means of maintaining and strengthening the cohesion of the population.[8] Moreover, loyalty was secured through an elaborate system of patriarchal rule.

> Women, young men and foreigners generally stood outside the centre of power. At best they were spectators, at worst they were exploited. The chief was a 'father' and the people he governed conveyed their respect by referring to themselves as his children. Closely allied to this hierarchical concept was the ethic of collective responsibility. In the absence of a strong centralised state, senior men were responsible for exacting social conformity from their subordinates. Patriarchal ideology, often transgressed in practice, rationalised a society where the rich distributed rather than accumulated wealth, and where the power of the state to extract wealth from the people it governed was weak. Political life was acted out in personal relations rather than in terms of depersonalised and rational law (Wylie 1990: 5).

The term patriarchy used by Wylie primarily connotes relations between men rather than relations between men and women. Older men could arrange strategic alliances by exchange of women and cattle. The patriarchal order was sustained at the *kgotla*, the chief's court and village council site. Women, uninitiated young men, poor people and serfs were not allowed to attend *kgotla* meetings and were all subjected to the patriarchal rule of the older men, both at the village level and at the ward and household levels.

The basic principle of physical organisation in Tswana society was the homestead. Its members could include one or more elementary units, i.e., husband, wife or wives and their offspring, married sons with their wives and children, and possibly other kin. This extended family group is commonly defined as a household, headed by the family patriarch (Schapera 1984: 39–40). It had its own *lolwapa*, compound, with several houses and a granary in the courtyard, surrounded by a fence of wood, reed or stones. Each married couple had its own house and, as a group, the household has its own fields for cultivation and usually also some cattle and small livestock. This extended family functioned both as a unit of production, reproduction and consumption. One or more closely related extended families formed a family-group and one or more family-groups formed a ward (ibid.: 39–40, 45–46).

In the 19th century the Botswana were almost self-supporting. They built their own houses, made their own clothes and household utensils from local natural materials and produced their own food by raising crops and breeding livestock, which was supplemented with game, wild fruits and vegetables. These economic activities were geographically dispersed, however, and most Batswana therefore had three homes: one in the village; one near their land, situated mostly a few kilometres, or as much as a day's journey, away from the village; and one at the cattle post, within a few days' walk of the village, sometimes as far as 50 to 100 kilometres away. Consequently, the household members lived a considerable part of the year apart, dispersed over the three homes.

This separation of household members was not only geographical, but also along gender lines, as the rather strict sexual division of labour illustrates. The land was the domain of women, who tilled the fields with the help of children, whereas cattle were the domain of men, who supervised the herding of cattle by young boys and serfs.

The women's provision of grains, wild fruits and vegetables was not a marginal economic activity. On the contrary, they supplied the family and community with staple foods, while men supplemented the diet with milk and meat.[10] But the women depended on the men for the allocation of land. The family heads allocated the land to their wives. This indicates that women's position in the community was different from the men's. Whereas men owned cattle and allocated land on an individual basis and, as such, enjoyed a rather autonomous position in the community, women depended on men for land and produced for the livelihood of the household.

The dissimilar socialisation of girls and boys began at an early age. At the age of 5 or 6, boys were given charge of small livestock and about the age of 9 or 10 they were stationed at the cattle post far away from the village. From about 6 years onwards, girls assisted their mothers in all the heavy work on the land, such as weeding, harvesting, storing and grinding the grain and, when somewhat older, in hoeing too. About the age of 10 or 12, girls were apparently supposed to be producers on their own account (Kinsman 1983: 47–48).

Thus, girls were already well equipped at an early age for their socioeconomic contribution to the community. The participation of boys and girls in all the tasks of men and women was the form of education employed by the Tswana, and this education was finalised during initiation rites. The two-month period of initiation took place between the ages of 10 and 13 about every four years. During the female rites, the obedience and servitude of women as food producers, housewives and mothers for the community was glorified and women were thoroughly prepared for their ultimate destiny: marriage. Senior women introduced girls to matters concerning womanhood, domestic and agricultural activities, sex and proper behaviour towards men. Young women who went through the ceremony were organised in women's regiments. These regiments could be called upon to work for the chief or the community, like the male regiments formed during the boy's initiation ceremony. By undergoing these initiation ceremonies girls and boys entered adulthood as proper women and men, obliged to obey the laws and customs of the community (Schapera 1970a: 176–77).

With the political arena virtually closed to women, they depended on the goodwill of men to defend their interests. The only area where women could express their communal involvement, opinions and concern was in religious activities like rainmaking, sowing and first fruit ceremonies.[11] Female dissatisfaction with the existing social order was expressed via songs and acts during the female initiation rites and sometimes on the sidelines during court meetings, scolding men for their laziness and their failure to work for their families. These acts of discontent, however, were merely symbolic and were hardly heard by men (Kinsman 1983: 49, 51). Individual women who rebelled against their subordinate position were severely beaten and sorcery was the sole means of effective female revenge. The only real escape from harsh and obnoxious circumstances was to flee and either return to the parental compound or live a life in destitution, leading to beggary. Ultimately, male hegemony in repressing women was more effective than female means of resistance and elderly women assisted men in disciplining younger women (ibid.: 52).

The whole complex of land allocation, socialisation, inaccessibility of the political arena and channels of repression forced women into a subordinate role as servants of the community. Although women had a secondary position, women's labour and procreative capacity were nevertheless highly valued. The prestige of a household rested on its size and, more importantly, on the number of workers it contained (Wylie 1990: 30). Women's work in the household fields and in those of the chief, was essential for the production of staple foods such as sorghum and maize and, hence, crucial for the survival of the community.

Marriage and the Regulation of Sexuality and Fertility

Women's lower status and servitude to the community was secured through the socialisation processes described and also the marriage system. Marriage in Botswana was a process which was completed when *bogadi*, the bride-price, was paid and the bride had moved to her in-laws' compound. However, to be able to marry, certain conditions had to be met. First, the boy and girl had to have passed through the initiation ceremonies; second, the two families concerned had to come to a mutual agreement through *patlo*, a series of formal negotiations; and third, *bogadi*, bride-price in the form of cattle, had to be transferred to the bride's family (Schapera 1970a: 127–30; 148).[12]

Marriage agreements established via *patlo*, negotiation, not only indicated a new relationship between a man and a woman, but also a strengthening of relations between two families. Cross cousin marriages, in particular, were preferred, as a means of keeping the cattle wealth within the family group. Marriage created a series of reciprocal obligations between the two families, such as assistance at work, exchange of food and gifts, and active intervention in the event of severe arguments between the married couple. If there were unsolvable problems a divorce was possible, provided that the cattle paid for *bogadi* were returned to the husband's family. As long as a woman stayed at her husband's compound he could not demand the return of the *bogadi* (Schapera 1970a: 140–55).

Before *bogadi* was transferred from the husband's family to the father of the bride, a period of living together called *ralala* was started in a hut specially set aside for the couple at the girl's parents' compound. The boy would return to his parents' home during the day and spend the night with his wife-to-be. Ideally, this period would last until a child was born and *bogadi* was paid. Only then did the couple move to the husband's home, finalising the marriage (Schapera 1978: 118). But *ralala*, of course, implied that the conditions for expression of sexuality had been fulfilled, while *bogadi* was crucial to the control of fertility.

In the old days, the child of an unmarried girl who was not betrothed would often be killed at birth or live a life full of humiliation and insults (Schapera 1970a: 171). Children born within wedlock were highly valued and all children, no matter who their natural father was, were considered legal offspring of the husband, since by the transfer of *bogadi* a woman's whole reproductive capacity was transferred to his family. If the husband died, the wife could be taken over by another male member of his family (levirate), because of the rights acquired over her by the payment of *bogadi* (ibid.: 164–65).

This patrilineal system was maintained through inheritance rules. The eldest son succeeded his father as the household head and inherited most of his cattle. The younger sons received a few heads of cattle whereas the widows and daughters none (Schapera 1984: 41–43). Consequently, male wealth to purchase women was guaranteed by inheritance laws. Fathers supplied their sons with bride-wealth and sisters brought in wealth, to be allocated by the father to purchase new wives for himself or his sons. Also, superiors provided subordinates with bride-wealth. In both instances, relations of debt and dependence were created, which sustained the cohesion and stability of the community (Schapera 1984: 34–35; Kuper 1982: 160).

If the concept of household and family is considered against the background of conventional Tswana society, the household had a specific meaning, both emotional and material. The extended family with mutual obligations of support was a unit of production and reproduction, organised around the male control of female fertility. Female fertility was transferred from the father's authority to the husband's authority during a long process of ceremonies and negotiations. The sexual division of labour within this family system was rather strict and gender roles fairly distinct. Women produced the field crops which were the means of subsistence, while men supervised cattle, the medium of exchange (Comaroff 1985: 62–74). Women were legal minors who could not take part in political affairs or hold a political position. Hence, women had a secondary position, households were headed by men and marriage was a woman's destiny.

However, the position of women changed under the influence of Christianisation and the introduction of a money economy, accelerated by migration. The confrontation with new norms and values, in particular, followed by the large-scale migration of young men changed the organisation of the society and its gender relations radically.

Christianisation and Commercialisation

In the mid-19th century, missionaries became the forerunners of colonisation. In that period all the Tswana rulers wanted weapons to protect themselves against the expansionist pressure of the Boers and other dominant groups competing for precious land. Since traders in guns and ammunition often accompanied the missionaries, the latter were requested to settle among the Tswana. Hence, missionaries from the London Missionary Society opened a mission post among the Bamangwato in the 1860s (Tlou and Campbell 1984: 110–13; 129–31).

To convert the Tswana to Christianity, missionaries like Mackenzie, who lived and worked in Shoshong, the royal capital of the Bamangwato during the 1880s, had decided that they first had to make the country British. By manipulating the chiefs of the major tribes, and through political lobbying in Britain, both by missionaries and chiefs, this attempt was successful and Bechuanaland became a protectorate from 1885 to 1966. The missionaries acted as protectors of the local interest, as interpreters and negotiators for the chiefs, and as intruders on behalf of the church, interfering in domestic and religious affairs.

The customary political system for administering the internal affairs of the indigenous people was left intact, whereas external affairs increasingly became a British colonial task.[13] It was in this political environment that missionaries acquired ample room to use their influence to obstruct traditional laws and customs at the local level.

With a Christian chief in power from 1872 to 1873 and from 1875 to 1923, missionaries could advance their message among the Bamangwato with little difficulty (Schapera 1970b: 267). The missionaries primarily opposed polygamy, initiation rites and bride-price. Most of the missionaries considered key customs like initiation rites as very immoral and most customs related to marriage were either abolished or discouraged.[14]

Bogadi was one of these 'pagan' customs to be abolished by the chief under pressure from the missionaries in 1875. They perceived the 'exchange' of women as humiliating. They especially opposed the law that a woman whose husband died was not allowed to leave her husband's compound. As stated earlier, her children born after his death and fathered by a male relative were still considered as those of her late husband. The same applied to a divorced woman. According to Christian morals, every man should be the father of his own child and the custom was therefore prohibited (Schapera 1970a: 145–46; 1970b: 138). The abolishment of *bogadi*, the most important means of establishing kinship bonds and regulating women's productive and reproductive labour, meant that men's regulating power over women and younger men weakened as did the ability to ensure fulfilment of social responsibilities.

Initiation rites, *bojale* for girls and *bogwera* for boys, were abolished in 1877. The last initiation ceremonies among the Bamangwato were held in 1876, though the age-set system persisted (Schapera 1970b: 127, 168). Instead, schools were started and religion-based Western education replaced the educational and socialising rites, which formerly prepared girls and boys for womanhood and manhood. Polygamy was prohibited in 1896. With the support of the chief, the missionaries forbade their converts to have more than one wife and a woman belonging to the church was not allowed to become the wife of a 'polygamist'. By 1889, inheritance laws were modified. From then on, women could ideally inherit cattle and daughters were to be given some cattle at marriage (ibid.: 135, 145).[15]

While fundamental changes in gender relations were initiated on the one hand, on the other hand the significance of cattle, land, and male and female labour power also changed. These changes could not of course take place without the combined effort of both the local leadership and the missionaries, the advance guard of colonial administration, to Christianise the Bamangwato and to bring sociocultural values and practices more in line with Western, Christian ideals.

The eradication or transformation of central Ngwato laws, customs and ceremonies occurred simultaneously with changes in the productive sources of Ngwato society. With the royal capital at the crossroads between Central and Southern Africa and the Ngwato nation as the 'Suez Canal' of colonialism, as Parsons (1974; 1977) so aptly calls the location of the Ngwato nation, cooperation with traders opened the way for economic reforms and commoditisation in this agro-pastoral society.[16]

First, long-distance trade with the Cape based on hunting products developed. Second, private ownership of cattle (and of the serfs accompanying it) offered large cattle owners and serf employers sources for the accumulation of cash. Cattle were no longer a means of strengthening kinship bonds and relations of dependence, but became a source of wealth on their own. This led to new patterns of socioeconomic stratification which threatened the cohesion of the community (Parsons 1974: 653–55). Third, new forms of local employment were generated by wage labour in the pay of European settlers. The wagon trade to the Cape and to the north, the construction of a road and telegraph line (1890–91) and of the railway line connecting Cape Town with Bulawayo in southern Rhodesia (1896–97), and the Anglo–Boer War in 1899 offered a range of new jobs, especially for men (Schapera 1947: 27). With the increase in income the Ngwato nation initially prospered. Local employment for both men and, to a lesser extent, women, as for instance, store assistant, cattle herder, domestic servant, workers in the railway road gangs and in the local administration apparently satisfied the demand for cash (ibid.: 137).

Until the end of the century the necessity to earn cash was limited, but the introduction of the 'hut tax' in 1899 by the colonial administration in cooperation with the local authorities, imposed on men of eighteen years and older, forced people to find a regular sum of money every year (Schapera 1947: 7). The income from wage labour was initially used to invest in tools, wagons, ploughs, and to acquire new commodities like Western clothes and household utensils. As early as 1902, however, many of the new income sources started to vanish as the railway replaced the wagon trade. With the decline in local labour opportunities and the growing demand for labour in the Union of South Africa, wage earnings through migration began replacing local income sources. The final result was that a fairly prosperous state was transformed into one of the labour reserves, exporting mainly male labour, with Native Reserves already being proclaimed in 1899 by the colonial administration for the major ethnic groups (ibid.: 4). In the early 1940s migration expanded and resulted in the absence of large numbers of young men for prolonged periods of time.

In the course of time, gender relations changed because of the above developments. Despite the lack of explicit references to gender relations in the literature, some conclusions can be drawn. In the first place, extensive trade with the Cape created new sources of income. Trade, as a new major avenue of generating income, changed the meaning of cattle. Before trade started to flourish cattle were a means of exchanging women, of regulating female labour power and fertility, and ensuring male dependants. It was not the production of commodities, but the preoccupation with the survival of the community which was the central characteristic of these agro-pastoral societies (Guy 1987; 1990). The social organisation of the society was balanced in such a way that organisation of production and reproduction, the latter referring to the arrangement of kin, labour and sexuality, secured the continued existence of the community (see also Rubin 1975). These characteristics lost significance, with labour and cattle in themselves becoming sources of income and surplus.

Because of these economic differentiations founded on commercial trade and the introduction of wage labour—which occurred more or less simultaneously with population growth, environmental deterioration, and recurrent droughts—agricultural production, the main task of women, lost its central importance. Although the introduction of the plough at the end of the 19th century gave men a more profound role in arable cultivation and potentially increased agricultural output, this technical innovation forced households without cattle to earn an income in order to be able to hire a span of oxen for ploughing. Consequently, trade, taxes, and wage labour brought about a whole chain of changes and differentiation, as will be elaborated in the following sections.

Here it will suffice to conclude that women's labour for the community as a whole diminished in importance, since women's agricultural production lost its central place. This did not mean that the process of change occurred smoothly; resistance to the abolishment and prohibition of bride-price, initiation rites and polygamy took place, but on a limited scale. The authority of the chief, combined with the influence of the missionaries, proved to be a powerful union.

Migration, Social Disruption and Unmarried Motherhood

Economic changes accelerated the transformation of the social organisation of the community and its gender relations. Large-scale migration, in particular, had a far-reaching and disturbing impact. The effects of migration have been two-sided, as it proved to be both an indispensable source of income and also detrimental to social life in the Protectorate (Schapera 1947: 156). For a clear understanding, the effects of migration have to be seen in relation with the religious, political, and socioeconomic innovations which disturbed the stability of conventional life.

Migration and Christianisation offered opportunities hitherto absent, such as an independent income, access to education, religious services and new lifestyles. Migration offered a spell of adventure for the youth and eventually developed into a form of initiation into manhood. Young women preferred men who had been abroad. Young people in general wanted to escape from domestic and tribal control. Moreover, young men especially found tribal life after the introduction of Christianity dull, as old forms of excitement and amusement, like initiation schools and rain ceremonies, had disappeared and even beer-drinking was prohibited. However, women were crafty in finding secret places to brew beer (Schapera 1947: 115–20).

Girls came more easily into contact with new norms and values through the church. More girls than boys followed modern education and became members of the Christian church, because boys, as herders of the cattle, were often absent from the village. Three-quarters of the children attending school were female (Schapera 1947: 183). Christian churches and schools offered women access to the Western ideals of individualism and personal autonomy. They also offered women an outlet for organisational talents and energies which was missing in their own society (Walker 1990: 15–16). Likewise, the experiences of men and women abroad provided new challenges.

Economic necessity, however, was the most important reason for migration. Taxes, clothing and other goods had to be paid for in cash. The Europeans had introduced new needs and taxes and the chiefs imposed levies for special occasions like the building of schools. Transport, education, Western medicines and fines, all had to be paid for in cash (Schapera 1947: 121–30).

Wage labour became an indispensable source of income. In the early 1940s, 34.2 per cent of the national income was derived from the sale of agricultural products, 19.2 per cent from employment inside the Protectorate, and 46.6 per cent from employment outside the Protectorate, excluding army pay. This illustrates that migration provided the most important source of cash for the population (Schapera 1947: 161).

One of the consequences of migration was that a fair proportion (roughly 6 per cent) of the men who migrated stayed away permanently, while the majority stayed away for prolonged periods of time. In particular, the absence of so many young men disturbed the customary process of marriage and led to a distorted sex ratio. The changing sexual mores caused by the absence and shortage of men of marriageable age, led to premarital sexual relations, promiscuity, unmarried motherhood and a rise in the average age at marriage. Furthermore, the intervention of family elders in domestic affairs became more difficult, with so many people abroad.

One of the outcomes of changing sexual mores was that unmarried motherhood became a widespread phenomenon. In a study on migration, Schapera states that the rise in the number of illegitimate children compensated for the decrease in the number of legitimate children. Since girls had to wait several years after puberty for marriage and it was considered to be against nature to remain chaste all the time, many had lovers or became concubines of married men, indicating deviate opinions on premarital sexual relations (Schapera 1947: 173, 188, 196–97).

A study, as early as 1933, reported an exceedingly high proportion of premarital births. Changes in moral values showed a decline in the use of sanctions when an unmarried girl became pregnant (Schapera 1933: 73).[17] A study published ten years later presented figures on unmarried motherhood of women between the ages of

15 and 44. The number of unmarried mothers among the Bamang-wato was 51 out of 266, i.e., 19.2 per cent (Schapera 1947: 173).

Thus a whole complex of factors contributed to the emergence of unmarried motherhood as a widespread social phenomenon. Migration as such had its disturbing impact on conventional life, but was not solely responsible for the changing attitudes and practices. The diminishing influence of elders and headmen, the growing impact of Western education and religion and the tempt-ations of new lifestyles, together with the economic necessity to earn cash, all contributed to the social disintegration of conventional life, its marital system and its organisation of kin, labour and sexuality. It will be clear from the above that production and reproduction, which were formerly organised and regulated within the community by the male family elders, headmen and chiefs, changed fundamentally. Production relations became increasingly determined by outside forces and, in their turn, undermined con-ventional reproduction relationships of kin, labour and sexuality, and the significance of subsistence agriculture. This has led to a different status of marriage, different gender relations and, in the context of Botswana, to the growing disintegration of the extended family.

Female-headed Households and Unmarried Mothers

The position of widows and unmarried mothers in the community was altered as a result of the economic and religious influences stated earlier. Women could inherit cattle, were no longer subjected to the levirate and were allowed to enter wage labour. Hence, they were able to live a fairly autonomous economic life. Nevertheless, their position did not change politically and legally, since they had to submit to the rules of the male elders in all major decisions, transactions and the allocation of land. For a long time, women could not manage independent households on an individual basis, since the change in their position was in conflict with conventional social and legal rules:

> There is often a conflict between traditional social forms and new ideas, between modes of behaviour and legal and conven-tional rules . . . . The *femme* sole has emerged, but there is as yet no place for her in the legal system, or in the political life of the community (Schapera 1966: 357).

After Independence in 1966, this situation of the 'femme sole' started to change and women obtained more legal and political rights: the right to vote, to occupy political positions and to hold land in their own names. Consequently, women could establish an independent household, since they were entitled to obtain a plot of land for arable cultivation as well as for a new compound.

Women also gained easier access to employment. Since the 1970s new opportunities for employment have expanded in Botswana's towns, as the hitherto stagnant national economy has undergone rapid growth. Recently, women have also migrated in increasing numbers to industrial and urban sites. The National Migration Study of the late 1970s indicates rising female migration. While the majority of urban migrants to the mining towns are male, women predominate in other towns. The capital Gaborone, for example, had a sex ratio of 80 males to 100 females at the end of the 1970s (Government of Botswana 1982a: 29–30).

At present, migration, both of women and men, is more prevalent within the national borders and is more permanent than in the past. This is caused by the discovery and exploitation of diamonds and other mineral resources in the 1970s and '80s, the decline of jobs in South Africa, and the growth of the governmental and service sectors. The logic of migration has turned full circle: cash needs dominate rural and urban society. The dependence on cash has been met with continued migration, while much of the exchange and non-cash system has fallen away (Government of Botswana 1982a: 15). As a result men do not need women as food providers, as they did in the past.

The diminishing importance of subsistence agriculture can be illustrated with figures on the distribution of the gross domestic product. A comparison of the structure of production at the national level in 1965 and 1988 shows the diminishing importance of agriculture—the percentage of both crop and livestock production in the distribution of the gross domestic product has declined from 34 per cent to 3 per cent during this period (World Bank 1990: 182).[18]

When we consider the percentages of female-headed households in Botswana and in Paje (as presented at the beginning of this chapter), it might be concluded that mounting numbers of women are managing their own independent households. In particular, the number of de jure female heads of households is outstanding in Paje compared with this category in other areas. In her study on women and income-generating activities, Narayan-Parker found that 50 per cent of the households were headed by women in four villages in southern Botswana. She classifies 33 per cent of the female-headed households as female *de jure* and 17 per cent as female *de facto* heads (Narayan–Parker 1983: 6).

In Paje, the category of *de facto* female heads of households is, as stated at the start, almost non-existent. Of the *de jure* heads, unmarried women outnumber widows as female heads. Single, unmarried women who head a household can marry at a later stage, however, and be replaced as household heads by their husbands and eventually become widows and take over their head-ships. Hence, households may fluctuate in composition. However, those households headed by single women in Paje represent a category of women who increasingly refrain from marriage. Temporary liaisons outside wedlock can replace marriage and offer women some economic support.

A closer look at the population structure, household composi-tions, and income sources in Paje shows clearly how profound this shift in the organisation of kin, labour and sexuality has been over the years and the extent to which female and male economic interests and roles have drifted apart. When we first look at the population structure, the higher incidence of male migration com-pared to female migration becomes apparent. According to the Census of 1981, the population in Paje numbered 1,216 persons and the sex ratio was 1.4:1. Migration is predominantly male and the distribution of the sexes is rather skew, particularly above the age of 20.

Looking more specifically at the income sources of Paje house-holds, we find an indication of the extent to which conventional support systems have changed and a new household development cycle has emerged. Cattle are still the main asset of wealth in rural areas, and can be sold in difficult periods. Among the female heads of households, 68 per cent have no cattle at all, while among households headed by single women, the percentage is even higher (80 per cent). Of the male-headed households, 18 per cent have no cattle. Hence most female-headed households lack access to cattle as an income source and as a repository of capital.

When we consider arable cultivation as a subsistence and income source, we find that this source of income has completely lost its central place. Looking at the yields in Paje over the last ten years,

it is clear that agricultural activities on the lands are no longer one
of the distinctive factors of rural socioeconomic position. In Paje,
arable cultivation was successful only in the 1987–88 season. Most
households need ten bags of sorghum (or more) a year, depending
on the size of the household. At least 42 per cent of the households
did not meet this required minimum quantity for their own consumption in 1988. This indicates that, during the last decade of
recurrent drought, women were unable to complete the full agricultural cycle in most years and to meet household food demands,
let alone produce for the market.

Despite the minimal economic significance of arable cultivation,
the sociocultural importance of this sector is still highly valued,
especially among older women. When asked whether they would
stop ploughing completely if they found another regular and secure
income source, half the women in the village very determinedly
stated that they would never stop ploughing, since it is part of the
culture. For young women, however, every opportunity to escape
this unreliable source of subsistence is welcome. They have experienced long periods of drought with no yields. Nevertheless, during
years of abundance, even employed women will, when allowed,
return to the lands to assist their female family members with
harvesting, processing and storing the crops in return for some
bags of sorghum.

Because of the uncertain agricultural output, women need other
sources of income. Those households without cattle, which include
most households headed by single women as indicated earlier,
depended mainly on beer brewing and, provided they have family
members in employment, on small amounts of remittances sent by
family members in wage labour. More female-headed households
is Paje lack employed family members as compared to male-
headed households. Households with family members in wage
labour, whatever their composition, mostly receive small amounts
of remittances, of little or no economic value. Of the 50 researched
households, 24 receive remittances. However, only seven households receive monthly amounts which make substantial economic
impact. This indicates that economic ties between family members
with wage labour in the towns and their kin in the home village are
rather weak. In general, women in households without cattle and
without remittance income are worse off.

The weak role of family support networks is further illustrated when looking at support arrangements for unmarried daughters with children. In the process of betrothal and marriage, the future husband should contribute to the maintenance of his wife-to-be and their offspring. If he fails to do so and a marriage is not expected, different systems of damage and maintenance payments can be applied, according to either customary law or modern law, to secure support for unmarried mothers (see Molokomme in this volume). Of the 50 households, nearly half, that is 27 households, have grown-up daughters. These households include unmarried daughters with children, indicating a high number of unwed mothers. The other households either have no daughters or have daughters who are too young to have children. In reality, the number of unmarried mothers is even higher; I came across five households with four generations: mother, daughter, granddaughter and her offspring. By including the second generation of unwed mothers, the total number of unmarried mothers was 59 out of these 27 households.

The number of unwed mothers who received damage payments according to customary law is very low. Damages, mostly in the form of a lump sum, were paid for only seven women in five households and maintenance is paid in six other households, for 10 unwed mothers in total. However, maintenance refers here to the amounts of money the father of the child(ren) pays voluntarily to the mother of his children, because they have ongoing relationship or friendship. These payments can be monthly contributions in cash or irreglar contributions in kind, such as food and clothing. Once the relationship ends, these payments and gifts stop too. In the remaining 16 households damages have not been paid for any of the unmarried mothers, all of whom are unwed daughters of households headed by single women. In a few cases the daughters had received some form of support for a short period of time, but not on an arranged or ongoing basis. These households headed by single women are among the poorest. The high number of dependent daughters with children increase the difficulties of providing for all of them, which in turn intensifies their poverty.

Examination of the number of civil court cases related to damage claims at the Paje *kgotla* reveals that only four cases were registered during 1990 and 1991. In two, the men paid the amount demanded without trial. In the two other cases, the court found the men guilty and they paid fines. These four cases concerned the first child of an unwed mother. This low number of 'seduction' cases confirms my findings that many unwed mothers do not report their cases to the court and, thus, do not receive damage payments. Moreover, it also indicates that damage payments according to customary law are still restricted to the first born. Whereas the customary damages and maintenance practice is rarely used by unwed mothers, the new maintenance law is not used at all. None of the unwed mothers sued the fathers of their children nor applied for maintenance specified through modern law. Most of the women do not know how the new law operates, some have not even heard of its existence.

The low proportion of maintenance cases at the magistrate's court in Serowe, which serves the whole of Central District, also confirms the minimal use of these provisions by unwed mothers. In the period from January 1990 to April 1992 a total of 224 requests for maintenance payments were made. Of these 224 requests, only 56 (25 per cent) had been brought before the judge, of which 23 were dismissed. The remaining cases were still pending. This means that only 33 requests were honoured, in which cases the men were summoned either to pay a lump sum or a monthly sum.

Among the 224 cases there was only one claim by a woman from Paje, who had her case settled and had received monthly payments since the beginning of 1990. How long this regular payment will continue is questionable, considering the high incidence of defaulters. In her study on maintenance cases of extra-marital children among the Ngwaketse at the *magistrate's court* of Kanye in the south of Botswana, Molokomme found that in less than a quarter of all cases the men paid in time, while almost two-thirds of them were between four months and five years in arrears with payment. Prosecution of the defaulters was rare and given low priority (Molokomme 1991: 267–69; also in this volume).

To summarise, of the 59 unwed mothers, seven received damages and ten another form of support, not legally arranged. It is questionable whether the support will be lasting and eventually result in marriage. These figures do not point to reliable economic security for an extended period. Forty-two unwed mothers received no substantial form of support for their child(ren). This seems not only to confirm the statement of Kossoudji and Mueller on the weakening responsibility of men in assisting women with the up-bringing of their offspring, but also indicates the weak role of the family in arranging damages and maintenance according to custom-ary law (1983: 834). It also indicates that most unwed mothers are not betrothed or otherwise linked to a future husband.

The majority of the unmarried female heads of households who own no cattle and do not receive remittances have dependent unmarried daughters with children. This confirms not only the prevalence of poverty among households headed by single women, but also suggests a growing number of dependents and the likeli-hood of this pattern reproducing itself. Here, we see a matrilinear trend parallel with the patrilinear trend. Unmarried mothers apparently follow two different strategies in order to cope with their situation. On the one hand, there is an increasing migration of female children, mostly unwed mothers, who are trying to support their mothers, who in turn look after the offspring of their migrant daughters. On the other hand, women compete for men who can support them.

When we consider migration of women in Paje, we see that women have gained easier access to employment, although they predominate in low-paid jobs as housemaids and cleaners and in informal sector activities. Looking more specifically at these migrant women, we have to distinguish between those with, and those without, reliable jobs. The migrant women with jobs have rather secure occupations in the formal sector such as wages clerk, prison wardress, senior cashier, teacher or cleaner in government or industrial institutions. Those women with reliable and better-paid jobs are all unmarried mothers, with no support from the fathers of the children. Moreover, they are better educated and come from families owning cattle, in contrast to the less fortunate women. The grandmothers take care of the children and the working women support their mothers in turn. This points to a transformation of the obligations of male relatives to support unmarried women and their offspring. Migrant unmarried mothers with 'good' jobs provide for themselves, their children and, if necessary, for their mothers.

Women from poorer households, however, have less education and more difficulties in finding a job. They often become part of the large group of unemployed, roaming around from town to town in search of paid labour. Often these women have to return

to the home village, disappointed and pregnant. The women who
stay behind in the village depend on the insecure income sources
described earlier and compete for the support of men. However,
the interests of men and women have diverged. With the more
insignificant economic position of women, the social and economic
importance of children related to marriage also diminished. Men
no longer need the products of women's and children's labour, as
these have been replaced by other income sources. While women
with young children need support from men, men only need children
to provide for them when they are old and retired. Unmarried
mothers have to find ways to support themselves and their children,
as a man's fulfilment of his responsibility for the upkeep of his
offspring cannot be counted on.

There seems to be no replacement of the old system of mutual
help and sustenance, such as damage payments, resulting in growing individualism. Young fathers increasingly enjoy a prolonged
youth, as sanctions on their undependable behaviour are lacking
or scarcely implemented, as the low occurrence of damage payments and maintenance arrangements illustrate. The weakened
responsibility of men makes unwed mothers who stay in the village
increasingly dependent on family members who, in turn, are rather
reluctant to support them, and on insecure income sources. The
final outcome is that these women very often must provide for
themselves and their offspring, not supported by anybody, with
the resultant poverty. The position of many women seems to have
changed from motherhood within marriage into motherhood
without marriage and an individual struggle for survival. Significantly, women have never been provided for by men; men, on the
contrary, who predominantly relied on the economic contribution
made by women, no longer do so.

Concluding Remarks

A review of the effects of religious and economic changes leads to
the conclusion that production and reproduction relations, and the
accompanying social organisation of society, have fundamentally
changed in the course of a century. With the most important laws
and customs opposed and prohibited, with a new code of conduct
propagated by the missionaries and supported by the chief, along
with the privatisation and commoditisation of cattle, gender relations have changed. The introduction of wage labour and migration

abroad accelerated the process of commercialisation and disintegration of the kinship-based community. The political and economic power, control and sanctions of the chief and elders diminished. The regimental system lost its disciplining and economic value, disturbing the social organisation of the society even further. Individual sources of income through wage labour and commoditisation of products and services replaced exchange based on reciprocal kinship bonds and diminished the economic significance of subsistence agriculture. As a result, female arable cultivation became an additional subsistence source for the more affluent and a meagre, unreliable income source for the poor.

Marriage lost its central, regulating character, both economically and morally. On the one hand, women's labour power needed less regulation, as most economic surplus was derived from other sources, such as trade in hunting products, cattle and finally, wage labour. The political and economic dependency between women and men changed because of diverging interests. At the gender structure level, however, the sexual division of labour did not change. Women retained responsibility for subsistence production, whereas men's participation in trade and wage labour gave them access to an independent economic life. Women are still food providers, whereas men have been able to escape their economic role. The ideology of women as social minors survived but the ideology of domestication did not materialise, resulting in diverging interests of men and women, instead of political and economic interdependency between women and men as in the past. On the other hand, women's fertility became more difficult to control. The marriage age rose and premarital affairs became the rule instead of the exception. Unmarried motherhood was less penalised and the number of unmarried mothers increased, with growing social disruption.

It is against this background that we have to consider the growing numbers of unmarried mothers and female-headed households. Whereas in the past the *femme sole*, as Schapera indicated, was unable to develop an independent life, except when (secretly) escaping to South Africa, this opportunity has become accessible to growing numbers of women in recent decades. Women who are not married and stay behind in rural areas establish and manage their own independent households in increasing numbers, either as single mothers, or when divorced, deserted or widowed. Women also have the option of migration, especially when young and educated, and thus to become economically independent and start their own households.

At present, two different household development cycles operate alongside each other: the conventional but modified household development cycle of an unmarried woman who chooses a husband and establishes a household with him; and a female-headed household development cycle, consisting of mother, daughter and granddaughter. The daughter and granddaughter might in due course establish their own independent households and continue this cycle. Women are still food providers, but their economic domain has lost its potential. Consequently, women use all possible means for raising their children and for securing their subsistence, with and without men. As a result, the interest in controlling fertility in Botswana seems to have shifted from the hands of men into the hands of women.

The increasing numbers of female-headed households in Botswana find their roots in the whole range of historical socioeconomic factors, which have transformed gender relations in such a way that a *contradictio in terminis* was able to materialise: the female-headed household.

Notes

1. Between 1989 and 1992, I spent a total of 13 months in the Central District of Botswana to study the impact of the rapid socioeconomic changes on the position of rural women. This article is a synthesis of two other articles (see van Driel 1992, 1993) and forms a part of my Ph.D. dissertation—'Poor and Powerful: Female-headed households and unmarried motherhood in Botswana', 1994.
2. See for example, Head (1981); Brown (1983); Kossoudji and Mueller (1983); Kerven (1984); Government of Botswana (1992); Molokomme (1991); van Driel (1994).
3. Botswana (Tswana-land) is the name of the country. A citizen of Botswana is called a Motswana. The plural is Batswana. The language of the Batswana is called setswana. All four words have the stem—tswana—referring to the same ethnic origin. When using the term 'Tswana', two different meanings are intended. First, it is the ethnological and linguistic classification of one of the three major divisions of the Sotho group of Bantu-speaking peoples of central Southern Africa, living in present Botswana and South Africa (Schapera 1984: 9). Second, the term is used to include all citizens of Botswana, thus also all non-Tswana groups (Molokomme 1991: 41). When using the term 'Tswana' in

this study, both meanings can apply; when dealing with the situation before Independence the first meaning will apply, while the second is intended for the situation since 1966.

4. According to the Census of 1981, households headed by women, both *de facto* and *de jure*, numbered as much as 58 per cent in Paje (Government of Botswana 1982b: 50–154). Of the 181 households in Paje, 105 were headed by women and 76 by men. Unfortunately, the census data do not distinguish between *de facto* and *de jure* female-headed households.

5. According to Molokomme, the two categories of female-headed households and unwed mothers should be treated as analytically separate from one another (1991: 60–61). I agree that these categories need analytical isolation, but unmarried motherhood and female-headship of household are not mutually exclusive categories. On the contrary, I have the conviction that these two categories are increasingly overlapping.

6. See Comaroff (1985); Kinsman (1983); Kuper (1982); Schapera (1970a, 1978, 1984); Wylie (1990).

7. The Bamangwato arrived in this region of southern Africa around 1780 and had their capital at several places. In 1902 they moved their royal town to Serowe.

8. This indicates that pre-capitalist Tswana societies were not static, as alternate compositions also influenced the political and juridical systems.

9. See van Driel (1994: chapter 1) for an elaborate discussion on the concepts 'household' and 'family'. There the term 'household' is exclusively defined as a dwelling unit in the village, in which whole or part of an extended family is living. Hence, I take the *lolwapa*, the compound (the physical entity), as the unit of analysis.

10. According to Guy, women's economic position was not fully recognised. He argues that women's subjugation in this region took a special form and although it appears that cattle were the central asset of wealth and status, they were just the means of obtaining it. Cattle were owned by men and were the means of serving the main goal of these societies: the accumulation of people rather than goods. Due to lack of material production these societies were centred around human reproduction: subsistence production and women's childbearing capacity (Guy 1990: 37–38). Concentration on the accumulation of people comes to an end when accumulation of things becomes a central feature of society. This implies that with the introduction of capitalism, the organisation of a society and its specific gender relations change accordingly (ibid.: 43–44). For an assessment and criticism of Guy's theory in the Botswana context, see van Driel (1994: Chapters 2 and 3).

11. Although some women were able to gain power as oracles and prophets, the executants of the conventional religious practices were male priests.

12. Molokomme (1991: 48–49) refers to a discussion on the essential requirements for a valid Tswana marriage, concentrating on the question whether the emphasis of Schapera on *bogadi*, bride-price, is not too legalistic. Here the standpoint is taken that, traditionally, all three conditions were as important for the marriage process to make the marriage valid.

13. In this section on Christianisation and colonisation I focus mainly on the implications of Christianisation and commercialisation, as part of the colonisation

process. Since Bechuanaland was a protectorate and not a colony, the external political implications of colonisation were of greater interest for the British than the internal affairs. Whereas this chapter deals with the internal changes, the external implications of colonisation are beyond its scope.

14. The extent of their resentment of the initiation ceremonies, especially those of women, can be read from the letters from Reverend J.D. Hepburn (see Lyall 1895: 11–12).

15. Since the different ethnic groups had their own independent political and legal machinery for incorporating or opposing new norms, values and customs, there were considerable differences between the eight major groups. Khama, the chief of the Bamangwato, was both a dutiful Christian and vigorous ruler who succeeded in directing and controlling social and economic changes with relatively little opposition (see for example, Head 1981 and 1984; van Driel 1994: chapter 3). Hence the differences among the Bamangwato and the Ngwaketse, when comparing changes in customs and laws in Molokomme, this volume, and in my contribution (see also Schapera 1937; 1966; 1970a and b; 1984).

16. Commoditisation refers to the process of goods and services becoming commodities primarily produced for and exchanged on the market.

17. In this study, Schapera also reports on the fine imposed upon the woman's lover. On the one hand, this fine was considered an innovation, referring already to the fact that they themselves were aware of the diminishing impact of the traditional sanctions. On the other hand, the fine indicated that the act of impregnating an unmarried girl was still considered an offence that had to be punished. Marriage was still the ideal (Schapera 1933: 84–85).

18. Note that the percentage of incomes derived from agriculture in the early 1940s, as supplied by Schapera, is similar to that of 1965.

References

Brown, B., 1983, 'The impact of male labour migration on women in Botswana'. *African Affairs 28 (328)*: 367–88.

Comaroff, J., 1980, 'Bridewealth in a Tswana chiefdom', in J.L. Comaroff (ed.), *Meaning of Marriage Payments*. London and New York: Academic Press.

———, 1985, *Body of Power, Spirit of Reistance: The culture and history of a south African people*. Chicago and London: The University of Chicago Press.

———, 1993, 'Commercialization of labour and its impact on gender relations in Botswana', in H. de Jonge and W. Wolters (eds.), *Commercialization and Market Formation in Developing Societies*. Nijmegen Studies 14. Saarbrücken: Verlag Breitenbach.

———, 1994, *Poor and Powerful: Female-headed households and unmarried motherhood in Botswana*. Nijmegen Studies 16. Saarbrücken: Verlag Breitenbach.

Government of Botswana, 1982a, *Migration in Botswana: Patterns, causes and consequences*. Final Report, National Migration Study, Volume 1, 2, 3 . Gaborone: Central Statistics Office.

———, 1982b, *Summary Statistics on Small Areas* (For Settlements of 500 or More People). 1981 Population and Housing Census. Gaborone: Central Statistics Office.

Government of Botswana, 1991, 'Population Census—Preliminary Results 91/4', *Stats brief.* Gaborone: Central Statistics Office.

———, 1992, *National Development Plan 7:* 1991–97. Gaborone: Ministry of Finance and Development Planning.

Guy, J., 1987, 'Analysing pre-capitalist societies in southern Africa'. *Journal of Southern African Studies 14 (1):* 18–37.

———, 1990. 'Gender oppression in southern Africa's pre-capitalist societies', in C. Walker (ed.), *Women and Gender in Southern Africa.* Cape Town: David Philip, and London: James Currey.

Head, B., 1981, *Serowe: Village of the rain wind.* London: Heinemann.

———, 1984, *A Bewitched Crossroad.* Craighall, South Africa: AD Donker.

Izzard, W., 1985, 'Migrants and mothers: Case-studies from Botswana'. *Journal of Southern African Studies 11 (2):* 258–80.

Kerven, C., 1984, 'Academics, practitioners and all kind of women in development: A reply to peters'. *Journal of Southern African Studies 10 (2):* 259–68.

Kinsman, M., 1983, 'Beast of burden: The subordination of southern Tswana women, ca. 1800–1840'. *Journal of Southern African Studies 10 (1):* 39–54.

Kossoudji, S. and **E. Mueller,** 1983, 'The economic and demographic status of female-headed households in rural Botswana'. *Economic Development and Cultural Change 31 (4):* 831–59.

Kuper, A., 1982, *Wives for Cattle: Bridewealth and marriage in southern Africa.* London: Routledge and Kegan Paul.

Lyall, C.H. (ed.), 1895, *Twenty Years in Khama's Country and Pioneering Among the Batauana of Lake Ngami: Told in the letters of the Rev. J.D. Hepburn.* London: Hodder and Stoughton.

Molokomme, A.L., 1991, 'Children of the Fence: The maintenance of extramarital children under law and practice in Botswana.' Leiden: University of Leiden, Ph.D. thesis.

Narayan-Parker, D., 1983, *Women's Interest and Involvement in Income Generating Activities: Implications for extension services.* National Institute of Development Research and Documentation, Working Paper no. 44. Gaborone: National Institute of Development Research and Documentation.

Parsons, Q.N., 1974, 'The economic history of Khama's country in southern Africa'. *African Social Research 18:* 643–75.

———, 1975, '"Khama & Co." and the Jousse Trouble, 1910–1916', Journal of African History 16 (3): 383–408.

———, 1977, 'The economic history of Khama's country in Botswana, 1844–1930', in R. Palmer and N. Parsons (eds.), *The Roots of Rural Poverty in Central and Southern Africa.* Berkeley and Los Angeles: University of California Press.

Rubin, G., 1975, 'The traffic in women: Notes on the "political economy" of sex', in R.R. Reiter (ed.), *Toward an Anthropology of Women.* New York: Monthly Review Press.

Schapera, I., 1933, 'Premarital pregnancy and native opinion: A note on social change'. *Africa 6 (1):* 59–89.

———, 1937, *The Bantu-Speaking Tribes of South Africa: An ethnographical survey.* London: George Routledge and Sons.

Schapera, I., 1947, *Migrant Labour and Tribal Life: A study of conditions in the Bechuanaland protectorate*. London: Oxford University Press.

———, 1966, *Married Life in an African Tribe*. Whitestable: Latimer.

———, 1970a, *Handbook of Tswana Law and Custom*. London: Frank Cass.

———, 1970b, *Tribal Innovators: Tswana chiefs and social change 1795–1940*. London: The Athlone Press.

———, 1978, 'Some notes on Tswana bogadi'. *Journal of African Law* 22 (2): 112–24.

———, 1984, *The Tswana*. London: Routledge and Kegan Paul.

Tlou, T. and A. Campbell, 1984, *History of Botswana*. Gaborone: Macmillan Botswana.

van Driel, F., 1992, 'Marriage in Botswana—From rule to rarity?' A discussion paper, presented at the Gender Network, University of Botswana, April 1992 and at the conference 'Changing Gender and Kinship in Sub-Sahara Africa and South Asia', 22–26 February 1993, University of Nairobi.

Walker, C., 1990, 'Women and gender in southern Africa to 1945: An overview', in C. Walker (ed.), *Women and Gender in Southern Africa*, Cape Town: David Philip and London: James Currey.

Wylie, D., 1990, *A little God: The twilight of patriarchy in a southern African chiefdom*. Johannesburg: Witwatersrand University Press.

World Bank, 1990, *Poverty: World development indicators*. New York: Oxford University Press.

3 State Formation and Transformation in Gender Relations and Kinship in Colonial Sri Lanka[1]

Carla Risseeuw

The impact of state actions on the intimate life arrangements of marriage, kinship and gender relations in colonial Sri Lanka is elaborated. Areas of social life which had remained outside the control of a centralised state or religion came under the purview of state governance with British colonial rule. Legislation and policy worked to institutionalise monogamous, virilocal, lifelong marriage; made women legal and economic dependents; created the category of bastards; and led to the devaluation of women labourers. The economic interests of the colonial rulers lay in the marketability of land and labour, which required clear-cut ownership rights to economic resources. While their actions facilitated this, their endeavours were tied also to their patriarchal and male-focused ideology. Furthermore, in the new competitive economic structures, the changes in marriage and family bolstered the attempts of both the old and new élite to limit the demands on their resources. The gradual and inexorable move in family relations went almost unnoticed due to a number of factors. It occurred over a long period, in small shifts, picking up on trends of male bias and inequality which were present

in precolonial structures. The interests of those involved were differ-
entiated and/or not seen as affected. Thus the 'margins of common
sense' were slowly pushed rather than openly challenged.

Introduction

Seventeen years ago, Rayna Rapp in a short article (1977) emphasised the need to undertake research into the origin of state formation and its impact on kinship structures and gender arrangements.
Much earlier, Engels (1884) in his famous work 'The Origin of the
Family, Private Property, and the State', had developed a framework which connected the growth of private productive property
to the decline of a communal kinship base. In the process, marriage
became more restrictive, legitimacy of heirs more important and
wives became means of reproduction for their husbands. Linked to
this was a privatisation of the household and of labour in the
household, curtailment of reciprocal relations among kin and a
growing unequal degree of access to the created productive
resources. Egalitarian, kinship-based societies were transformed
into those based on hierarchy and class.

The hypothesis closely linking the formation of class-based societies to the creation of the patriarchical family has yet to be
examined through detailed research. Rapp makes a plea for such
work:

> State formation and penetration is processual; its form and
> force are highly variable, both within and between societies . . .
> but . . . the power of the state to penetrate and reorganize the
> lives of its members is clear (1977: 314).

Although Rapp's article could not be other than tentative, its
value lies in framing questions on the conditions under which
gender and kinship are transformed, questions which may otherwise be erased before they can be addressed. Social science inquiry
continues as if state formation, large-scale economic change or the
effects of colonial rule are disconnected from changes in gender,
family and kin relations. This hinders an analysis attempting to
pose questions not only in relation to changes in people's degree of
wealth or poverty, employment, or education, but also into the
nature of their intimate life arrangements and support networks.

This chapter discusses one case of state interventions in the intimate life arrangements of marriage and family affecting gender relations and the position of the more vulnerable family members vis-à-vis those who gained in power within their kin networks. In describing this process, the chapter points to the influence of decisions which were being taken partly on the basis of the 'common sense' of the policy makers. While colonial policy and rule changed the life conditions of the subject people, neither the implementors, nor the leading élite members of the colonised seemed fully aware of the consequences for women or other vulnerable family members. This was possible as, for both parties, the belief in so-called 'natural' gender relations meant non-recognition of the fact that in practice they are to a large extent shaped by economic and political factors and thus also subject to change.

The example discussed here is that of the Sinhalese in Sri Lanka under British colonial rule (1795–1947). British colonialism differed from its European predecessors (the Portuguese and the Dutch) in that it established rule over the whole island. This had seldom occurred in the nearly 20 centuries of documented Sri Lankan history. Colonial rule also established its brand of capitalism, which reallocated land-ownership and reshaped avenues of social mobility, through the redistribution of existing, and the creation of new, resources. In the process, families, family members, and men and women found themselves confronted with differing opportunities and developed varied strategies in response.

The basic thrust of the discussion is the emphasis on the deteriorating impact of colonialism on the position of women and the degree of security offered by kinship relations. My findings correlate with those of other feminist writers, who have elaborated on the theme of devaluation in the position of women in societies under European colonialism (Etienne and Leacock 1980). In highly differing cultures in North America, Africa and Asia, imported economic forms and ideology affected not only the access to resources such as land and labour, but also the degree of women's participation in decision-making structures within their marriages, families and communities. Such changes have to be related to the complexity of total change the societies have undergone, which requires a detailed historical analysis. The colonised societies of the 19th and 20th centuries were extremely varied and often had virtually no more in common than foreign domination itself. The degree and length of colonial domination was also subject to great variation.

However, the mutations in the position of women which took place prior to colonisation should not be underestimated. Leacock has pointed out that the enthusiasm to expose the destructive effects of (neo)colonialism, at best divided into different economic phases of European expansion from mercantilism to full-fledged industrialisation, also caused a neglect of precolonial history.

> Indeed, there is almost a kind of racism involved in the assumption that cultures of Third World peoples have virtually stood still until destroyed by the recent mushrooming of urban industrialization (Leacock 1981: 17).

This point can be further worked out in societies with an extensive written history prior to colonisation, as in Sri Lanka. The colonial history of Sri Lanka, especially the south coast of the island, is relatively long; almost four centuries of successive invasions by the Portuguese, the Dutch and the British. The formation of hierarchy mentioned by Rapp had largely taken place before the advent of the first European colonialists. It can be surmised that there were several shifts in gender relations during these centuries. Therefore, I start with a short elaboration on precolonial Sinhalese Sri Lanka, before continuing with the processes engendered by the only European coloniser who established an island-wide colonial state.

The Position of Sinhalese Women Before Colonialism[2]

Long before the advent of European colonialism, Sinhalese society had developed apparent characteristics of stratification, including hereditary kingship, aristocracy, a central religion sanctioned by royalty, military powers, tax collection, trade and the use of currency (de Silva 1981; Hettiarachchy 1972). At the same time, a degree of 'upward mobility' was possible and could even become pronounced when new forms of economy, such as sea trade, gained influence. The uneasy equilibrium between forces striving for central control and those attempting to break through, or rather into, the system, resulted in a society of conflicting interests and subsequently, struggle (Kulasuriya 1976). This struggle occurred mainly within the élite, both traditional and newly founded, and centred primarily on its male members.

Several writers have noted the relatively better position held by women in Sinhalese society in earlier centuries (fifth century BC to fourth century AD) when compared to the Middle Ages (Dewaraja 1980; Goonatilleke 1982, 1983; Horner 1978; Law 1927), although much research still remains to be done. Their findings are based on the position of women in the fields of religion and the state, and the manner in which they are portrayed in the literature and plays of that period in history. No information is available on a change in their position in marriage, as Buddhist marriage remained a lay affair and relatively few written references were made on the subject.

As far as religion was concerned, the Buddha allowed women to enter their own orders, which was a revolution in his day. When Buddhism came to Sri Lanka, women established their own religious orders and gained exceptional prominence.[3] Women were thought capable of attaining the high spiritual state of *Arahatship*, while the highest state of Buddhahood could only be achieved if she was first reborn a man. Despite occasional ambivalence, the Buddha was known to speak highly of women. Early Buddhist literature is said to be less denigratory of women than the mediaeval writings of a later date (Goonatilleke 1982: 35). It is significant that the oldest chronicle of Sri Lanka, the *Dipavamsa*, was written by nuns and describes the history of Buddhism on the island. It is known to give greater prominence to women and their role in bringing Buddhism to the island than the later chronicle, the *Mahavamsa*, which was written by monks. Currently, it is the latter chronicle which is more frequently referred to, this being but one example of the imperceptible ideological shift from a female to a male perspective. In the course of time, there was a clear decline in women's religious status from approximate parity with men. After the destruction of Anuradhapura[4] and the Buddhist orders in the 11th century, only those of monks were reinstated. Since then, nuns never regained their own orders and have had a low status in Sinhalese society. Several historical accounts refer to their unsuccessful resistance to this situation, and currently new efforts are being undertaken (Goonatilleke 1983).

In affairs of the state, references to women are rarer as kingship, aristocratic and military leadership were mainly male domains. Nevertheless, in early history there are references to women being trained in warfare and science (Ellawala 1969: 88) and, in the 1st century AD, there are still references to women who held titles in the feudal hierarchy in their own right.[5] Women were also known to be involved in trade and travel to the coast for this purpose (ibid.: 82).

In the literature of almost any period there is a recurrent theme emphasising the evil side of womanhood and the necessity for males to curb her power, lest she lead to their spiritual and/or social downfall. However, a difference in emphasis can be detected. For instance, in the first chronicle, the *Dipavamsa*, women are described as having played an active part in bringing Buddhism to the island, especially through their access to the supernatural. In the well-known Jataka Kata (Cobwell 1957), which has been re-written by monks over at least twenty centuries, women are often depicted as evil, scheming beings[6] who can nevertheless be admired for their cunning and cleverness. The literature of the Kotte period (preceding the Portuguese period), profoundly influenced by the contemporary Hindu culture, depicts a similarly evil woman, but here her passive, beguiling beauty receives far more emphasis than her active, scheming qualities.

These shifts in emphasis become all the more interesting when set against the pre-Buddhist cultures of Ceylon. These are described as being centred on a female ancestor, tracing descent through the female line (Nagas) or as having been matrilineal, and having practised polyandry (Yakkhas) (Paul 1929: 278). Although these cultures are now completely forgotten, the first Buddhist monks incorporated some of their beliefs in order to hasten the acceptance of Buddhism among the people. For instance, the worship of spirits living in trees is said to be transformed currently into a recurring worship of certain trees in parts of the island and in reverence for the Bo tree in Buddhist philosophy (Paranavitana 1929: 315). Examples are also found of deities of the Yakkha period, which have been transposed into central figures of Buddhist mythology (de Silva 1981: 50; Saratchandra 1952).

In studying the distant past, one also stumbles on two versions of the myth depicting the origin of the Sinhala race (Paranavitana 1931: 310). In the version accepted today, a prince named Vijaya (or Simhala) is the mythical conqueror of Lanka. The second version accorded a role to his sister as well as to him. Vijaya's sister left her father's palace in a boat, as had her brother, and founded a civilisation on another island. She became known as the ancestress of a race of Amazons or 'Western women'. According to Paranavitana, this woman, known as the Sister of Simhala, was venerated among the Sinhalese as the 'Western Queen' (ibid.: 309).[7] Mediaeval travellers, like Marco Polo and Ibn Batuta, referred to the existence of an island to the west of India, which was inhabited by a race of Amazons. Although references to these 'Western queens' are found in the Buddhist chronicle, the *Maha-vamsa*, and also in Sinhalese folklore,[8] and a place of worship is said to have been reserved for them near the Western Gate of Anuradhapura (Geiger 1908), in later periods this version of the myth seems to have disappeared. It is virtually unknown nowadays.

At this stage these findings must remain speculative, but they do justify the research Rapp had called for into the relationship between the dimming of a female presence in history and the rise of a centralised state and religious power. They also indicate a society undergoing deep-felt changes, in which women venerated for their fertility were slowly transformed into beings feared for their evil and fickle character[9], long before the advent of European colonialists.

Turning now to a more specific period in history, the 19th century, this chapter attempts a concrete and documented analysis of a process of change in which women and less influential family members lost socially and economically. As the society was already highly stratified and feudal, I first concentrate on the access of women (particularly of the more privileged sections of society) to land and property through marriage and inheritance. In the second part, I focus on peasant women's degree of access to labour and trade.

Colonial Impact on the Position of Women

The Portuguese (1505–1640) and the Dutch (1640–1795) ruled only in the coastal areas, but had a profound influence on the economy and social life of those regions. The brands of Christianity introduced to the island, including concepts of sex and marriage, conflicted deeply with those of the local people and, to an extent, with the Hindu-coloured ideology of the élite. As is found in the literature of the Kotte period, for the local people marriage did not necessarily take the monogamous form preferred by the colonialists. There is an amusing anecdote recorded by a Portuguese officer at the beginning of the 16th century, who encountered a

Sinhalese woman complaining about her eight husbands. He gallantly offered to chase away or even kill seven of them. The woman, however, replied that she wished to retain at least four. This had mystified him sufficiently to remark on it in his writings, leaving us with one of the few comments on Sinhalese women made by the Portuguese military (Peiris 1909).

Later writers in the Dutch and British colonial periods elaborate a picture of a society in which sexual relations in general, and marital relations to some extent, were not made much of, but 'considered rather as casual and inevitable incidents in a person's life' (Peiris 1956: 197). Initial reports concentrated on the aspects of the marriage systems encountered which, to them, seemed shocking and chaotic. This led them to overlook the importance of family bonds, which gave men and women greater economic security than marriage itself. Apart from fraternal polyandry and the practice of infanticide, group marriage was practised (Davy 1821; Knox 1911; Le Mesurier 1860). A man could be married in a fraternal polyandric union and also have a monogamous union with a wife in a separate home. Instances of polygamy are also recorded. These facts, and the observation that people often entered into four or five marital unions during a lifetime (Knox 1911: 171–79), completed the European judgement of horror and amazement.

The Portuguese could not induce even their own personnel to enter into permanent monogamous unions, as, during their period of domination in Ceylon, a process leading to such marriages sanctioned by the state was only just being introduced. At a later stage the Dutch faced similar problems, although a negative judgement on sexual relations outside marriage had become more pronounced. A judgement on sexual behaviour became an important indicator of a person's morality. Leading Sinhalese were forced in growing numbers to marry officially and monogamously within Dutch churches, if they wished to pursue a career in the Dutch colonial service. Public power and morality thus became fused, while the position of a wife under Dutch law became equated to that of a minor. Obviously, the vast majority of the population still remained unaffected by such laws.

It was only under British colonisation (1795–1947) that the traditional forms of family and marriage were systematically attacked and brought under degrees of state control, which in themselves formed a fundamental break with a tradition where neither the state nor religion interfered with marriage and family life. In the course of time, under the influence of British attempts to change the 'traditional' and Roman–Dutch laws of marriage then prevailing, detailed studies were undertaken to obtain a better understanding of how the system worked (Hayley 1923; Jayewardene 1952). Two forms of marriage were recognised in relation to residence and property: the virilocal *diga* marriage, in which the wife went to live on her husband's land, and the uxorilocal *binna* marriage, where the husband lived on his wife's family land and the children took the mother's family name. In the latter case, the husband acquired no right to his in-laws' land and was liable to expulsion or divorce by the wife or her parents (Peiris 1956: 204).

In this system the phenomenon of a bastard child was not recognised. All children born to a woman were accepted by her family, provided they were fathered by men of similar or higher rank/caste (Hayley 1923). A child became a bastard only if a woman had mated beneath her caste, in which case her male family members (including her husband if she was married) had the right to chastise and even kill her in order to restore the dignity of the family. This last practice was in conflict with British concepts and they tried to curb these male rights within the family and replace them with marriage laws, whereby a man could be brought to court for killing his wife.

One of the most significant consequences for women in the earlier system was the great importance of the family as a social unit, which implied that even after marriage they could fall back on their family of origin. In practice, this meant that a woman who returned to her father's or mother's family from a *diga* marriage would regain her right to own the land and could be married in *binna* by her family. In *binna* marriages similar rights were accorded to the husband within his family of origin.

The complex rules of inheritance of hereditary and acquired property, of divorce by the consent of either party, of the relative lack of maintenance obligations for a husband towards his wife— as they were unnecessary—of the strong economic position of the widow, as well as the custom on divorce by which the husband's family could take the sons and the wife's family the daughters cannot be elaborated upon here. I can only summarise three trends which developed with the implementation of the British marriage laws (see also Goonesekere in this volume).[10]

In the first place, the legislation worked towards a monogamous, lifelong union, sanctified by the state and/or the church, with preferred virilocal residence and patrilineal inheritance.

Second, a woman's relative independence in marriage, provided by her lifelong access to land and property and the right to divorce, shifted to the position of a legal and economic dependent with limited divorce rights, to be protected by her husband and, on his default, by the state. Her position became one which was at best secure but lacked economic potential. Even as a widow her rights to land and property were curtailed (Hayley 1923: Ch. 5). The fact that the British extended the wife's rights compared with the prevailing Roman–Dutch law, in which her degree of dependency on her husband was comparable to that of a child (Jayewardene 1952), does not contradict this basic trend.

Third, legislation reduced the number of persons for whom older family members could be legally held responsible, by creating a category of 'bastards' and by altering 'adoption' from a family decision into a legal procedure (See Goonesekere in this volume). The new system thereby created a greater inequality of access to family land and property among family members, coupled with a reduced responsibility of the newly privileged for the less privileged—the former being found only among selected male members.

British Legislation on Marriage and Inheritance

The reshaping of the marriage and inheritance laws was a process covering most of the 19th century. The first laws passed made the practice of infanticide a crime (in 1823 and in 1842) and also required the registration of every birth. In 1846, bigamy was made unlawful; in 1859, polygamy and polyandry were mentioned by name and prohibited, and a marriage had to be registered. Non-registration was punished with a fine. Possibilities for divorce were severely curtailed and divorces were only legal if the decree was passed by a District Court. Under the new laws it was easier for a man to claim divorce from his wife than vice versa (Books of Ordinances 1823; 1842; 1846; 1859).

In 1869/70, debates arose between Government Agents and the Governor, when it became apparent that the majority of the people were ignoring the new legislation, leading to an 'alarming rise in bastardisation of the population' (Sessional Papers 1869/70a: 1). In 1870, the law was further amended (Book of Ordinances 1870); while in 1919, the payment of alimony and maintenance of children in the case of divorce was regulated by the Provincial Register.

These new laws raised a great deal of passive and active resistance from the Sinhalese and it is by no means certain that the British were totally successful, even by their own standards. Nevertheless, monogamous marriage has become the rule and today, about 80 per cent of marriages are said to be registered. *Diga* marriages are on the increase in preference to *binna* marriage. Polyandric unions have become relatively rare occurrences. Earlier marriage customs are forgotten by many sections of the Sinhalese population; at best they are remembered as quaint, at times embarrassing customs of the past, especially amongst the élite and middle class.[11] That this could take place in a relatively short period of just over 100 years poses several questions in relation to socialisation, family networks and relations between spouses, to which I return later.

To further understand how such drastic changes in the relationships between the sexes could take shape in such a relatively unnoticed manner, two factors may be considered:

1. The reasons underlying the British implementation of this policy and its association with their strategy regarding the main resource involved, namely land.
2. The response of different layers of the Sinhalese population to the implementation of these new policies.

British Land Policy

When analysing the dynamics of change, it is evident that it will not suffice to explain it at an ideological level alone by emphasising the moral indignation felt by the British and, to a degree, shared with the earlier colonisers. A more crucial factor emerges in explaining the policy on marriage laws during the period 1800–1870 when one looks at what happened to the most important inheritance, namely land.

The commercial land policy of the British, with the development of plantations, has been well documented. To implement this policy the British concentrated initially on alienating vast tracts of land on behalf of the European capitalists. The way was prepared in 1833, with the Colebrooke Cameron Papers (Mendis 1956), while in 1840 the Waste Land Act was passed, which claimed all land for the Crown unless property rights by individuals could be proven. Several additional ordinances followed between 1841 and 1907, all consolidating the initial policy outlined. Much of this alienated land was utilised in the so-called 'Coffee Boom' of the 1840s and was sold mainly to Europeans.[12] Tea and rubber plantations were to follow.

The process of changing land-ownership in the non-plantation areas has not been well documented. In these regions, a Sinhalese Revenue Officer, the Mudaliyar, was installed, who had far-reaching powers to reallocate and divide land between Crown property and property belonging to villagers. The Mudaliyar was the official tax-collector and, as a principal government informant, he also decided when a villager could not pay taxes and thus had to sell his land. In areas of the country with the highest population density (the southern and western parts of Sabaragammuwe provinces), this included sales of undivided shares, which meant that if one shareholder could not pay tax the whole field was sold. This highly intricate process is well analysed by Obeyesekere (1967) who, in this context, speaks of dramatic and serious consequences to the Sinhalese social structure, giving not only European capitalists, but also local village headmen, Mudaliyars and those with capital, great opportunities to expand their landed property.[13]

With the introduction of the Waste Land Act and the Crown Land Ordinance, land had not only been taken out of Sinhalese hands, it was also redistributed on a new basis of individual ownership and monetary purchase. Land became concentrated in fewer hands, but including those of rising élites. Mobility between and within castes became a reality. This new mobility did not result in an easy accumulation of wealth. Every financial or social mistake was dearly paid for. A misguided marriage alliance could inhibit absorption into the sought after élite. Endless struggles in the form of petitions had to be waged to enter public service, in competition with the British as well as the traditional élite for the higher posts (Peebles 1973). It was within the context of these new forms of land tenure and ownership that the revised marriage legislation gained momentum and reduced women's access to landed property, by means of the altered marriage laws.

When seen in the light of this land policy, it becomes clear that a form of enduring monogamy, preferably limiting economic power to one of the spouses and reducing the responsibility networks from a large extended family to a smaller unit, is a necessary prerequisite for a successful transition to the private initiative and ownership envisaged by the British. This is not the same as saying that the British officials were consciously changing the marriage patterns in order to fit their economic policy. On a conceptual level, economic policy and land-ownership were logical components of one design, but it is doubtful that a similar correlation was made consciously to reduce the economic power of women within their families. Most British officials probably felt this to be too minor a matter to require specific attention. It is important to realise that modifications in the position of women could thus be effected while remaining relatively unnoticed among the many changes taking place.

I now explore the reactions of the Sinhalese, mainly that of the male élite, who served as informants and intermediaries for the British, to the changes in marriage legislation.

The Sinhalese Response

Initially, most Sinhalese ignored the legislation passed in 1846, in which divorce options were limited and subject to a court decision and polyandry as well as polygamy were forbidden. Their refusal to adopt the British marriage laws became clear from the many government agents' reports of 1869/70:

> It is probably within the mark to assume that 65 per cent of the existing unions are illegal and that 80 per cent of the rising generation born in the last 8 or 9 years are illegitimate (Sessional Papers 1869/70a: 1).

Although registration of marriage was not widely practised, it could suddenly show fluctuations, as for example, when there was a rumour that, via the Census, young *unmarried* men would be selected and sent to Europe to replace casualties in the Franco–German War (Administration Report 1872). However, as time passed, more serious problems cropped up when inheritance conflicts arose within a family and the new laws had been ignored.

When family members disagreed, they could try to involve the new rulers to achieve what they conceived of as their rights; however, if divorce had to be registered many difficulties arose, since usually the marriage had not been registered in the first place.

> Nearly all the squabbles and crime among the villagers have their origin in the present difficult and expensive way of getting separated. Their old customs admitted divorce by mutual consent in cases of unconquerable aversion or utter incompatibility of temper, and this generation cannot eradicate this from their minds (Sessional Papers 1929: Entry No. 17).[14]

At times, British officials wrote expressing their disagreement with the new legislation and even noted the detrimental effects it was having on the inheritance rights of women and children. One of them, an Irishman and an Acting District Judge named Berwick, stood up for his convictions that neither 'uncertainty of paternity' nor the wife's ownership of land and property was connected to a high rate of instability in marriage. On the contrary, he foresaw that the changes planned would lead to increased violence, both in the *diga* and *binna* forms, while the position of the wife and children would be marked by growing insecurity, including violence. Although he called compulsory registration 'a bitter gift of bastardy' to the people, his writings received no response worth mentioning from the British colonial authorities (Sessional Papers 1869/70b: 2). It also became clear that 'high people' and headmen were more amenable to registration, while the mass of people were far slower (Sessional Papers 1869/70c).

At this point, it is important to look into the specific reactions from the élite, members of whom could benefit by the new land registration. In 1855 (nine years after the British declaration that bigamy was unlawful; fifteen years after the Waste Land Act and five years after the Coffee Boom), the Governor received a petition from the chiefs of Kandy 'praying for the abolition by legislation of polygamy and polyandry', which was described as a 'grievously wrong custom and one exceedingly unsuited to the present state of the Memorialists' (meaning the writers of the petition). The problems they encountered centred around:

> . . . the great barrier which now exists for a deceased person's rightful heirs succeeding to his Estate can be traced to the lax

state of the law of marriage; and all Judges and Magistrates conversant with the business of Kandyan courts will bear ample testimony to the truth of this statement (Ward 1864: 451).

As they continued, it became clear where they located the problem of their existing marriage system—in the right of (divorced) daughters to return to their brothers' homes and reactivate their land claims—

> That in numerous instances parents are reduced to poverty solely in consequence of their *married daughter*, and her issue, being thrown upon them for support and maintenance, and this the Memorialists submit, is a clear result of the existing law regulating the marriage contract among them (Ward 1864: 451).

The document ended with a plea to the Governor to 'adopt some measures' so that 'the present grievous state of things may be averted'. As this petition had no effect it was followed by a second one in 1858 and later that year by a Memorial, signed by 8,000 'Kandyan chiefs, headmen and people' (Roberts 1975: 29).

The British were initially reluctant and mystified by what they termed as a 'golden opportunity' (Roberts 1975: 30) and, after further questioning, decided that the Kandyan petition, although claiming to speak for the whole population, had in fact spoken for the élite only (ibid.: 31). Nevertheless, they did make use of the apparent change in attitude and implemented the 1859 Marriage Ordinance referred to earlier, an ordinance described by the Governor as:

> A novel and curious attempt in Eastern legislation and the outcome of a spontaneous attempt on the part of the Kandyans to elevate and purify their institution of marriage (Roberts 1975: 31).

Although historians have described this process and noted the connection between marriage customs and land disputes, they have not yet looked at it from the perspective of women (Roberts 1975: 72). However, it is clear that these petitions were a thinly disguised assault on the independent position traditionally held by women within marriage, the rules of inheritance and, more generally, the structure of responsibilities in kinship networks. It remains unclear in what number and to what extent the Memorialists were aware of this.

In the implementation of a widow's rights, the pressure of the male élite is clear as well. The British seemingly grasped this extremely alien marriage system from the information supplied by male Sinhalese intermediaries, but in relation to the rights of the widow, persistent confusion occurred. Either the Sinhalese informants were less clear on this issue for reasons of self-interest, or the British officers remained unable to grasp this part of the traditional law.

Women traditionally held substantial rights to dispose of their own property, both ancestral and acquired. In principle, this could lead to a situation where a widow could alienate her husband's lands from his family by remarrying in *binna*. Though she passed his land to her children by him, if there were only daughters married in *diga*, the land went into another family. How far this occurred in reality we will never know, but it is significant that the confusion regarding a widow's rights persistently cropped up in terms of the degree of independent use she could make of her inheritance.

The process was gradual, but inexorably towards the British concept of a widow's maintenance, implying that, at best, she could only have a life-interest in the landed, inheritable property, as a guardian of her minor children (Hayley 1923: 352).

It is submitted that in cases of doubt . . . the soundest course is to adopt that view which restricts rather than which enlarges the widow's interest. It is clearly most in accordance with the spirit of the law to keep property in the family as far as possible, and, so long as the widow is well provided for during her life, there can be no equity which calls for an enlargement of her interest so as to enable her to transfer land to her own or a second husband's family (Hayley 1923: 368).

In this context, the findings of Obeyesekere (1967: 173) are relevant. When tracing cases of inheritance over several generations he came across the phenomenon of 'females being consistently excluded', of which he gives several detailed examples. The shift had been diffuse and long drawn out, as exceptions to this rule occurred even in the beginning of the 20th century.

This trend to limit women's rights in marriage also becomes apparent in the British analysis of the frequency of *diga* and *binna* marriages, as they assumed the latter to be dying out. With the shift to monogamous lifelong unions, the traditional marriage patterns of *diga* and *binna* assumed a different character, in the sense that they became lifelong arrangements. Earlier, not only did people enter into more than one union, a union could shift between *diga* and *binna* forms. Thus, the same numerical frequencies at these different points in time had very different social implications.

If a man married in *binna* he would be socially inferior to his wife's relatives, who held the land and whose name the children would bear. The same case applied to women in a *diga* marriage. As the new avenues of mobility were open mainly to men, one can expect a trend among them to avoid *binna* marriage, and for brothers to opt for a *diga* marriage for their sister in order to terminate her rights to the family property. In the 20th century when statistics became available, we indeed see that *binna* marriage was on the decline (Vital Statistics Reports 1946; 1956; 1962). Furthermore, an increasing number of marriages were taking place under the General Marriage Law (originally introduced by the Dutch), whereby Kandyan Marriage, in time, came to appear more like an aberration than a norm. By 1962, statistics no longer incorporated the distinction between *diga* and *binna*.

Marriage and Inheritance Legislation in Retrospect

A prerequisite for the British overall economic policy was the changing of the land tenure system from one which incorporated the interests of all, to one in which land-ownership became individualised and marketable on the basis of monetary purchase. This policy deeply affected the distribution of land among the Sinhalese and resulted in a loss for the poorer sections, while sections of the élite managed to survive or better their position. Within the family too, the British policy created a conflict of interests. Although this does not adequately explain the trend to exclude women from access to land, it does explain the pressure to reduce family responsibility. The British economic policy required swift decisions on land transactions, taken preferably by one family member. However, on paper it should have made no difference whether this was a man or a woman. In theory, one can visualise a system of individual land-ownership existing within a system which included *binna* and/or *diga* marriage forms (but as lifelong unions), and in which men and women of the élite could both strive directly for land-ownership, depending on their position in the marriage. That such a system was not encouraged by the British is explained by the extreme male domination in British colonial society. This was not only in their outlook, based on the existing concepts of gender relations in Britain where state-controlled monogamy and primogeniture were a reality, but also in the fact that the British colonial service was open only to men. This was in contrast to the former colonialists, who, while only relying on male staff, could not enforce monogamy even among their own soldiers and sailors.

However, the fact that women lost their traditionally advantageous position cannot be solely explained by the British policy. Part of the explanation must be sought in the fabric of the society in which the British policies were implemented. In the Sinhalese society of that time, public positions were already mainly in male hands and the men were the obvious persons to deal with the British. Family relations had remained relatively equitable and free from state control, although, earlier in history, marriage alliances had become one of the platforms on which the struggle for greater influence in the Kandyan kingdom had been fought. Thus, although male domination in British and Sinhalese societies at this time were of a fundamentally different character, women held a socially weaker position in both. This made it possible for a deterioration of women's rights in marriage and inheritance to take place relatively unnoticed at the policy level. Women did resist loosing control of their land and property. Government Agents' diaries and even a short look at the registration-lists of petitions, bring this to light (Risseeuw 1991: Ch. 1 and 2). However, they fought as individuals at particular phases in their life-cycle, with little opportunity to gain a public platform.[15]

The process of change whereby there is a shift of power between individuals within a group seems to gain momentum in situations of scarcity, leading to intensified struggle. The struggle among the leaders of a threatened community or family becomes paramount and the interests of others have a lower priority. In this case, not only did the poorer sections of the population suffer but also the weaker family members, among whom women paid a high price.

The Case of Peasant Women: Labour and Trade

In relation to marriage and inheritance legislation, the position of landless and poor peasant women initially remained relatively unaffected compared to the position of women in families with substantial property and other resources. The majority of the poorer classes ignored the demand for registration of marriage as there was no incentive to respond, except in relation to land-ownership.

Over several decennia of British rule, the peasantry was confronted increasingly with land-scarcity and degrees of landlessness, aggravated by the rise in population in the 1920s. Towards the end of the 19th century, landlessness was still recorded occasionally in the registers of the Government Agents. In areas where land-shortage was acute, the high incidence of litigation was explained as a peculiarity of the 'nature' of the inhabitants correlated to the local, disproportionately high crime rate. In 1905, this area was introduced to the newly arrived government agent of the Southern Province as being the 'most criminal province' in the whole of the British empire (Sessional Papers 1897).[16]

A first suggestion to curb the land-shortage was to change the 'multiple inheritance' to primogeniture as was practised in England. However, the Governor himself disagreed with the suggestion as the sudden introduction of such a measure would deprive three-fourth of the population of their property. The upsurge of crime it would result in would burden the judiciary to a degree they would not be able to handle. In developing his argument, the Governor even pointed out several 'minor' issues, which are relevant to my current argument. He refers to the resulting insecure position of the dependants (for example, unmarried females and males under 18) of a single heir.

> . . .what is to become of them if the heir in possession sells the property? . . . It is difficult to believe that peace and good order will be secured by a system under which the heir in possession is obliged not only to maintain, but to keep living in the house with him and his wife, a number of maiden sisters . . . (such) proposals are out of the question . . . . After all the rule under which brothers and sisters inherit equal shares is one which prevails . . . over the greater part of the civilised world (Sessional Papers XL 1910b: Part 8).

Government officials articulated the consequences of changing the inheritance system when it affected the younger brothers in a family and not only the women. One feared implementing legislation which could increase crime as 'sons might as well buy a knife and stab each other, as has happened in so many cases' (Sessional Papers XL 1910c: 8/9).

Until 1927, the government had taken the view that land-scarcity and rising crime were but consequences of 'the irreversible process of development'. However, a series of locally formulated petitions and hesitant reports from (Assistant) Government Agents, who were regularly confronted with the rural population, finally alerted the higher authorities to the seriousness of the issue. The Land Commission was installed, which reported in 1929 that 'there is a serious danger of this class (the peasantry) going to the wall' (Sessional Papers XXXV 1929: 2). This led to a series of land settlement schemes, where land-ownership was circumscribed such that when an allottee died, it could not be passed on to 'a minor, a woman or some other person not capable of developing the land' (Sessional Papers 1941: 44). Upto this day, land settlement schemes, for example, the current large-scale Mahavelli Scheme, has not made adequate provision for women owners.

Outside the settlement schemes, the vast majority of the poor were confronted with minute land-shares and family members who could now apply several law systems to make their ownership claims. This led to cases, recorded extensively in the entries of Government Agents' diaries as 'hotbeds of undivided shares', whereby women were at times openly accused of 'being at the bottom of all quarrels' (Government Agent Diaries, Southern Province 1910). By this time, quarreling family factions were often basing themselves on the 'customary law' introduced by British legislation, selecting for themselves the most beneficial law.

In retrospect, one can say that the British administration mis-recognised the growing land-scarcity, as they lacked an economic incentive to give priority to the problem. In a later study, it was found that between 1871 and 1946 there was a fourfold increase in the number of landless/surplus families on the land, and that by 1937 over 65 per cent owned none or less than one acre of land, of which 40 per cent seemed to have no obvious occupation (Sarkar 1957: 217–22).

It is against this background that the peasantry increasingly turned to labour and trade as a source of income, and men and women were confronted with different opportunities. Between 1871 and 1946, statistics were regularly collected on labour activities, which provide several relevant insights:

- From the earliest statistics (1901), it is significant how often women are mentioned as participating in the agricultural sector, where they are noted as paddy cultivators and unspecified labourers.[17] Thus at the start of the 20th century, women participated substantially in agriculture as well as land-ownership.

- Second, an increasing number of occupations were listed in the Censuses of 1870, 1884 and 1901 in the category 'industrial class', indicating the involvement of the population with non-agricultural activities. Initially, women seemed to have found growing access to this sector and were represented in occupations which nowadays appear to be totally part of the male domain: carpenters, watch repairers, building contractors, mechanics, iron and steel workers, brass and copper bell workers, butchers, etc., although men were in the majority.[18]

- It, however, also becomes clear that while women initially penetrated a wider range of jobs than they do nowadays, they frequently landed up in the lowest-paid sectors. In the figures for trade, termed the 'commercial class', this impression is confirmed, as well as for the professional class, where women entered new avenues in medicine and education. Nevertheless, here also they occupied the lower-paid sectors.

- A fourth finding is that women were more firmly entrenched in those occupations considered their domain in the pre-colonial sexual division of labour. It is also in these sectors (for instance, all kinds of weaving, and food and drink processing) that women managed to maintain a relatively higher degree of control when their product became commercialised. However, it is striking that as the most profitable sectors of the 'female domain' were commercialised, male ownership increasingly penetrated them (See Risseeuw 1991: 108–10).

- Finally, most of the new occupations created by the colonial economy were considered masculine by the colonisers, thus providing most labour opportunities for males.[19]

Summarising, one can probably say that both sexes were confronted with immensely harder work conditions. There were advantageous opportunities for a minority, which was predominantly but not exclusively male. The tendency was for men to take over female domains if they became lucrative, a phenomenon which did not apply vice versa. Thus, slowly women found themselves in the least beneficial sectors of paid labour and trade.

Although with difficulty, changes in the position of men and women can be traced and it is evident that family and kinship relations were also greatly affected. First, in areas with high levels of landlessness, unemployment and population pressure, such as the Southern Province and Jaffna in the north, land disputes were most frequent and involved conflicts between family members. Second, in these areas, migratory labour became the norm and even before 1900 the Southern Province has always recorded more female than male inhabitants. Migration was induced by a lack of land and jobs, especially along the coastal strip of the South.

The constant wars during the Portuguese and Dutch colonial periods which had caused local people in the coastal areas to flee to the hills must have seriously disrupted their (family) lives. Men were frequently taken away to fight battles, often without payment, leaving women to fend for their families and themselves. In the British colonial period this process continued in a different form, as labour became a marketable entity for which a wage was paid. In such a situation married women, who in contrast to unmarried ones could not migrate easily, were forced to rely on jobs available in their village, with a growing dependence within families on women's economic contribution. One of the home-industries which grew in importance in this situation is the coir industry, which currently still provides a (meagre) income for over 25,000 women (Risseeuw 1987). Women from both the South and the North entered domestic service in large numbers and also left their homes for long periods at a stretch.

Family-specific information is rare. Government records only noted the high incidence of poverty during periods of recession, at times voicing the view that the 'teeming masses of the poor classes of Asia . . . (have) been accepted as a more or less necessary evil' (Sessional Papers XXIX 1937: 1). Social workers and their relief organisations regularly emphasised the fact that many families were breaking up. Men were absconding from their familial duties and their wives were left solely responsible for their families (Sessional Papers VII 1937). Likewise, a government committee on the situation of domestic servants highlighted the flourishing exploitative practices as linked to the inability of employees to return 'home' (Sessional Papers 1935). Finally, the casual but regular entries in Government Agents' diaries are revealing. One of them is the repeated mention of local women waiting outside their offices for a chance to speak to them on the issue of their missing daughters, supposedly employed as domestic servants (Risseeuw 1991: 115).

Misrecognition of the Female Worker

Elsewhere, I have elaborated on the hypothesis that, in a fashion comparable to their élite peers, male peasants were in a mounting struggle between themselves to gain access to meagre and changing resources. In the process, they marginalised their women in society as well as in the family (Risseeuw 1991).

Referring to the earlier described mystification of the relation between British land policy and the legislation on marriage and inheritance, I would like to draw a parallel in relation to the peasantry. In the first case, the interests of women were not much contested in that they somehow never seemed to surface as an issue. A similar phenomenon occurred with the definition of the 'female worker' in the various Census reports of 1870, 1884, 1891, 1901, 1911, 1921, 1930 and 1946.

While the initial census reports noted each occupation in detail, later ones increasingly made use of summarising categories of labour. In the process, certain unformulated assumptions on male and female labour predominated. The concept of 'female worker' never gained a high legitimacy from a state-determined perspective. It was defined differently at each census, leading to huge disparities in the supposed female participation rate in the paid labour force. Before 1946, they fluctuated between 30 and 48 per cent.

After 1946, census reports 'professionalised' their categorisation system even further, leading to a growing invisibility of female labour, which thereafter seldom reached more than 20 per cent of the total labour force. During the period 1953–71 for instance, the percentage of 'own account' or 'unpaid family' labour dropped from 45 to 13. Instead of interpreting this as a negative, if not threatening development, it was seen as a result of progress; where most displaced workers were female and therefore 'less likely to seek alternative employment' (Census Report 1971).

When analysing the shifts in definitions, one finds that they are based on three persistent misconceptions, which census officials could seldom have encountered in the field, but which they nevertheless regularly reported. These misconceptions arose from a 'common sense knowledge' which enumerators applied without thinking. These faulty conceptions were the singular focus on 'formal sector' activities, the notion of the man being the sole breadwinner and the notion of one job per person. These conceptions likewise rendered invisible changes between family members and their earning capacities. In certain respects the mechanism was similar to that employed when analysing the scarcity of land. By discounting the female half of the population in search of land, land pressure was reduced. By the 1950s, labour opportunities had diminished (as the supply of land had earlier) and a reduction on paper of the number of people seeking work was one way of keeping rising unemployment figures down. Again, we cannot say that this was done from a conscious strategy to exclude women. The effectiveness of the policy was based precisely on the fact that it seemed like 'common sense' and required no further explanation.

Common Sense and the Transformation in Gender Relations

Although this chapter cannot fully address all the questions cited at the outset, it brings out several characteristics of the changing relations between the sexes and family members during the British colonial rule of Ceylon. I speak of a transformation in gender relations as these changes apply not only to the access to society's resources, but also to the manner in which they were conceived. In Sri Lanka, 'marriage', 'divorce', 'adoption', 'offspring' and the 'rights of the widow', all gained new meanings, incorporating the new reality and facilitating a misconception of the women's position (see Goonesekere in this volume; 1987; 1985; 1984; 1982; 1980). At a later stage, the concept of 'female worker' was added to the list.

To understand the extent of this transformation, one has only to place oneself in the position of a woman in a polyandric or *binna* union to realise how different her outlook on human relations, and more specifically family relations, must have been from that of a woman married in a monogamous, lifelong *diga* marriage among her in-laws. Her perception of her worth for her own relatives and her children, and her position vis-à-vis her husband(s) would have had a radically different emotional content. In the first case she possessed a source of active economic power to protect and influence the lives of her children, who would subsequently have regarded her in a different light unlike the children in the later case. The latter's relationship with her children had to depend more on 'love' since she could do little more than manipulate/ influence their father and his relations on their behalf. A comparable difference must have applied to men in the two marriage systems. Both, women and men, are likely to have had totally divergent perceptions of self, of each other and their relationships, and will have created entirely different processes of socialisation. Children will have grown up with transformed interpretations of what women and men could 'do' or 'be' in the family and society at large.

Such transformations in the content of human relations are seldom recorded. Examples, however, can be traced. Tambiah for instance, noticed in his study on polyandry in Ceylon, that older males would calmly explain the system of wife-sharing and 'sexual jealousy was not considered the ground for keen friction or disruption' (1979: 293). In contrast, the younger men would be amused and embarrassed if questioned, while firmly stating never to consider marrying in polyandry, 'I wouldn't like to eat off the same plate as another man' (ibid.: 296–97). Here, one sees a shift in emotional experiencing of intimate relations in a relatively short time-span. Unfortunately, none of the (male) researchers on polyandry have ever thought of interviewing women and children on the same topic.

Summarising, the main elements to be kept in mind when analysing this process of changing gender relations:

- Changes seem to take place through a process of increasing inequality of access to resources between the sexes.
- Further, these changes seem to take place most effectively if they can take place over a substantial period of time—a century or more. In the described case-study, the time span facilitated mystification of the process. The implications of change for women could remain diffused. Decisions and counter-decisions seem to have taken place in the sphere of 'common sense', at intervals of 10 to 20 years or more.

- A woman's interests appeared unrelated to the central issues being debated and thus could not be raised, while slowly and imperceptibly she became an outsider in her own world.
- With the growing degree of state control with its—in this case—capitalist and individualised market relations of land, labour and capital, one sees the concept of 'a person with certain rights' emerge. This had consequences: family life, initially outside the political and religious sphere, was transformed as the state gained basic control. However hypothetical at first, people acquired a dual position. One was within their kinship and marriage system, the other was as a citizen with a different set of rights and duties. In the case of women especially, this could lead to widely divergent positions. While on paper the colonial state, however contradictory, articulated a philosophy of 'equal opportunities for all', in practice it often eroded the more balancing access to resources between genders in the kinship system. It also eroded the degree of support family members could ideally expect from their wealthier and more powerful members.
- Precolonial gender relations influenced 'the margins of common sense'. The position of women prior to European colonisation, although in many respects preferable, had not been on par with their men. The relatively secure and comparable position was confined to kinship arrangements. As mentioned in the beginning of this chapter, there are substantial indications of a gradual dimming of their presence in the nineteen centuries of written history before colonialism. This precolonial process of changing gender relations facilitated the further loss of ground during British rule. If women had retained a share in public authority and religion, and if the female principle had been more pronounced in the religious/cosmological world, the promotion by British colonialism of exclusively male participation in certain sectors may at least have resulted in an articulate conflict.
- The transformation process was characterised by a rising struggle for resources and increasing possibilities of upward and downward social mobility created by British macroeconomic policy. The colonised resisted and confused their coloniser, but they also faced an increased conflict between themselves, in which the weaker members of the society and family stood to lose.

- This was not a straight process of the all-powerful dominating and reshaping the lives of the dominated. This view would simplify the intricate levels of resistance by various levels of society and the genders. The powerful had the dubious privilege of remaining (partially) unaware of the consequences of their policies. In situations where common sense notions are not contested, they influence decision-making without being noticed. In this case one can, for instance, argue that capitalism was not gender-blind in its thrust for economic development. To succeed as a policy, the new colonial economy required hierarchy in families, reduced familial responsibility and swift decision-making. It did not require males to take precedence over females. The expanding avenues of agriculture, trade and employment could have held equal benefits and equal obstacles for both men and women. In reality they did not. However, this was not due to the demands of the economic policy but to it being implemented by people who, acting from their own gender perceptions, were only partly aware of the implications of their actions for gender relations.

- A final point I would like to make is the need to understand how such macro, partially state-controlled processes of change influence not only the intimate life arrangements, but also the emotional experience, of the actors involved. In this case, the number of people for whom responsibility of different kinds was held was modified. But also, the most intimate and 'natural' or common sense parts of these marriage and kinship relations appeared liable to change. This case-study demonstrates the need for further research into the dynamic relations between such seemingly disconnected processes.

Notes

1. My grateful thanks to Rajni Palriwala and Savitri Goonesekere for their thorough and stimulating comments on earlier versions of this chapter.
2. In this section, I focus on the position of women with little reference to the family, due to paucity of data.
3. For example, in the 5th century AD, Sinhalese nuns were invited to China to assist in the ordination of women there (Goonatilleke: 1984).
4. The kingdom of Anuradhapura ended in the 11th century AD.
5. The title of *paramuka* was held by women in their own right in the 1st century AD (de Silva 1981: 23). Gentry can be equated to the title of *paramuka*.

6. See, for example, the following legends in Cobwell's work (1957: 32, 61, 62, 63, 64, 66, 102, 106, 120, 147, 318, 374, 402, 433, 436, 537).

7. Geiger (1908) also mentions the 'Western Queens', although he has no further knowledge of these figures.

8. Paranavitana (1931) has come across the name Stripura, city of women, in Sinhalese folklore.

9. 'When does the shift take place from "Female" as a symbolic of positive fertility to "Female" as temptation to evil?' (Leacock 1981: 28).

10. For a full discussion, see Risseeuw (1991: Chapter 1).

11. In economically poorer circles, the new norms are regularly ignored, as is shown in the powerful documentary film *Illegitimate* (Lal 1985).

12. In 1840, 78,686, acres were sold; by 1843, this had increased to 230,000 acres of which 2/3 went to European buyers. In 1850–57, the area used for coffee plantations tripled and after 1860, a new era of massive land sales began (Snodgrass 1966: 22).

13. For example, between 1880 and 1888, in six of the nine provinces where the Ordinance was implemented, 29,899 sales of paddy land in default of tax payment were effected by the Crown. Between 1878 and 1888, in five provinces, one in every 26 acres was sold. In Galle and Matara districts, these figures were even higher (Obeyesekere 1967: 120–22).

14. See also Sessional Papers XL 1910: 8–9, the response of Mr. C.M. Lushington, Government Agent, Southern Province, in this respect.

15. Although the statistics of the time are by no means reliable, it is striking how frequently women are mentioned as owners, planters or higher staff. In the Census of 1884, for example, 1,525 women are noted as landed proprietors, compared to only 425 men. However, the majority of owners of modern plantations were men. In 1901 nearly 34 per cent of the landed proprietors were recorded to be female. Nowadays land-ownership statistics are not recorded, but such a high proportion of female landowners seems unlikely (Risseeuw 1991: 89).

16. The highest crime rates on the island were found in the most densely populated areas where land-scarcity was most pronounced: the south of the island and Jaffna in the north.

17. See Risseeuw (1991: 102–12) for a more detailed account.

18. In 1871, women workers in the industrial class appear in 16 of the 44 listed occupations; in 1884, in 48 of the 71 mentioned; and in 1901, in 120 of 172 (Risseeuw 1991: 106).

19. An exception being formed by teaching and nursing, which the colonial gender ideology perceived of as female.

References

Administration Report, 1872, *Section: Report Registrar General of Marriage, Birth and Death on Figures of 1871*. Colombo: National Archives.

Books of Ordinances, 1823, Ordinance No. 9; 1842, Ordinance No. 2; 1846, Ordinance No. 7; 1859, Ordinance No. 13; 1870, Ordinance No. 3. Colombo: National Archives.

Census Reports, 1870, 1884, 1891, 1901, 1911, 1921, 1930, 1946, 1971. Colombo: Department of Census and Statistics.

Cobwell, E.B., 1957, *The Jataka Stories: Stories of Buddha's former births*. London: Pali Text Society.

Davy, J., 1821, *An Account of the Interior of Ceylon and of its Inhabitants: With travels in that island*. London: Longman.

de Silva, K.M., 1981, *The History of Sri Lanka*. Colombo: Ceylon University Press.

Dewaraja, L., 1980, *The Position of Women in Buddhism*. Kandy: Wheel.

Ellawala, H., 1969, *Social History of Early Ceylon*. Colombo: Department of Cultural Affairs.

Engels, F., 1884, *The Origin of the Family, Private Property and the State*. Edited by E.B. Leacock. New York: International. Reprinted in 1972.

Etienne, M. and E. Leacock (eds.), 1980, *Women and Colonization: Anthropological perspectives*. New York: Praeger.

Geiger, W., 1908, *The Mahavamsa*. London: Pali Text Society.

Goonatilleke, H., 1984, *Contemporary Buddhist Nuns of Sri Lanka: Intellectual and spiritual struggles within an unequal framework*. Colombo: University of Kelaniya.

——, 1983, *Female–Male Relationships in Buddhism*. Colombo: University of Kelaniya.

——, 1982, 'The position of women in Buddhism from a historical perspective'. *Logos*, (Centre for Society and Religion, Colombo) 21(4): 33–41.

Goonesekere, S., 1987, *Sri Lanka Law on Parent and Child*. Colombo: Gunasena.

——, 1985, 'The impact of the UN decade for women on the legal status of Sri Lankan women', Unpublished paper.

——, 1984, 'The application of the personal laws in Sri Lanka: A reappraisal', in H. Claude (ed.), *Sansoni Felicitation Volume*. Colombo: Cave and Co.

——, 1982, *Law and the Status of Women*. Women's Bureau of Sri Lanka, Colombo.

——, 1980, *The Legal Status of the Female in the Sri Lanka Law Relations*. Colombo: Annasena.

Government Agent Diaries, Southern Province, 1910, *July No: 58*. Colombo: National Archives.

Hayley, F.A., 1923, *A Treatise on the Laws and Customs of the Sinhalese, Including Portions Still Surviving Under the Name of Kandyan Law*. Colombo: Cave and Co.

Hettiarachchy, T., 1972, *History and Kingship in Ceylon*. Colombo: Lake House.

Horner, I.B., 1978, *Women in Early Buddhist Literature*. Kandy: Buddhist Publication Society.

Jayewardene, C.E., 1952, *The Roman Dutch Law of Divorce with Special Reference to Ceylon*. Colombo: Apothecaries.

Knox, R., 1911, *An Historical Relation of Ceylon*. London: Chiswell.

Kulasuriya, A.S., 1976, 'Regional independence and elite changes in the politics of 14th century Sri Lanka'. *Journal of the Royal Asiatic Society of Great Britain and Ireland* 2: 136–55.

Lal, I., 1985, *Illegitimate* (16 mm documentary film). Colombo: Centre for Ethnic Studies.

Law, B.C., 1927, *Men in Buddhist Literature*. Colombo: Bastian.

Leacock, E., 1981, *Myths of Male Dominance: Collected articles on women cross-culturally*. New York: Monthly Review Press.

Le Mesurier, C.J.R., 1860, *Niti Nighanduwa or the Vocabulary of Law as it Existed in the Last Days of the Kandyan Kingdoms*. Colombo: Government Printer.

Mendis, G.C. (ed.), 1956, *The Colebrooke Cameron Papers: Documents on British colonial policy in Ceylon: 1796–1833*. Oxford: Oxford University Press.

Obeyesekere, G., 1967, *Land Tenure in Village Ceylon: A sociological and historical study*. Cambridge: Cambridge University Press.

———, 1963, 'The great tradition and the little tradition in the perspective of Sinhalese Buddhism'. *Journal of Asian Studies* 22 (2): 139–54.

Paranavitana, S., 1931, 'Pre-Buddhist religious beliefs in Ceylon'. *Journal of the Royal Asiatic Society* XXXI (82): 302–28.

Paul, S.C., 1929, 'Pre-Vijayan legends and traditions pertaining to Ceylon'. *Journal of the Royal Asiatic Society* XXXI (82): 263–85.

Peebles, P., 1973, 'The transformation of a colonial elite: The mudaliyars of the 19th century Ceylon'. Unpublished Ph.D. thesis, University of Chicago.

Peiris, P.E., 1909, *Ribeiro's History of Ceilao*. Colombo: de Conto.

Peiris, R., 1956, *Sinhalese Social Organisation*. Colombo: Ceylon University Press.

Rapp, R., 1977, 'Gender and class: An archeology of knowledge concerning the origin of the state'. *Dialectical Anthropology* 2: 301: 308.

Risseeuw, C., 1991, *Gender Transformation: Power and resistance among women in Sri Lanka*. Delhi, Manohar.

———, 1987, 'Organisation and disorganisation: A case study of women coir workers in Sri Lanka', in A. Menefee Singh and A. Kelles Viitanen (eds.), *Invisible Hands*. New Delhi: Sage.

Roberts, M., 1975, *Facts of Modern Ceylon History through the Letters of Jeronis Peiris*. Colombo: Hansa.

Saratchandra, E.R., 1952, *Folk Drama in Ceylon*. Colombo: Department of Cultural Affairs.

Sarkar, N.K., 1957, *The Demography of Ceylon*. Colombo: Government Press.

Sessional Papers, 1869/70a, Papers Relating to the Operation of the Kandyan Marriage Ordinance No. XIV, Minute by the Governor. Colombo: National Archives.

———, 1869/70b, Further Papers Relating to the Kandyan Marriage Ordinance 1869, from Mr. Berwick, Acting District Judge, Colombo, to the Honourable Colonial Secretary, 11 October 1869. Colombo: National Archives.

———, 1869/70c, Government Agents of Sabaragammuwe and Matale.

———, XL, 1910a, The Response of Mr. C.M. Lushington, G.A., Southern Province. Colombo: National Archives.

———, XL, 1910b, Proceedings of Low Country Chiefs, Answer of Governor to Mr. Kindersley, A.G.A., Matara, Part 8 . Colombo: National Archives.

———, XL, 1910c, Proceedings of Low Country Chiefs, No. 11. Colombo: National Archives.

———, 1929, Papers relating to the Kandyan Marriage Ordinance 1869, No. 3. Entry no. 17, Response from G.A., Matale. Colombo: National Archives.

———, XXXV, 1929, Former Reports on No. 8 Waste Land Ordinance 1927. Colombo: National Archives.

Sessional Papers, 1935, Report of the Joint Sub-committee of the Executive Committees of Home Affairs and Education on the Employment (Domestic Service) of Women and Children and the Control of Orphanages. Colombo: National Archives.

———, VII, 1937, Unemployment in Ceylon. Comments on Social Service League. Colombo: National Archives.

———, XXIX, 1937, February. Report on Nutrition in Ceylon, Part 2. Colombo: National Archives.

———, V, 1941, Report to draw up a Scheme for Settlement of educated young men on the land through the medium of existing schools. Colombo: National Archives.

Snodgrass, D.R., 1966, Ceylon: An export economy in transition. Homewoods, Illinois: Irwin.

Vital Statistics Reports, 1946, 1956, 1962. Colombo: Department of Census and Statistics.

Tambiah, S.J., 1979, 'Polyandry in Ceylon', in C. von Fürer-Haimendorf (ed.), *Caste and Kin in Nepal, India and Ceylon*, London: East West.

Ward, H.G., 1864, 'Speeches and Minutes of the late Sir Henry G. Ward, 1855–1860.' *Sessional Papers*. Colombo: National Archives.

4   Gender, Kinship and the Control of Resources in Colonial Southern Ghana[1]

Dzodzi Tsikata

Prior to the passing of the 1985 Intestate Succession Law, inheritance rules favoured the lineage over the conjugal unit in both matrilineal and patrilineal groups in southern Ghana. The law was enacted in response to demands pertaining to the difficulties faced by widows and children. The lineage had survived a range of socioeconomic developments following the establishment of a (colonial) state and cocoa dominated economy, but with a diminished role in the acquisition and distribution of resources. Simultaneously, the conjugal family had also been strengthened. Along with intra-lineage stratification and the concentration of lineage resources in fewer hands, this resulted in competing claims over an individual's self-acquired resources and conflict—within the lineage, between the lineage and conjugal family, and within the polygynous conjugal family. This clash of interests carried implications for gender relations and limitations on legal reform on the part of the post-colonial state. Women, as wives, responded through various non-legal strategies. Their attempts at legal redress were limited by confusion in the law, different interpretations by various adjudicators, contradictions between coexisting laws, and gender discriminatory concepts and notions carried within the law and by its implementors, particularly the assertion that customary law was unchanging and irreversible.

Introduction

This chapter discusses aspects of the economic, political and social processes in parts of southern colonial Ghana,[2] and their effects on existing social relations. Specifically, it explores the establishment of a state and cocoa dominated economy and the responses of the lineage and the conjugal family in both patrilineal and matrilineal kinship systems. The discussion explores the competing claims between the lineage and conjugal family, and within the conjugal family itself, on the individual's cocoa derived resources and its implications for gender relations in these institutions and in the society as a whole. Also of interest are the attitudes of the colonial state, and the various interest groups in the Colony, to the responses of the lineage and the conjugal families to these developments.

Colonial Ghana was formally colonised by the British between 1901 and 1957. However, the economic, social and political processes under discussion, began with the first European (Portuguese) contact with the Coast in 1471. It was an area of about 9,200 square miles, made up of a group of territories: the Gold Coast Colony in the south, Asante in the middle belt, the Northern Territories, and the British administered portion of the trust territory of Togoland in the east, which became a part of the Gold Coast after the first World War (WW1) (Hinden 1950).

This exercise is to contribute to a deeper understanding of the nature of gender inequalities in access to, ownership and control of resources in Ghana today; illuminate the difficulties encountered by the post-colonial state in its attempts to reform these inequalities and; hopefully, aid future policy reform. These concerns are important in the light of the limitations of the Provisional National Defence Council's (PNDC)[3] Intestate Succession Law, PNDC Law 111 of 1985. This was the first successful attempt in Ghana's history to explicitly acknowledge changes in the character of lineage and conjugal relations.[4] Law 111 was passed in response to demands that the hardships suffered by widows and children as a result of their lack of property rights under customary law be modified.

Before this law, inheritance rules in Ghana favoured the lineage over the conjugal unit. In both patrilineal and matrilineal societies, traditional political office, property and descent were transmitted through the lineage. Spouses, in both patrilineal and matrilineal groups, could not inherit property from each other and children in matrilineal areas could not inherit their father's property. Children from patrilineal groups, on the other hand, inherited from both parents. In both patrilineal and matrilineal groups, persons were succeeded by particular categories of lineage members, preferably of the same sex. Among the matrilineal Akan,[5] a successor was a *de jure* trustee, but the *de facto* chief beneficiary of the estate (de Graft–Johnson 1974), whereas among the Ewe[6] and other patrilineal groups such as the Larteh,[7] succession was distinct from inheritance (Brokensha 1966; Nukunya 1975). A successor's task was to distribute the property of a deceased man or woman among the latter's children, when they were of age. In the distribution of landed property, among the Ewe, sons received larger portions than daughters. No such inequality has been reported for the Larteh (Brokensha 1966; de Graft–Johnson 1974; Nukunya 1975).

Of significance is the fact that widows and children were inherited, along with moveable and immoveable property and liabilities, among both patrilineal and matrilineal groups. The successor was expected to take responsibility for the children[8] and the widow. If she elected not to marry the successor, she was given a customary send-off. The point here is that the widow's right to refuse to be inherited was compromised by the real danger that she and her children would not benefit from her deceased husband's estate. The successor, on the other hand, was free to refuse to inherit the widow.[9] The checks on the conduct of successors was largely moral and anecdotal evidence indicates that their neglect of the conjugal family had become an issue since the colonial period.

It is almost anomalous to describe with such certainty the customary law rules which governed intestate succession and inheritance before 1985. However, the exercise is useful in so far as it is a statement of the rules which were applied to disputes and which were the bedrock on which variations were made in everyday life. Since the colonial period, individuals have increasingly varied these rules in practice. For example, in early post-colonial Akwapim, some (patrilineal) Guan, probably under the influence of their matrilineal Akan neighbours, reportedly gave their matrilineal kin portions of self-acquired property (Brokensha 1966). More significantly, there was a strengthening of the conjugal family's claim to resources as a result of greater urbanisation and the increase in virilocal residence. These developments were manifested in the increased incidence of joint conjugal property among the urban élite and the making of statutory wills. Also, Christian churches[10] in both urban and rural areas developed rules for distributing intestate property which gave specific portions to wives, children and lineage members (ibid.). It has been observed that inheritance depended on factors such as the 'age and sex of the deceased, the presence of a will, number of widows and children, ages of the children, relationship between the deceased and his lineage, size and composition of the estate, encumbrances on the estate and the ability and honesty of the successor' (ibid.: 218).

In spite of this situation on the ground, post-colonial attempts at legal reform of the customary rules of inheritance were unsuccessful[11] until the 1985 PNDC Law 111, which sought to unify the rules governing the inheritance of property of individuals who died intestate, irrespective of the character of their marriages and the customary succession rules of their communities. Both, the spouse(s) and children, were given independent portions of the bulk of self-acquired property of a deceased intestate. The Law is only a recent and limited acknowledgement of the contributions of the conjugal unit to the acquisition of conjugal resources. For example, there is no law to address the distribution of resources in customary divorces. The customary law,[12] of both patrilineal and matrilineal groups, does not recognise non-monetary contributions to the acquisition of property during married life. What a man is required to do after a customary divorce is to give the woman a 'send-off' if the divorce is through no fault of her own. The value of this 'send off' is discretionary. Both parties can demand the repayment of debts and some of the expenses incurred on each other's behalf during the marriage, including the bride-price (Brokensha 1966; Economic Commission for Africa 1984).

The courts have similarly maintained—in relation to ordinance marriages[13]—that housekeeping is a marital duty and therefore does not bring rewards such as a share of the property acquired by the husband while the marriage lasted. In order to succeed in any such claims, spouses must show a substantial contribution beyond the call of duty. Under the Ordinance, maintenance provisions are made for a needy spouse and her children.

Another limitation of the Intestate Succession Law is that, eight years after its passage, its enforcement is still hampered by disputes about the applicability of its provisions to different categories of persons. The early cases had to address the question of whether or not Law 111 applied to the estate of persons who had died before its present passage and estates which did not have cases concerning their distribution pending before any forum at the time the law was passed. In *Ampoma (deceased): Oppong and others v. Oppong and Another*, H.C. 1987, the High Court held that Law 111 was not applicable, while in the 1989 and 1991 High Court and Appeal Court case of *Armah (deceased): Armah v. Armah*, both courts declared that the law was applicable to cases where the intestate had died before the passage of the Law and there was no matter pending at the time of its passage.

When Law 111 was passed, together with the Customary Marriage and Divorce Registration Law of 1985—Law 112—the non-registration of a marriage became a criminal offence, but it did not invalidate the marriage. A related issue was what constituted a valid marriage within the terms of the law?[14] In the case of *Re Pratt's Caveat: Bentil v. Pratt*, H.C. 1987, the judge suggested that non-registration of a marriage would render Law 111 inapplicable to the estates of both parties. In *Neequaye (deceased): Re Armah v. Annan*, H.C. 1988, *Essilfie v. Quarco*, H.C. 1991, the court was of the view that non-registration of a marriage was not a bar to the application of Law 111.

Another area of dispute has been the status of children born outside an ordinance marriage during its subsistence. While some courts have held them to be legitimate children under Law 111, which establishes a criterion of recognition (*Mensah v. Mensah* H.C. 1992), the judges of the Supreme Court, the highest court of the land, did not agree on the status of such children. Some have ruled that they were illegitimate and therefore with no locus, while others accepted them as surviving children within the terms of Law 111.[15]

Resistance to the law is reflected in these cases. In addition, with the lukewarm attitude of the enforcement agencies and inadequate knowledge about its provisions, there have been indications of non-legal forms of resistance, sometimes violent, to the law from those who stand to lose. The limits of the Intestate Succession Law and the patterns of resistance to past and present attempts at law reform are not simply cases of the law lagging behind social reality. They illustrate the difficulties in tackling inequalities in gender relations through legal reform in a complex situation of competing claims and interests within institutions and in the society at large.

This chapter is based on information from earlier anthropological and legal studies of the Asante empire (Arhin 1982 and 1983; McCaskie 1980; Rattray 1923 and 1929; Reynolds 1974; Wilks 1975), more recent gender sensitive perspectives (Hill 1963; Mikell 1989; Okali 1983; Phillips 1989; Vellenga 1974 and 1986) and records of the colonial administration and court proceedings.

Asante and its Southern Neighbours Before Colonisation and After European Contact

The discussion focuses on the sections of the Gold Coast Colony and Asante which were home to the matrilineal Akan and to which patrilineal groups migrated for economic reasons. The groups considered are the sedentary matrilineal Asante and Brong cultivators in Asante, migrant patrilineal groups such as the Guan and Akwapim, and the Krobo, Shai, Ga,[16] and Ewe from other parts of the Colony for the purposes of comparison. The Gold Coast Colony and Asante are of interest because the gold mines and the cocoa farms which were very crucial to the colonial enterprise were found in the two territories. They were also areas to which members of neighbouring communities from the north and south migrated in search of work. Therefore, economic and social processes in Asante and the Gold Coast Colony affected colonial Ghana as a whole.

Since Asante and its neighbours were largely subsistence agricultural societies,[17] land was the most basic resource. There was also some mining and trading across the Sahara that predated European contact. European commercial contact with the Coast in the 15th century displaced this trade and speeded up the development of a generalised exchange economy.

Precolonial Asante and its neighbours, though lineage based, had significant class and gender differences which were clearly visible during the 19th century (Rattray 1929: 341; Wilks 1975: 443). In Asante in particular, state formation and centralisation in the 17th and 18th centuries deepened the process of stratification. In addition, patrifilial[18] offices based on achievement emerged as a complement to the matrilineal lineage based ones.[19] The stools and offices inherited through the male line were created for economically and socially prominent male members of the society

(Arhin 1982: 4–8; McCaskie 1980: 23–24). In the late 19th century, the rise of the Asafo companies (urban based military organisations of young men) as defenders of the state during this period of wars and uncertainty was another significant development.

Mikell argues convincingly that these two developments posed a challenge to the matrilineal inheritance lines and the political, economic and social importance of women in traditional society (Mikell 1989: 17). It is important to point out that apart from patrifiliation, practices such as the mother's brother's control over his sister's children and the husband's rights in relation to his wife (ibid.: 110–12) show that matrilineality in Akan society was not synonymous with female dominance.[20]

The process of state formation also affected land relations. In Asante, a confederacy of states headed by a king (*Asantehene*), who was also head of the Kumasi State, was established. The states were composed of divisions which were made of villages, each level with its own ruler. The chiefs at each level of the hierarchy owed allegiance and paid tribute to the office holder immediately above them (Tsikata 1984).[21] Tributary relations developed between the rulers (the stools) and the ruled (the subjects). Obligations which became customary were extracted from individual cultivators by the family head[22] or village head, and portions transmitted upwards in the hierarchy (ibid.: 13–16). The development of tributary relations did not affect the strong ideology of communal ownership and the inalienability of land.[23] As developments in the colonial period showed, customary rules and institutions were not immutable. This view of land as being communally owned and inalienable was selectively used by the colonial state in response to rampant land sales by the chiefs.[24]

One important aspect of land rights was the rights of individual household member. In precolonial and colonial Ghana, among both patrilineal and matrilineal groups, the male headed conjugal family was an important unit of production. There were, however, variations in the organisation of production and consumption in the unit. Post-marital residence was usually virilocal in patrilineal areas. In matrilineal areas, spouses usually lived separately in their natal compounds with their mother/sisters, although virilocal residence was widely practised in larger communities (Mikell 1989: 110). In both kinship systems, post-marital residence depended on factors such as whether or not the union was polygynous, whether the parties lived in the same or in different communities, the youth of the bride and her situation in her natal family.[25] The point is that women lost access to lineage land for long periods in their lifetime.

Even where the spouses lived together, the customary rules ensured a strict division of property and resources. In addition to helping husbands on their farms, it was customary for wives to be given smaller adjacent plots by their husbands for their own use and benefit. In cases where wives had their own means of livelihood, whether as separate farms or in different lines of business, they owned the fruits of their labour and contributed to the provision of household and children's needs from those resources.

Rights in land and the ability to exercise them were affected by many factors. While both men and women did have access to lineage land in patrilineal as well as matrilineal groups, among some groups, women's rights were limited by marital residence and gender bias in the size of land given to them. The rights of spouses in each other's lineage land were inferior to those of one's own lineage members, since it depended on marital residence, the continued existence of the marriage, the goodwill of the spouse and the size of land s/he was entitled to.

The most crucial determinant of men's and women's rights in land was the sexual division of labour in both patrilineal and matrilineal areas. The clearing of land—the mode of establishing usufructuary rights in lineage land—was assigned to men, thus preventing the majority of women from acquiring such rights in forest land. A wife's duty to labour for her husband, without any reciprocal duty on his part, tended to sabotage women's attempts at farming for themselves and therefore their use of available land. These customary rights and duties, which were established before the colonial period, contributed to the problematic character of men's and women's relationship with the changes that colonialism and European ideology brought to Ghanaian society.

Colonial Policy After the Establishment of the Colonial State

It has been suggested that colonial policy was 'necessarily makeshift' because the state had to respond to situations it could not completely control (Phillips 1989: 11; see also Lovett 1989). This insight is supported by the important shifts and contradictions in policy during the lifespan of the colonial state. Two broad phases of colonial policy in Ghana have been identified. The first, from the 1890s until WW1, saw attempts to introduce wage labour and private property into the Colony (Phillips 1989: 11). Shifting cultivation and 'communal' land-ownership were considered detrimental to 'development efforts'. The period was marked by two failed attempts to pass Land Bills and colonial court decisions such as *Lokko v. Konklofi* (1907 *Ren* 450), which declared that a subject could acquire exclusive ownership of stool land through long occupation.[26]

The second phase, between the two World Wars, saw the adoption of the 'peasant road to development' (Phillips 1989: 85). In this period, the pace of land privatisation was considered problematic by the state for a number of reasons. The successes of cocoa had shown that production was safe in the hands of the peasantry on small plots of lineage and stool land. This circumvented the concentration of labour and capital required for plantation agriculture. It also shelved the need for land reform, thus averting the risk of alienating the chiefs and land owning groups.

Again, this phase in colonial policy was reflected in court decisions. In the landmark Nigerian case of *Amodu Tijani v. Secretary of Northern Nigeria* [1921] A.C. 399, the Privy Council, the highest colonial appeal court for all British colonies, decided that the traditional usufruct was an interest giving indefinite rights of beneficial use which fell short of ownership. Thus, precolonial land relations were reaffirmed in spite of earlier acknowledgement of changes. Ghanaian cases in this period followed this trend.[27] This denial of the growing privatisation of land was important in reinforcing lineage ownership of land.

Colonial ideology was an important influence on policy. Of interest here are elements of this ideology which promoted institutions and practices such as the nuclear family, monogamy and the housewife over the lineage and polygamy. The colonial courts, the educational system, the bureaucracy and the Christian missionaries worked actively to get these practices accepted. The notion of the nuclear family as consisting of a working man, a housewife and their children came to influence education and employment policies to the detriment of women and gender equality.

Colonial Administration

Native administrations were set up for chiefs, under the supervision of the colonial state, in both rural and urban areas in the Colony (Hinden 1950: 95–120). These institutions were responsible for law and order in areas under their jurisdiction. In addition, native courts, closely supervised by the central government, and native treasuries to finance native administration, were set up. Thus the day-to-day control of subjects was left to the chiefs.

For the chiefs, the economic and institutional changes under colonialism presented both new opportunities for accumulation and challenges to their hegemony. Quite early on, they were locked in a struggle with the colonial state about the basis of their powers, which the state resolved in its own favour by the passage of the Chiefs Ordinance of 1904. This law established the state as the source of authority of the chiefs, thus putting an end to their claims about their inherent traditional powers.

Another source of friction was the challenge posed by new influential groups—the intelligentsia, the merchant classes and the Asafo companies. The rapid alienation of land, excessive demands for communal labour and the imposition of taxes eroded the legitimacy of the chiefs. As a result, the traditional remedy of destoolment and the colonial court processes were invoked against them. The colonial state was very concerned about the high incidence of actions for destoolment (Mikell 1989: 88–89; Tsikata 1984: 90–91). There were also land disputes among migrants and chiefs, and between chiefs, for the control of cocoa land (Mikell 1989: 84–87).

Economic Policy

Colonial economic policy was centred on agricultural exports, trade and mining. Jobs were created in the mines, the bureaucracy and the construction industry. Formally educated persons were able to take advantage of the job opportunities in the bureaucracy. Keeping women out of the bureaucracy was explicit colonial policy (Economic Commission for Africa: 1984: 56; Mensah-Kutin 1986: 39). The few women who went to school were trained in home-making, thus disabling them from applying for clerical and administrative work (Prah 1992: 1–4). Initially, only men were recruited by chiefs for the mines and construction work. Later, women became part of the labour force that built the colonial infrastructure.

The colonial authorities were very active in the development of the cocoa industry, supplementing the efforts of the Basel missionaries by sponsoring selected males for training in cocoa culture, distributing seedlings, setting up demonstration farms, providing extension services and allowing the export of cocoa duty free. Most of the beneficiaries were male because women were not regarded as proper farmers (Mikell 1989: 101). The merchants supported the state by escalating buying prices and offering large advances and credit to cultivators. These measures contributed to steering peasant cultivation towards specialisation in cocoa, rapidly increasing cocoa exports.[28]

The earliest cocoa trees were cultivated in the Colony, particularly the Akwapim areas and the eastern Asante, by matrilineal farmers on lineage land. Matrilineal Akwapim farmers also cultivated cocoa on land purchased from local lineages (Hill 1963: 15–16). In the 1890s, many matrilineal Akwapim farmers migrated to neighbouring Akyim Abuakwa in the Gold Coast Colony to purchase land. By 1900, a scramble for land had developed in Akyim Abuakwa, which later spread to Asante. Patrilineal groups such as the Larteh, Krobo, Shai and Ga in the main, but also, Ewe, Dangme and Osudoku, formed companies made up of groups of male friends and purchased land as 'stranger' farmers (ibid.: 25–37).[29]

For both the conjugal family and the lineage, these developments had consequences. The contribution of the matrilineage in particular, to the production of cocoa, has been documented (Hill 1963: 16). On the other hand, cocoa cultivation required labour over and above what was needed in subsistence production and the conjugal family was a very important source of labour (Hill 1963: 16, 170; Vellenga 1986: 65). The labour of wives and children was put to use on cocoa farms, by both migrant and sedentary farmers. Polygyny provided labour for males who owned multiple cocoa farms (Mikell 1989: 68–69).[30]

Cocoa, a perennial crop, deepened the process of change in land relations because it could not be cultivated successfully within the old precolonial systems of land relations and agricultural practices such as shifting cultivation. The fears that chiefs would never willingly alienate land proved unfounded. Instead, as early as

1981, there was anxiety that some chiefs were disposing of land in a manner contrary to customary law (Kimble 1963: 332). As land became more valuable due to the expansion of cocoa cultivation and gold and timber extraction, there was an increase in the outright sale of land to 'strangers', both community members beyond the land owning lineage and migrants from outside the community. In addition, tributary relations, that had been established with state formation, were transformed into various tenancy arrangements between land owning lineages and 'stranger' individuals and groups. The most widespread of these tenancies were the *abunu* and *abusa* tenancies.

The excessive rents on the above tenancies became a matter of concern to the colonial state. Its inability to control land tenure weakened its ability to address the problem of high agricultural rents. State officials sent warning circulars to chiefs and fixed rents in some areas to no avail.[31] High rents were considered one of the major causes of rural indebtedness, particularly among cocoa cultivators, along with the fluctuating prices of cocoa.

Indebtedness during the colonial period was an important issue. Of particular significance was its connection to the institution of pawning.[32] Whereas in the past, both males and females were pawned, by the 19th century, females—because of their reproductive capacities—became highly valued as pawns. Also, the practice developed of females being married off to rich creditors in settlement of debts. Apparently, female pawns were particularly desired among matrilineal groups by men seeking total control of their wives and children (Mikell 1989: 17). Since the colonial state outlawed pawning of human beings, cocoa farms came to be pledged to repay debts (ibid.: 111). For small farmers, it meant the loss of their only source of livelihood for long periods.

Responses to Changes

Changes in Lineage and Conjugal Relations

For the peasantry, cocoa was a new source of income and also of stratification. Class differences emerged, based on creditor/debtor relations and ownership/labour arrangements. A complicated network of farm owners, tenants and various types of labourers came to characterise cocoa cultivation (Hill 1963: 11; Vellenga 1986: 64).

The emerging differences were complicated by gender based ones. Women formed what has been described as a 'parallel hierarchy to men, in owning farms and employing labour' (Vellenga 1986: 71). However, they mostly owned food crop farms or had smaller cocoa farms than male farmers did. The reasons for this included their duty to labour on husbands' farms without reciprocity and their general lack of resources to hire labour (ibid.: 76). As has been pointed out already, there were gender inequalities in access to land before cocoa cultivation spread. However, the process of commoditisation and privatisation promoted by cocoa deepened the social and economic implications of these inequalities.

The significance of cocoa for the lineage and the conjugal family receives different emphases in studies on the subject. While Mikell (1989) and Vellenga (1986) point to changes in the lineage's continued access to the property of its members and the attempts by cultivators to circumvent such access in favour of the conjugal family, Okali (1983) has stressed the resilience of the lineage and its continued usefulness in property acquisition. Both points of view are important in that the lineage has survived, but with some changes.

There is general agreement that cocoa had different implications for women as lineage members and as wives. As lineage members, they were involved in the distribution of resources through the lineage, whereas as wives, they had no property rights in resources acquired with their labour (Vellenga 1986: 63). Even as lineage members, women suffered disadvantages. They were adversely affected by the customary law dichotomy between women's property and men's property in both patrilineal and matrilineal areas which, in apparent equality, favoured men inheriting from men and women from women. However, self-acquired property of significant value passed through males, even in matrilineal societies (Mikell 1989: 124).

There were tensions between the conjugal family and the lineage over property questions, especially among matrilineal groups (Vellenga 1986: 76). Mikell argues that another equally potent source of tension was among potential heirs within the lineage itself. This was a result of the trend towards concentrating property in fewer hands, exemplified by the inheritance of farms by brothers instead of nephews (Hill 1963: 128; Mikell 1989: 121–23). Roberts (1987) has also noted the tensions between co-wives in polygynous unions.

Among matrilineal groups, male cocoa cultivators responded to the increased importance of the labour of wives and children by making gifts of farms to them and also to their lineages before farming for themselves. Among patrilineal groups, the practice of a customary successor distributing property among the children of the deceased was increasingly dispensed with and self-acquired property passed directly to the children (Hill 1963: 113).

Women's Strategies

In the conjugal family, women were known to withdraw their services from husbands cultivating cocoa, in cases where their chances of gaining property for their services were not promising, because of competition from the lineage or a co-wife/wives. During the depression and collapse of cocoa prices in the early 1930s, female migration to urban areas for trading and other service sector work increased dramatically. There was anxiety and accusation on the part of men about the role of migrant women in the spread of prostitution, witchcraft and venereal disease. The chiefs responded with bye-laws to restrict the movement of women, to combat prostitution and restabilise marriage.[33] Increased rates of divorce and remarriage were recorded in Asante, particularly after WW2 (Mikell 1989: 120).[34]

Another response, of a more limited nature, in the struggle over resources between the conjugal family and the lineage within and outside the cocoa growing areas was litigation, mainly by urban wives (Vellenga 1974: 19). It has been observed that before the 1940s, many of the cases concerning women had been brought by aggrieved male relatives against other men seeking compensation on issues such as adultery and seduction. After the 1940s, more women brought actions on their own (Mikell 1989: 116). Inheritance issues were only one of the different classes of marital complaints brought to the courts.[35]

A number of cases on appeal from the Native Tribunals indicate some of the issues related to succession and inheritance which arose in different parts of the Colony and the colonial courts' attitudes to claims of widows and lineages.[36] Women brought actions claiming immoveable property as their share of the deceased husbands' properties. A comparison of the 1888 case of *Swapim v. Achuwa* and the 1938 case of *Effuah Kwakuwah v. Effuah Nayenna*

([1938] 4 WACA 165–67) showed how little the customary law, as pronounced by the courts, had changed over a span of almost half a century. In *Swapim v. Achuwa*, the court stated categorically that the wife of a deceased matrilineal husband had no interest in the house, which both she and her husband built on lineage land, except as a mere occupant who could be ejected by the family[37] of the deceased if they so wished.[38] In *Kwakuwah v. Nayenna*, an Akan widow brought an action for a piece of land and a building on it claiming that she had rendered monetary and other assistance to her late husband during the building of the house, as a result of which she had been given part of the building during her husband's lifetime. The appeal court rejected her claim on grounds that even if it was the deceased's intention to give her the piece of property, it had not been properly done according to customary law.[39] Thus, customary gifts[40] made by persons to circumvent customary law rules were not upheld by the law if they did not strictly follow customary procedure.[41]

Marriage under Ordinance did not automatically defeat the interests of the lineage because of the presumption in favour of 'family' (lineage) property. In the 1938 case of *Dadzie v. Dadzie* ([1946] *D.C. Land*, 38–47), an Akan widow who had been married under Ordinance sued for her share of a house acquired by her deceased husband. Her case was that from 1901 to 1934 when he died, her husband had treated the house as his self-acquired property to the knowledge and consent of the family members. The defendants for their part claimed that the house was family property. However, there were other cases involving lineages where the courts had no difficulty distinguishing individual property from lineage and stool property even in situations where the deceased, as head of the family or as chief, in his lifetime had administered such properties together. In the case of *Ankrah v. Allotey* (1944), the new head of a Ga family and beneficiary of the will of his predecessor brought an action against the executors of the estate of the deceased claiming the title deeds to some of the properties. The defendants argued that the property was self-acquired, which the plaintiff could only claim as a beneficiary of the will and not as family head, as he was attempting to do. The courts held that there was not a merger of property in cases where the family was aware that the head was conducting his own business and acquiring properties with his own money. The same judgement was made with respect to stool property in the case of *Yaw Kwarteng v. Yaw Assabill* in 1944 in Ashanti.

Some lineage groups gave the children part of their father's property as a compromise between competing claims and the courts upheld such measures, as happened in *Clerk v. Okai*, 1950. However, the courts asserted from as early as in 1871 that children from a matrilineal lineage lived in their deceased father's house only with the agreement of the head of the family and subject to their good behaviour (*Amamoo v. John Clement*, 1871 Ren; *Mary Barnes v. Chief Mayan*, 1871). In *Williams v. Esson Payin*, ([1946] *D.C. Land*, 38–47), the principle of good behaviour was put to the test. The customary successor tried to eject children who had occupied their father's house for 35 years on grounds of their bad behaviour. The court rejected the successor's action on grounds that he could not prove that the acts complained of constituted misbehaviour, and even if they did, it was a native custom repugnant to natural justice, equity and good conscience to eject them. It is difficult not to form the impression that the courts were better at protecting the interests of the lineage than those of wives.

Summary and Conclusion

From the foregoing discussion it emerges that the inability of the post-colonial state to give full effect to the increased importance of the conjugal family through law reform has its roots in the socio-economic developments of the colonial period as they affected social relations within the lineage and conjugal family. Tensions arose between the two institutions in the competition for the new resources generated in the colonial economy.

The incapacity of the post-colonial state was reflected in the limits of the Intestate Succession Law passed in 1985, after decades of unsuccessful attempts to reform the rules of inheritance. Most of the cases arising from the Law have concerned the property of men and have been between women with various types of unions with them, between wives and the men's lineages and between children of different unions, and have also involved attempts to circumvent its provisions.

The application of Law 111 has been characterised by disagreements at all levels of the judiciary from the High Court to the Supreme Court. While some sections of the judiciary have interpreted the law to widen its scope of operation, others have tended to restrict its application. The law's implementation has been complicated by the limitations of the larger legal system. For example, the customary law marriage regime, which allows poly-gyny, operates together with the Ordinance Marriage system, which is monogamous. This has in some cases resulted in legal and practical complications in the nature and status of the various unions a man can contract in a lifetime. Also, customary laws and statutory provisions governing marriage and divorce continue to be biased against non-monetary contributions to the acquisition of property. Thus, in a number of disputes, parties have tried to tailor their circumstances *ex post facto* to fit the provisions of the Intestate Succession Law by claiming, unsuccessfully, in some cases to be spouses and in others the joint owners of the property. The situation demonstrates the complications of applying piece-meal remedies to changes which require major legislative reform.

This chapter has argued that the lineage survived the colonial period as an important player in the acquisition and distribution of resources. The nature of land relations, the predominance of peasant agriculture, the practice of indirect rule and the resultant accommodation of traditional practices of interest to the chiefs and women's structural subordination, all played a crucial part in this. However, the lineage did undergo some changes due to conflicts between itself and the conjugal family, and some equally significant tensions within both institutions themselves, in the assertion of property rights during the colonial period. Within the conjugal family, the tensions have been a result of the polygynous character of customary marriage.

In cocoa growing areas, especially, these changes varied and reduced lineage control over resources. Individual cultivators, in recognition of the contribution of both the conjugal family and the lineage to the acquisition of cocoa farms and to ensure the conti-nuation of these contributions, gave farms as gifts to various lineage and conjugal family members in their lifetime. It has been suggested that the lineage was more tolerant of gifts to children than gifts to wives. The predominance of children's property rights in patrilineal groups was strengthened by increasingly dispensing with the role of the customary successor. Another change was that the category of potential beneficiaries of a matrilineage member's property shrunk in size to the closest relations and resulted in an increasing concentration of lineage resources in fewer hands.[42]

Women, as wives, responded to these pressures by migration, divorce and remarriage to improve their chances of acquiring some resources for themselves and their children. The changes in the control of resources were supported by Christianity and the colonial educational system which were biased in favour of monogamy and the conjugal family. However, the legal system, made up of the hierarchy of native, provincial and divisional courts employing traditional rulers as assessors,[43] continued to assert the rights of the lineage to the self-acquired property of a deceased intestate against wives and children. The opinions of assessors were not verified outside the court processes, but nevertheless entered the legal system as the true state of customary law, becoming precedents which were applied in all subsequent cases, even where they contradicted actual practice.[44]

The colonial courts did not apply equity and good conscience clauses to disputes between wives and the lineage as it had done with other customary practices. However, they banned practices such as trials by ordeal, the pawning of persons and ritual murders on those grounds. This selectivity is striking. Laws of succession and inheritance remained untouched and could only be affected by marrying under the Marriage Ordinance of 1989 or making custom- ary law wills (*samansiw*) and gifts inter vivos. Even then, they could be challenged, with the courts insisting on strict customary procedures to assess the efficacy of such practices.

Farm labour, housework, biological reproduction and other forms of marital support were not considered as contributions which created rights in the self-acquired property of a spouse. Customary rules governing marriage and the sexual division of labour thus worked to deprive wives of resources in situations of divorce and the intestate death of husbands.

Thus, the colonial courts did not give voice to the changes in the socioeconomic role of the conjugal family in relation to the lineage and continued to assert customary law as unchanging and irrever- sible. In spite of legislative reform, this attitude to the customary law continues to influence the decisions of post-colonial courts, partly because of the limited reform and the contested nature of changes in social relations.

Notes

1. I am grateful to Rose Mensah-Kutin, Dotse Tsikata, Yao Graham and the editors of this book for their useful comments on the drafts of this article.
2. To avoid confusion between the terms 'the Gold Coast'—which stands for the entire colony—and 'the Gold Coast Colony'—which is one of its component parts, 'colonial Ghana' and 'the Colony' will be used throughout the paper to refer to the entire colony.
3. Ghana's coup d'etat government, from January 1982 to January 1993, was headed by Flt. Lt. J.J. Rawlings. Since 7 January 1993, Ghana has been ruled by an elected 4th Republican government whose president is Flt. Lt. Rawlings.
4. In the preamble to the Law, the growing importance of the conjugal family was clearly stated.
5. The Akan consist of the Asante, the Brong, the Sefwi, the Akyim, the Akwapim and the Fanti. In the colonial period, they lived mostly in Asante and the Colony. They are the single largest language group in Ghana—44 per cent of the population according to the 1960 population Census. Information of ethnic composition has not been collected since then.
6. A group found in South–Eastern Ghana (13 per cent of the population).
7. A Guan group from Akwapim. There are 28 Guan groups spread throughout Ghana. They are believed to be the aboriginal people.
8. Among the Akan, children lived in their deceased father's house, subject to good behaviour.
9. The practice of widow inheritance is becoming symbolic, although a 1974 study asserted that it was very much in force in some rural areas (de Graft-Johnson 1974).
10. Although these rules are not binding, 50 per cent of Ghana's population practices Christianity.
11. In 1963, Ghana's first post-colonial government tried unsuccessfully to pass a Marriage, Divorce and Inheritance Bill which was withdrawn because of the controversy about its provisions (Vellenga 1970).
12. Customary law divorces, in consonance with customary marriages, are a matter between the natal families of both parties or can be secured through arbitration in the traditional courts presided over by chiefs. Although customary law marriages could be dissolved under the Matrimonial Causes Act of 1971, most customary marriages continue to be dissolved at home. In the colonial period, disputes arising from customary divorces were heard by the native tribunals (Economic Commission for Africa 1984; Roberts 1987).
13. In Ghana, since the colonial period, there have been two legal regimes—customary and ordinance—under which marriages could be contracted. The customary regime, which accounts for over 80 per cent of all marriages, consists of unwritten laws of the various language groups in the country under which potentially polygynous unions are contracted. The ordinance regime has two pieces of legislation: the Marriage Ordinance (Cap 127) which results in monogamous marriages and the Marriage of Mohammedans Ordinance (Cap 129) which allows polygynous marriage. It is the norm for customary marriage rites to precede Ordinance marriages, thus transforming a potentially polygynous union into a monogamous one.

14. See *Prempeh v. Agyepong*, Court of Appeal, 1990 and *Essilfie v. Quarco* H.C. 1991.
15. In the matter of the estate of Major (Retired) Kwame Asante (deceased), S.C. 1993.
16. These groups belong to the Ga-Adangme people, who were found in the south–eastern part of the Colony (8 per cent of the population).
17. Agriculture employed technology such as shifting cultivation, fire, hoe, machete and long blade.
18. Patrifiliation in the Asante kinship system is the social and ritual recognition of a father's role based on the belief that a person's spirit (*ntoro*) came from her/his father, while blood (*mogya*) was from her/his mother. The father thus named the child, and in the case of sons provided professional training, and played a key role in the marriages of children. Children in turn were members of his totemic group and observed the rites and taboos of the group and provided the coffin for his burial.
19. See Wilks 1975: 371; also Mikell 1989: 108–9 for a discussion of the decline in women's rights.
20. The role of colonialism in the decline of the ritual and political powers of queen-mothers in Asante has been observed (Arhin 1983). These powers, though important, were exercised by only a minority of women. The queen-mother among Akan groups is the female counterpart and lineage member of a male chief and a member of his council. She was a key player in the enstoolment and destoolment of the chief and could become a chief herself. She was in charge of women's affairs and had her own court and linguist, wherein disputes among women and spouses were settled (ibid).
21. Along with this hierarchical structure, there was a particular kind of multiple ownership in land, which Ghanaian legal scholars have described as a series of customary law interests existing simultaneously, the highest being the allodial title, the King's title. Others were the usufructuary interest which granted indefinite rights of beneficial use and the individual cultivator's rights (Asante 1975).
22. Family, in this paper, is the lineage, a group of persons related by blood, who trace their ancestry through a male or female line back to a single person. The conjugal family is a smaller group which consists of a man and his wife/wives, children and dependents, who together form an important unit of production. Both, the lineage and the conjugal family, are juridically and socially recognised as performing particular roles in the society.
23. The rationale was that land was communally owned by the living, the ancestors and the unborn. Therefore, chiefs and family heads were only trustees.
24. These beliefs about land are still very current in Ghana, in spite of overwhelming evidence to the contrary. Hill argues that customary law has for a long time allowed the outright sale of land and cites an ancient *Guaha* custom as proof of this (1963: 109).
25. Marital residence could change in a woman's lifetime. Older Akan women sometimes returned to their lineage home after child-bearing years.
26. Other decisions in the same vein were *Sam v. Tham* (1924 DC: 63) and *Kodadja v. Tekpor* (1931 DC: 31).

27. See *Hammond v. Randolph* 5 W.A.C.A. 42; (1939) and *Abinabina v. Enyimadu* 12 W.A.C.A. 61 (1953).
28. From a figure of 80 lbs. in 1891 and 536 tons in 1900, cocoa export figures rose progressively to 113,195 tons in 1921 and 231,000 tons in 1926 (Tsikata 1984: 49).
29. Cocoa country today covers 3.6 million acres which is 56 per cent of cultivated land in Ghana.
30. Labour from the conjugal family was very important because of competition from the mines for hired labour (Hill 1963: 187; Vellenga 1986: 67).
31. See Native Affairs Department Circular to the Central Province Chiefs, 25 August 1910, signed by Francis Crowther, Secretary for Native Affairs: File No. ADM 11/184, Letter No. SNA. 89/10.
32. Pawning was a practice whereby the head of a lineage gave away a member in servitude as a means of paying off a debt. Pawns could be released on full payment of the debt with interest, or absorbed into the lineage of the creditor eventually (Mikell 1989: 17).
33. An example of such a law, The Free Women's Marriage Proclamation of 1929, was passed by the chief of Sefwi Wiawso in the early '30s (Roberts 1987: 48–69).
34. It has been suggested that women and their lineages used divorce and remarriage as a strategy to cut their losses and seek a better deal elsewhere (Mikell 1989: 120; Roberts 1987: 54–55).
35. Other issues were slander, divorce, compensation claims against seducers and adulterers, and maintenance of the wife and children (Vellenga 1974: 94–99).
36. The discussion is limited because the cases were chosen at random and no statistical computation or classification have been attempted. It is important to bear in mind the limitations of court processes as indicators of trends in society since only disputes, and very few of them, end up in court.
37. Family here refers to lineage.
38. See also *Barnes v. Mayan*, 1871: *Owoo v. Owoo*, 1944 in the Eastern Province.
39. In the lower court, the widow's claim to property she had aided her husband to acquire was rejected on grounds of lack of proof.
40. An old accepted practice put to new use in the colonial period.
41. The steps include seeking the consent of the lineage, publicising the gift and thanks giving by the donee. See also (*Bonsam v. Edubia*, 1948, D.C. Land, '48–51; *Yakoah v. Egya Koom*, 1948. D.C. Land, '48–51).
42. A post-colonial study in an Asante village found that 18 out of 39 farms had gone to children and spouses (Benneh 1970).
43. Native assessors were usually traditional rulers whose role was to inform the court about the position of customary law in a case.
44. See Woodman (1974) on the limits of court-pronounced customary law; Also see Chanock (1982) for an account of the invention of customary law in northern Rhodesian courts.

References

Arhin, K., 1982, 'Rank and class among the Asante and Fante in the 19th century'. *Africa* 53 (1): 2–22.

Arhin, K., 1983, 'The political and military roles of Akan women'. In C. Oppong (ed.), *Male and Female in West Africa*. London: George Allen and Unwin.

Asante, S.K.D., 1975, *Property Law and Social Goals in Ghana, 1844–1966*. Accra: Ghana University Press.

Benneh, G., 1970, 'The impact of cocoa cultivation on the traditional land tenure system of the Akan of Ghana'. *Ghana Journal of Sociology* 6 (1): 43–61.

Brokensha, D., 1966, *Social Change at Larteh, Ghana*. Oxford: Clarendon.

Chanock, M., 1982, 'Making customary law: Men, women and courts in colonial northern Rhodesia, 1897', in M. Hay and M. Wright (eds.), *African Women and the Law: Historical perspectives*. Boston: Boston University Press.

de Graft-Johnson, K.E., 1974, 'Succession and inheritance among the Fanti and Ewe', in C. Oppong (ed.), *Legon Family Papers No 1: Domestic rights and duties in southern Ghana*. Accra: Institute of African Studies, University of Ghana.

Economic Commission for Africa, 1984, *Law and the Status of Women*. Prepared by T. Manuh, Addis Ababa.

Hill, P., 1963, *The Migrant Cocoa Farmers of Southern Ghana*. Cambridge: Cambridge University Press.

Hinden, R., 1950, *Local Government and the Colonies*. London: George Allen and Unwin.

Kimble, D., 1963, *A Political History of Ghana: 1850–1929*. London: Oxford University Press.

Lovett, M., 1989, 'Gender relations, class formation and the colonial state in Africa', in J. Parpart and K. Staudt (eds.), *Women and the State in Africa*. Boulder and London: Lynne Rienner.

McCaskie, T., 1980, 'Office, land and subjects in the history of the Manwere Fekuo of Kumase: An essay in the political economy of the Asante state'. *Journal of African History* 21 (2): 189–208.

Mensah–Kutin, R., 1986, 'Women in wage labour: A study on Ghana'. M.A. Development Studies Research Paper. The Hague: Institute of Social Studies.

Mikell, G., 1989, *Cocoa and Chaos in Ghana*. New York: Paragon House.

Nukunya, G.K., 1975, 'Land tenure and agricultural development in the Anloga area of the Volta region'. Legon: University of Ghana. (mimeo).

Okali, C., 1983, *Cocoa and Kinship in Ghana*. London: Kegan Paul International.

Phillips, A., 1989, *The Enigma of Colonialism*. London: James Currey.

Prah, M., 1992, 'Women and education in Ghana', Paper presented to the Gender Analysis Workshop of the Development and Women's Studies (DAWS) Programme of the Institute of African Studies at the University of Ghana, July, Legon.

Rattray, R.S., 1929, *Ashanti Law and Constitution*. Oxford: Clarendon.

———, 1923, *Ashanti*. Oxford: Clarendon.

Reynolds, E., 1974, *Trade and Economic Change in the Gold Coast: 1807–1874*. London: Longman.

Roberts, P., 1987, 'The state and the regulation of marriage: Sefwi Wiawso (Ghana), 1900–1940', in H. Afshar (ed.), *Women, State and Ideology—Studies from Africa and Asia*. London: Macmillan.

Tsikata, E., 1984, 'Agricultural rent control in Ghana: Colonial and post-colonial attempts'. LLB Dissertation. Legon: University of Ghana.

Vellenga, D.D., 1986, 'Matrilinity, patrilinity, and class formation among women cocoa farmers in two rural areas of Ghana', in C. Robertson and I. Berger (eds.), *Women and Class in Africa*. New York: Africana.

——, 1974, 'Arenas of judgement: An analysis of matrimonial cases brought before different types of courts in the eastern region of Ghana in the nineteen thirties and nineteen sixties', in C. Oppong (ed.), *Legon Family Papers No. 1: Domestic rights and duties in southern Ghana*. Legon: Institute of African Studies, University of Ghana.

——, 1970, 'Attempts to change marriage laws in Ghana and the Ivory Coast', in P. Foster and A.R. Zolberg (eds.), *Ghana and Ivory Coast: Perspectives on modernization*. Chicago: University of Chicago Press.

Wilks, I., 1975, *Asante in the Nineteenth Century*. Cambridge: Cambridge University Press.

Woodman, G.R., 1974, 'The rights of wives, sons and daughters in the estates of their deceased husbands and fathers', in C. Oppong (ed.), *Legon Family Papers No. 1: Domestic rights and duties in southern Ghana*. Legon: Institute of African Studies, University of Ghana.

5   Women's Rights and the Decline of Matriliny in Southern India

K. Saradamoni

Features indicating that women in the state of Kerala have a better position than in other parts of India are often linked to the region's matrilineal past. However, this was a changing and varied past, denied by the model of Kerala matriliny based on Nayar practices, particularly of the middle decades of this century. Between the 1910s and 1930s, a series of legislations dealing with the rules of inheritance and succession, marriage and the joint family irretrievably altered the marumakkathayam system. These laws closely followed changes in land relations and economic opportunities, the emergence of the conjugal family under colonialism, as well as the spread of notions of progress, civilisation and orthodox Hindu practice, which had a strong male bias. The legislative reforms were the result of prolonged demands by a section of the male élite. The major points of discussion were, and in analyses of Kerala matriliny still are, the powers of the family manager, the nature of marriage, and women's inheritance and succession rights. The individualisation of property worked in conjunction with alienation, fragmentation and male bias in employment to eliminate women's security base. Factors explaining the lack of opposition from women to the proposed legal reforms which worked against them are explored.

Introduction

A series of legislations passed during the second and third decades of this century brought about major changes in the numerically strong communities, including the Nayars, Izhavas and Vellalas, which practised *marumakkathayam* or matriliny in Kerala. These laws were the Travancore Nair Acts passed in 1912 and 1925; the Ezhava Act and Nanjanad Vellala Act, 1926; the Cochin Nair Regulation, 1919–20 and 1937–38; the Madras Marumakkathayam Act, 1933 and the Moplah Marumakkathayam Act, 1993. As the state of Kerala was at that time composed of the princely States of Travancore and Cochin and the Malabar province of the Madras Presidency, legislations were separately enacted in the three regions. The new laws were comprehensive and dealt with all the major aspects of matriliny. They were the result of prolonged demands from a section of the male population. The legislation closely followed changes in land relations and specifically dealt with the institutions of joint family and marriage, and rules of inheritance and succession.

While making brief mention of the non-propertied sections of society, this chapter deals mainly with the propertied sections of matrilineal communities in Travancore.[1] It summarises the import-ant aspects of Nayar matriliny, especially what they meant to women, using the writings of commentators at the turn of the century. In looking at the processes of change, it examines how and why these legislative measures were demanded and how women perceived the changes, contextualising their reactions in the history of that period. The changes in matriliny, brought about during the late 19th and early 20th centuries, have often been overlooked in anthropological writings. However, the attempt is not to glorify or exaggerate the past. My position is that these changes, which were largely seen as 'progressive' and 'forward-looking', were on the whole, not so for women.

The noted historian Sreedhara Menon stated that the changes in matrilineal practices in Kerala had ushered 'in a new and progress-ive society in Kerala, following the natural laws of inheritance and marriage and the code of conduct observed by progressive societies elsewhere in India and abroad' (Menon, 1979: 92). Further he added, although the *marumakkathayam* system had become a relic of a bygone age, some of the traditional bonds which had governed the relations between brothers and sisters and their children continued to operate. Menon, it appears, was prompted to add the latter part of his observation mainly because of certain special features of matriliny, which lingered even after the legislations had been passed.

Similar observations can be found in other writings. T.K. Velu Pillai, who was instrumental in no small way in bringing about the legislation to end matriliny, noted that it was a matter for special gratification that women were playing a prominent part in public life. He wrote that the number of girls enrolled in schools rose from 1,019 to 2,69,444 between 1874–75 and 1934–35 (1940: 43). A large number of women had already entered the liberal professions of pedagogy, medicine and law and had also joined the cooperative movement. Pillai reproduced a speech of Maharani Sethu Parvathi Bayi, mother of the last Maharaja (king) of Travancore, which was delivered while addressing the tenth session of the All India Women's Conference at Trivandrum. She said that in Kerala, women faced no restriction in the matter of holding and disposing of property. They faced no inequalities regarding education and social and cultural practices (ibid.: 43).[2]

Even today, one comes across references to Kerala's matrilineal past, especially in the context of some distinct and positive features of the state, as shown by the figures from the 1991 Census given here:

	Kerala	India
Sex ratio (F:M, 1991)	1040	942
Literacy (% all ages):		
Women	66	25
Men	75	47
Life Expectancy:		
Women	68	56
Men	64	57

Kerala has remained the only state in India with a sex ratio favourable to women for several decades, a factor recognised in linking female literacy and the acceptance of the small family norm. Such observations lead one to argue that if Kerala is distinctly different from the rest of India and one factor for this distinctiveness is its matrilineal past, surely more needs to be known about that past. A study of the changes that have taken place in Kerala is relevant today when most changes that are being introduced, particularly in the socioeconomic realm, are being described as inevitable and 'progressive'. Does the past, when women experienced a slide back, have any lessons to offer?

Matriliny in Kerala had been specially noticed by visitors and travellers for a very long time. Early administrators and scholars, including sociologists and anthropologists, made descriptive records of their observations and studies. It remains a fascinating topic for research and continues to attract scholars from different disciplines. Most of the studies have focused on the Nayars, who were a numerically strong and dominant community with interest in land. Though Gough (Schneider and Gough 1961) dealt extensively with the Izhavas and Mappilas, Nayar practices in Malabar had become a model of Kerala matriliny for many researchers and scholars. It is not easy to get an idea of the depth and spread of matriliny in Kerala from these studies. The reference is always to women's rights over property. While this is in marked contrast to the position of patrilineal women, the emphasis on property-owning groups obscured the fact that several other communities who did not own property also followed matriliny. That matriliny and patriliny coexisted in Kerala and that in the actual practice of matriliny there were differences between castes/communities and regions is not considered in the literature describing and analysing matriliny. An observation from the Census of Travancore, 1931, is worth noting in this context. In that year, i.e., after the Nair, Izhava and Vellala Acts were passed which covered the three major matrilineal communities, 28 per cent of the Hindu population was declared to be patrilineal, 30 per cent matrilineal and the remaining to be following a mixed or 'doubtful' system. Furthermore, it has also to be noted that major changes had come about in matriliny and its practices. Critically, many of the studies on Kerala matriliny, including Gough (Schneider and Gough 1961), were based on fieldwork undertaken much after the legislations mentioned earlier were passed.[3]

Matriliny is described as the system by which descent, succession and inheritance of property are traced through women. The important aspects of Kerala matriliny were the joint family, marriage, inheritance and succession. It has already been mentioned that most of the literature on Kerala matriliny relates to the Nayars and it is the latter system which is first discussed.

Property and Authority: the *Taravad* or Joint Family

In his memorandum submitted to the Marumakkathayam Committee, Travancore, 1908, K.P. Padmanabha Menon, member of the Committee and renowned historian, described the constitution of a *marumakkathayam* family.

> It is known as a Tarawad and consists of a group of persons, male and female, all tracing descent from a common ancestress; living under the control and management of the eldest male, who is called the Karanavar. In its simplest form, a family would consist of a mother and her children living together with their maternal uncle, that is, the mother's brother, as Karanavar. In its complex form, it would include a mother, her children, both sons and daughters, the children of such daughters, and their descendants in the female line, however distant, all living together under the control of their common Karanavar who would be the one senior in age to all the males in the family. A Malabar Tarawad is, perhaps, the best type of a matriarchal family. In this, the mother forms the stock of the descent, and kinship as well as rights to the property are traced through females and not through males. Each of the mothers and her children and descendants in the female line form of Thaivazhi (Thai means mother and Vazhi means line), meaning a mother's line. The Tarawad property is owned by all its members jointly. None can predicate to himself or herself that any portion of it belongs to him or her; nor can any one claim separate possession or enjoyment of any portion. The groundwork of the system is that the Tarawad estate is held in trust for the support of the females and their descendants in the female line (Travancore Marumakkathayam Committee 1908: Annexure B).

Practically every author points to descent from a common ancestress and that *taravad* property was held in trust for the support of women and their descendants in the female line. Not surprisingly, kinship was traced through women. According to many books and documents, matrilineal property was impartible, and division or alienation was possible only with the consent of all its members. Such views overlook the fact that separate families could and were set up by a senior woman and her children. These were established either very near the original *taravad* or at a distant place where that *taravad* had properties. Sometimes, they were known by the name of the original *taravad*, otherwise, a new name was adopted, but they all belonged to the same *taravad*. Most writers also highlight the presence of a *karanavar*, generally the maternal uncle to the majority of the members of the *taravad*. The *karanavar* was said to control and manage the family property, though the latter passed through women.

Nagam Aiya, a non-Kerala Brahmin who had held several senior positions in the Travancore government and bureaucracy, after describing the same features as Padmanabha Menon had, and noting the ability of the system to conserve property, added that the 'Nayar system of life' gave their women greater freedom and independence than the rest of Hindu society. Nayar women were free from many of the 'conventional restrictions, such as child marriage, a demure life in the husband's house, widowhood . . .' (1906: 363). Family name and property, which could not be divided without the collective agreement of all adult members of the *taravad*, passed through women. A female baby was eagerly welcomed in every *taravad* and if no such baby was born, a baby girl was adopted. Census data showed that more boys were born in Travancore but girls showed a greater survival capacity (Census of Travancore, 1875: 140). Nagam Aiya, the then Census Commissioner, hazarded the opinion that this phenomenon was because among the *marumakkathayam* people a female child was prized more highly than a male one.

Though *taravad* is generally used as a synonym for the Nayar family house, it literally means an extended family and evokes togetherness and rootedness.[4] In the context of this chapter, the important aspect is that the *taravad* offered women a lifetime security, both material and emotional, the degree of which may have differed according to circumstance. Women belonging to *marumakkathayam*, whether they were of upper or lower caste or tribals, had a sense of belonging and not one of displacement (See Dube, in this volume).

Both Padmanabha Menon and Nagam Aiya have highlighted the overall authority and power of the *karanavar*, the eldest male member, which has led many to assert that Nayar women under matriliny were virtually dominated, if not oppressed, by their maternal uncles. However, Ananthakrishna Iyer, the noted anthropologist, wrote in 1912 that the senior-most woman in age used to be the head of the *marumakkathayam* family. Her eldest daughter was the 'prime minister' and orders were transmitted to their little world through her. The son recognised the priority of the mother before whom he did not venture even to seat himself, unless she had given him permission. The brother obeyed the elder sister and respected the younger ones. 'In fact, the affection between the brother and sister was a feeling that endured, while conjugal love was but a passing sentiment' (Iyer 1912: Vol. II, 47).

Iyer was aware of the changes that were taking place in Nayar families. He added that 'many of the old time-honoured customs have already disappeared or begun to disappear. The senior woman is no longer the head of the family, and she has given place to the eldest male who is known as the *karanavar*' (ibid.: 48). In contrast to the views of Padmanabha Menon and Nagam Aiya, what Iyer implied was that women's position was certainly higher and more important during an earlier period and that it had declined over time. It has been argued that the custom of the eldest male becoming the *karanavar* was institutionalised only after British rule was established (Arunima 1992).[5] There is written evidence to show that female managers were not absolute rarities. In the families of the Zamorin of Calicut and other notables, and in all cases where there were no adult male members, the senior female was the manager. It has to be seen whether this last stipulation was in vogue before 'modern' courts were introduced. However, there are verdicts from the same courts decreeing that a female manager could exercise all the powers vested by law in the *karanavar* and that no distinction was to be made between a male and female *karanavar* nor any restriction placed on the powers of the latter.[6] In another judgement, it was stated that there was no reason to suppose that a female manager/*karanavars'* powers would be less than those of a male *karanavar* (Aiyar 1922: 34).

Sambandham/Marriage[7]

The *Gazetteer of Malabar and Anjengo* (Innes 1908) described *sambandham* as a loose form of 'marriage' obtaining among castes following *marumakkathayam*, entailing no responsibility or legal obligation whatsoever on the part of the husband towards his wife or children. According to this system, which was followed by the upper castes of the Kshatriyas, Samantans, the Ambalavasis, the

Nayars and partially by other castes, children belonged to the same caste or sub-caste and family as their mother, not to that of their father. Neither party to a *sambandham* union became thereby a member of the other's family. The offspring of the union belonged to the mother's *taravad* and had no claim, so long as the law of *marumakkathayam* applied, to a share of their father's property or to maintenance there from (Innes 1908: 95).

Sambandham, which means alliance or binding, has been viewed with curiosity. It is common to find words like 'concubinage' and 'promiscuity' in writings on Kerala marriage by early travellers and chroniclers from foreign countries and also others. In fact, many were thrilled by the exoticism they imagined they saw in Kerala.[8] True, *sambandham* as a conjugal relation between a man and a woman was different from a Christian marriage or one prescribed under the Hindu Dharmasastras, but it had to have the sanction of the elders of the family and society. It was in the nature of a contractual relation and, in theory, either party could repudiate it at will. According to Logan, the author of the *Malabar Manual* (1887/1951), it was this part of the existing law which led 'ignorant commentators' to morally condemn the people of Malabar. Nagam Aiya made special mention of divorce, which he described as being generally the result of 'misconduct' and incompatibility of temperament, and the mother getting custody of the children. Further, in the event of separation from their husbands by divorce or death, women were free to remarry (1906: 358–59). However, according to Logan, 'conjugal fidelity', and according to Aiya, 'permanent attachment', was the general principle in conjugal relationships, although freedom was sanctioned (Logan 1951; Aiya 1906). Ananthakrishna Iyer found that most marriages effected through *sambandham* were as happy and enduring as the more formal and ceremonial unions (1912: vol II, 32).

None of the authors cited here belonged to matrilineal communities. Whatever one makes of their writing, it can be said that matriliny and its institutions of joint family or *taravad*, inheritance and marriage were logical in their organisation and functioning. However, it must be noted that the Nayars were divided into several sub-castes between all of whom intermarriage and interdining were not possible; that caste rules were very powerful; the honour of the family was firmly guarded; and that the system was not an egalitarian one as we understand it today. Yet, women had more freedom and rights in the *taravad* than under patriliny, where they had only a temporary living right. A woman and a man who entered into *sambandham* did not lose their individual identities. In most cases, the woman did not change her residence or her name or lose her right in her natal home. The husband was not obliged to maintain the wife. It was the responsibility of the *taravad* to provide for her and her children. Divorced or widowed women were not considered unlucky, inauspicious or looked down upon as in patrilineal Hindu society (See also Dube, in this volume).

Inheritance Among Non-Propertied Matrilineal Groups

Matrilineal inheritance worked differently among some landless, low caste and tribal people. In *Travancore Tribes and Castes*, published in 1937, i.e., more than a decade after the passing of the major Marumakkathayam Acts, the anthropologist Krishna Iyer, found many of the people he studied adhering to matrilineal practices. Writing about the inheritance practices of the Kanikkar, whom he described as a 'wild but inoffensive' tribe of south Travancore, Iyer said, 'Property includes clothing, implements, utensils, weapons, livestock and crops. A deceased man's property is divided—half to his nephew and the other half to his sons. In the absence of a nephew, the property devolves on sons. In no case does it go to his wife. Even the hut goes to his nephew. The widow with her children goes back to her brother' (Iyer 1937: vol. I, 27). He observed that descent was reckoned in the female line among the Kanikkars.

Another community, the Mannan, which also followed *marumakkathayam*, passed on property which consisted of bill hooks, vessels and cattle to nephews, two years after the demise of a person. During these two years, the property remained in the custody of the sons, who did not have a share in the property (ibid.: 213). About Pulayas, the main body of agricultural labourers, he wrote that inheritance was through the female line. Property was divided equally between a son and a nephew, in the case of self-acquired property. Ancestral property went to the nephew (Ibid.: 153).

Thus, matriliny in Travancore (or Kerala), could not be reduced to one single or uniform practice, and was more widespread than generally recognised. According to the author of the *Principles of*

Marumakkathayam Law, some Christians and Muslims in pockets
of Travancore also followed matriliny in its 'pure, unadulterated'
form (Joseph 1918: 10). He remarked that even Nambutiris—
Malayalee Brahmins—had adopted Nayar customs in matters of
family management.

However, the demands for change came from the dominant
matrilineal communities. It came in the form of representations
from the English educated young men, first among the Nayars,
and later among the Izhavas and Vellalas in Travancore. The fact
that the Maharaja of Travancore had by then set up a representative
body[9] encouraged young men who were keen for changes to make
the appeals.

The Emergence of Demands for Legislative Reform

The Travancore Marumakkathayam Committee,[10] which was
largely a response to the demands of the Nayars, had ten points as
terms of reference. One was to give 'legal' validity to the customary
practice of *sambandham*. Most of the other points related to the
management of *taravad* properties, controlling the *karanavar's*
powers, the rights and obligations of junior members and the
rights of a branch of a family to demand partition. The terms
included the declaration that the self-acquired property of a
marumakkathayee dying intestate should go to his wife and children.
The last item was a major departure in the hitherto followed
practice of a *marumakkathayee* male not having a legal responsibility towards his wife and children. Along with other points, the
implication was that there were *karanavars* who squandered away
taravad wealth, failing in their responsibilities as managers and
custodians of the welfare and prosperity of the *taravad*.

As has been noted earlier, legislation regarding matriliny was
passed in all the three regions that later constituted the present
state of Kerala. A section of the English educated matrilineal men,
who had by then absorbed new ideas about themselves and their
social institutions, were largely responsible for bringing about
these changes. One example is that of A. Govinda Pillai, Dewan
(Prime Minister) of Travancore. In his submission to the earlier
Malabar Marriage Commission, he said that as the father, more
than anyone else, was responsible for 'multiplication', it was primarily his duty to make a provision for the children. This, according

to him, was a dictate of natural law (Malabar Marriage Commission 1896).

It is not clear how sizable a section of the Nayars were owners of large properties or could amass large amounts of self-acquired wealth to bequeath to their wives and children. Ward and Conner, who surveyed Travancore and Cochin in the early 19th century, did not find a significant number of big farmers in the state. They wrote that the lower classes rarely possessed sufficient rice land (Ward and Conner 1863: 61). There is data showing large-scale, and even community-wise, transactions of land in the years following the *marumakkathayam* legislation.[11] However, there is no authentic information on the socioeconomic consequences of the spurt in land transaction. Varghese thinks that it caused a reduction in land concentrations in the hands of the 'superior' castes (1970: 105). At the same time, another view also prevailed that there was no serious deterioration in the economic condition of the Nayars (Pillai 1945). Obviously, this referred to the minority at the top level of the land holding, educational and employment structure.

While talking of the 'modern disintegration' of matriliny with reference to the Malabar, Gough was of the opinion that the British administration brought about major changes in the structure of production and occupation. The immediate result was the emergence of private ownership and marketability, not only of produced goods, but also of land and labour (Schneider and Gough 1961: 643). The alien rulers' interpretation of customary land practices resulted in the dissemination of ideas about private gains, in a way hitherto unknown. Few of the new economic undertakings proved practicable in the long term for joint enterprise on the part of the matrilineal descent groups. The collapse of the descent groups was strongly felt by the poorest, landless wage workers and small tenants (ibid.: 645).

A combination of various factors undoubtedly worked towards the shake up of the *taravad*. The advent of the British as rulers, administrators, educators and missionaries certainly had its impact. This period witnessed a new linkage of the Kerala economy to world market forces. Kerala is said to have had trade relations with countries far and near for many centuries in the past. But the impact of the new linkage was different. There was a shift from subsistence cultivation to cash crop cultivation, in order to meet the growing export demands, and people were affected by the economic crises in the advanced countries—the World Wars and the Depression. New schools and colleges began to cater to large numbers of students, but the openings to absorb them as employees fell behind the demand of the growing population.[12] Many scholars, including Kathleen Gough (Schneider and Gough 1961), have highlighted these aspects as major factors in the decline of matriliny.

In addition to the socioeconomic and political developments, profound changes took place in the realm of ideas. One such shift related to the father's duty towards his children. Some fathers were already providing for their children's upkeep, especially as the costs of education and clothing were increasing. When the question of giving legal sanction to the fathers' responsibility was raised, the argument was:

Apart from the question of personal duty, as a matter of public policy too, a deceased man's property should go to those who are nearest to him, and nearness is to be measured by the degree of affection which may be presumed by the nearness of relationship. To give a man's earnings not to his son, who was only one degree removed, but to his sister's son who was removed by three degrees, was opposed to the above principle (Travancore Marumakkathayam Committee 1908: 66).

These ideas had already surfaced in Kerala. Logan, who was not derogatory about *sambandham*, had different arguments about the law of inheritance through females. He stated that the time had come to institute some legal mode by which a man could pass on his self-acquired property to his children, for whom he had natural affection, and their mother. Unless this was done, he argued, a Nayar would not be motivated to exert himself, as the 'fruits of his labour went to persons for whom he had but little sympathy' (Logan 1887: 61–62).

British opinion emphasised individual effort, private gain and 'natural' affection. Their actions led to concrete changes in areas vital to our discussion. Referring to Malabar, Arunima writes:

The changes in the fluid structure of the Nayar household under [East India] Company rule thus altered relations between kin and non-kin in several ways. Gendered rights began to emerge within the household in relation to property and authority, with men gaining greater legitimacy than women in the exercise of control over both spheres (Arunima 1992: 77).

Responses to and Perceptions of Change

A question that arises at this juncture is that of women's reactions to the proposed changes. The official view was that either the women did not have an opinion of their own or that they did not respond. The fact, however, is that there was no concerted effort to elicit the responses of women, through whom property rights were traced. The Travancore Marumakkathayam Committee collected opinions only from a section of the landed and educated men. The Committee reported that an attempt was made to question a few ladies (at least in the capital), but only 11 out of 52 women were willing to be interviewed. The Committee remarked that it was practically impossible to speak to these women because they insisted that it should be done at their respective homes.

From the evidence available, we know that only an insignificant number of men and women responded to the Commission.[13] It is not known what the vast majority of people thought and whether they would have reacted differently had they been given the opportunity. However, there are reasons to believe that there was a small group of educated and articulate women and men who seriously discussed changes in matriliny and related issues, as well as women's freedom and status. This can be deduced from articles that appeared in journals at that time.

A number of women's journals were published in Kerala from the late 19th century onwards.[14] Some of them were owned and edited by men, some were edited by women. A number of prominent women of the period were associated with the journals[15] and there were women subscribers and contributors. Women's contributions to these journals varied. They included articles, comments, reactions or replies, short stories and plays. The journals would carry felicitations to the Maharajah and other members of the palace, articles—on women's status and movements in other countries, women and society, women and religion, and ethical and moral questions—book reviews, philosophical and spiritual discourses and poems. Many well-known and influential men of the period contributed regularly. They consistently wrote on topics such as *bharyadharmam* (wifely duties), *pàtivrityam* (marital devotion to the husband), domestic work and its importance, and the influence of western models. Though women too wrote on spiritual matters, household management, and child and health care, they also wrote, and sharply too, on women's rights and the inequalities they faced. It has to be noted that there were men who espoused the cause of women, but by and large most men wrote to keep women in a lower position.

A few articles discussing matriliny and related issues are discussed in this chapter, to give the reader an idea of the range of views on, and reactions to, changing *marumakkathayam*. An article entitled 'Marumakkathayam', written by a man (Udayabhanu) in the monthly *Sarada* in February 1908, will be examined first. His comment on the legislations which were being considered was that 'the whole world was jubilant at destroying woman's freedom'. He, however, gave credit to the service women rendered to the family, and thereby to society, without expecting rewards. According to him, the property and inheritance rights enjoyed by women in Kerala were a recognition of the heavy burden they shouldered. Unlike in the rest of the world, in Kerala, women were not separated at a young age from their mothers and natal homes to be made subservient to outside men. He repeated that men were only the managers of the land women owned. Matriliny did allow women to go and live with their husbands, but they were received back on widowhood. In response to debates regarding *marumakkathayam* practices, he argued that matriliny also allowed its members—women and men—either to merge their personal wealth with that of the *taravad's* or to set up separate families. On *sambandham*, he opined that marriages did not depend on rituals and that the *marumakkathayam* marriage was like any other marriage in the world. While he was agreeable to some legislative reforms in the areas of property division and inheritance rights, he was against the weakening of the *taravad* and introducing reforms in the *sambandham*. With their rights in the natal home along with their right to private wealth, either through earnings or through gifts from a husband, matrilineal women were certainly in a better position than their sisters under patriliny.

Another prominent writer, Kannan Nair,[16] who was a relentless fighter for patriliny, frequently contributed to these journals. In his article, 'A comparative study of matriliny and patriliny' (*Lakshmi Bai* 1919), he summarised the salient points of both matriliny and patriliny, presented here in tabular form.

	Under Patriliny	Under Matriliny
Family or *taravad*	Descent through father, son remains in father's family	Descent through mother, son remains in mother's *taravad*
Wife	Joins husband's family	Does not merge in husband's family
Daughter	Joins husband's family after marriage	Remains in natal *taravad*
Rights over family property	Married son can get his share	None can claim his/her share without the consent of all *taravad* members
Family wealth	Not equal between man and woman	Equal between man and woman

From a woman's point of view, matriliny offered her a better status and security. However, Kannan Nair used the Dharmasastras and other Hindu religious texts, as well as notions such as 'civilised' (*nagarikata, parishkaram*), which were being used by the English courts in dealing with Hindu marriages, to argue for patriliny. Whereas the first author was pro-woman and pro-matriliny, Kannan Nair was prejudiced against both. His opinions regarding the daughter under patriliny, where without marriage she had no place, makes this clear. In going through the salient points, it is evident that matrilineal women enjoyed greater equality and independence than women under patriliny. However, Kannan Nair argued that those who believed in the Smritis, particularly the Manusmriti,[17] would not ask for this equality and freedom. The system under which men had the right to control and protect women was considered superior and more civilised.

This in effect was the demand of men who agitated for legislation to alter and end matriliny. With the changes brought about in the institutions of matriliny, the man was obliged to provide for his wife and children. However, the ability to do this did not come about automatically as many men were impoverished after the *taravad* was partitioned. However, the notion of provider or bread winner gave them a new importance. Two years prior to the passing of the Nair Regulations, an article entitled 'Nair's Patriliny' appeared in the periodical *Service* (July–August 1923), the mouth-piece of the Nair Service Society. The author, K.N. Nair, a man, wrote that a Nayar woman who had perennial rights in the *taravad* from where nobody could send her out was being moved to the refuge of a husband, of which there could be no certainty.

Turning to a woman writer, Mrs. Raman Thampi wrote a series of articles on *marumakkathayam* in *Sarada* from June 1908 onwards, in favour of legislative intervention to modify matriliny. At the same time, she took great pains to show that matriliny was prevalent in many parts of the world and that its customs should not be seen as uncivilised or immoral. Another woman, K. Padmavathi Amma, who was not an ardent supporter of matriliny, also wrote several articles in the same journal. She talked of the tension and disharmony prevailing in the *taravads* at that time. The practice of giving maintenance only to those who lived in the *taravad* prevented persons from choosing to live elsewhere. She suggested that the share of those who did not stay in the *taravad*, and were not maintained by the family, had to be kept aside and given to them later. This applied to both men and women. Regarding the division of family property, she thought it should be effected when a sizable number of family members demanded it and not only when all members agreed, as was the practice. Padmavathi Amma wanted the unquestioned powers of the *karanavar* to be curtailed and financial help, in the form of loan or advance, to be given to those members who wished to start independent work.

Yet another woman writer challenged the newly emerging discriminatory social ideas regarding marriage, in the periodical *Lakshmi Bai* (Nov.–Dec. 1908). She said that women had to ignore the criticism that *sambandham* was not a proper marriage. She asked why a man who took more than one wife did not become an object of ridicule, while a woman who had more than one husband was considered 'fallen'. She questioned the Puranas[18] which declared that women have no other role in society beyond serving the husband.

In an article which also appeared in *Lakshmi Bai* (Nov.–Dec. 1913), one year after the Travancore Nair Act was passed, Karthiyayini Amma expressed happiness in the great victory which Nayar women had won. This Act had allowed partition between branches of families and paved the way for individual branches to partition. But this did not take away 'women's rights over property'. According to her, women had gained rights in their mothers', fathers' and husbands' properties. She was aware of the legislation and also the demands on the state from different quarters for the enactment of necessary laws. She ended the article by making a comparison of women under patriliny with those under matriliny. A woman under patriliny had maintenance rights in her father's home till her marriage; after marriage the same continued in her husband's family. She wrote:

> We, Nayar women, are up in the educational ladder and hence can enter government service and the like, we can make independent earnings in addition to the three shares to which we are now legally entitled . . . . Malayali woman's importance has risen . . . (Karthiyayini Amma 1913: 315)

Karthiyayini Amma was theoretically correct. Women's property rights were not taken away. However, with division, fragmentation and alienation, property was depleted. Also true was that women were not formally barred from education and employment. Yet, there was an 'invisible hand' working against them. The public sphere absorbed men rather than women. In a famous example, Lakshmi N. Menon, who was later to become a member of Nehru's cabinet, had to accept a teaching job in Madras, because the Travancore Government denied her a position on her return from England on completing her education.

A very interesting article appeared in another issue of *Lakshmi Bai*, entitled 'New fashioned Malayali marriage'. The woman author described the changes that had taken place which included greater demands from bridegrooms, the increasing worth of men and the emergence of dowry. She sarcastically classified men into different classes or gradations according to their educational level, employment and earnings.[19] She remarked that there were some clever men who ensured that their wives' families paid for their college education. 'Some of them go to Calcutta, Bombay and Madras in the name of higher studies and enjoy life there'. She saw these as new tricks that men played on innocent women.

There are any number of articles which make it clear that there were women who had independent views of what was happening around them. They would have been a small minority. Unfortunately, the number of these women, their families and their educational or occupational backgrounds are not known. Some of them rose to high positions in the educational field; some remained active in social work or politics; but most of those who contributed these provocative articles remain unknown. At the same time, one can see that all these women writers had a freedom which allowed them access to education, employment and public life. Yet the matrilineal *taravad*, which had given women maintenance rights throughout their lives, could not satisfy the aspirations of the changing times. Thus, one recent observer of Kerala society and the Nayars wrote that with the dismantling of matriliny, women lost at least as much as they had gained (Jeffrey 1992).[20]

Conclusion

It must be remembered that matriliny to the women under that system at the beginning of this century was not what is discussed today academically. They would most probably not have seen anything special about matriliny. At the same time the world around them was changing. Ideas about equality and freedom found expression in the struggles of the lower castes to gain their rights, in the Travancorean fight against the rule of Tamil Brahmin Dewans and their coteries and in the national struggle against British rule. The First World War and its economic consequences, such as the fall in prices of cash crops, rising food prices and unemployment, had a direct impact on matrilineal *taravads* which were preparing for individual partition. The changes were too many and took place at a speed unprecedented in Kerala society uptil then. Demonstrations and protests were unknown at that time.

There were also other reasons which explain why women did not oppose the changes or suggest modifications in the proposed laws which could protect their interests. First, matrilineal *taravads* were not replaced by patrilineal joint families, in which case women would have easily felt the difference. The provision for partition did not deny women their place in the *taravad*. This was aptly captured by a sociologist in the '50s. He observed that the altered nature of property inheritance did not completely transform the matrilineal character into a patrilineal system. 'Only certain aspects of patriliny are accommodated' (Rao 1957: 137).

This occurred over a period of several decades, and with fragmentation and alienation many big propertied *taravads* withered away. Nuclear families have become the accepted norm in Kerala today. The Kerala government passed the Hindu Succession Act, 1956 (HSA) and the Kerala (Hindu Joint Family System Mobilis- ation) Act, 1975. As the ramifications of all these acts are not known to most people, there is confusion in the minds of many. One comes across instances when both Keralites and outsiders talk of matriarchy (confusing the term with matriliny) in Kerala as if it is still prevalent there. Though the present generation does not appear to have nostalgic memories of the past, a matrilineal culture is believed to be still lingering in Kerala.[21]

Another reason could be that the opportunities and exposure women obtained as a result of education, employment or even marriage with highly placed men were new, and set in the context of the national movement and other awakenings, even exciting at times. It was a period when lifestyles, including food and dress, changed. As against the earlier spartan approach, this was wel- comed. However, this applied only to a minority from the well-to- do households.

A third reason could be the formation and effect of community- based organisations which have come to be termed as social reform movements. The Nair Service Society, the Sree Narayana Dharma Paripalana Yogam of the Izhavas, and the Unni Nambutiri and the Yogakshema Sabha of the Nambutiris have brought about changes in Kerala society in a way that was unimaginable earlier. Women in large numbers may not have taken an active part in the move- ments, but it is likely that they would have developed community- based affiliations. Has this obstructed the emergence of a collective voice of women? Was this a period when women began to listen to the 'commands' of male leaders? This is an area which needs serious examination.

Above all, it must be emphasised that this period witnessed a spate of new ideas, whether it related to the question of freedom and equality, science and technology, women's roles and place, or philosophy and spiritualism. Women were constantly and consis- tently exposed to ideas which extolled their *dharma*[22] to the family, particularly to the husband, and glorified female virtues based on orthodox Hindu or Brahmanical texts. Coupled with this, notions such as progressive, civilised, fashionable, modern came to be associated with the ways of the alien rulers, as against the natives who were considered to be traditional, backward and old-fashioned. The voice of the individual 'radical' woman against this background was feeble.

Thus, it is not wrong to think that by default women supported the shift in the balance of power in favour of men. Both material and ideological developments led women to accept a less than equal place within the home and outside. The period under discussion initiated a new gender hierarchy which was more beneficial to men. As far as women were concerned, they experienced a slide back from which they are yet to recover.

Notes

1. This chapter is based on a larger, on-going study on matriliny in Travancore. For Malabar, see Saradamoni (1983) and Arunima (1992).
2. It has to be noted that the remark of the Maharani (Queen) referred to the upper strata of matrilineal communities, and even then, there can be an amount of exaggeration.
3. Mayer (1952), Rao (1957), Gough (Schneider and Gough 1961) and Fuller (1976) are among the anthropologists who studied Kerala matriliny. While Gough has written extensively, only Fuller concentrated on Travancore. Shortage of space does not permit a discussion of their inquiries. This is being taken up in the larger study on which this paper is based. However, it has to be noted that their assumption was that women in these households were under the overall control of the male head or *karanavar*.
4. *Taravad* is a term used by non-Nayars too, and the renowned Malayali poet Vallathol called the whole world a *taravad*.
5. This argument needs to be explored further.
6. Appeal suit numbers 47 and 65 of 1905, *Travancore Law Report*, Vol. XXI, 1911.
7. *Talikettu* or ritual tying of *tali* is not discussed here. There are many writings available on it. Polyandry and polygyny are also left out of the discussion as not being relevant here.
8. Fuller (1976) gives detailed descriptions of Nayar marriages as observed by several of the early visitors to the area. He notes in the postscript of his book, 'Lovers of the exotic may well find cause for regret in the history of the Nayars'.
9. Called Sree Mulam Popular Assembly.
10. The Travancore Marumakkathayam Committee was formed by the government to investigate and report on the *marumakkathayam* system and on specific points of reform in order to design and enact legislation.
11. A.N. Thampy, (1941), *Report of the Enquiry into the subdivision and fragmentation of agricultural holdings in Travancore, 1941*; Quoted in Varghese, (1970).
12. The population of Travancore, estimated to be 906,857 in 1820, rose to 2,311,379 in 1875, to 2,401,158 in 1881 and 2,557,736 in 1911 (Ward and Conner 1863; Census of Travancore 1875, 1881 and 1911).

13. The Committee itself stated that a fair percentage of the educated and land-owning classes gave their views on the points raised for consideration. They also had informal discussions with a few chosen gentlemen at different places. One can conclude that the vast majority of people were not part of the discussions.

14. Kerala has a long tradition of newspapers and journals. The first women's journal, *Keraleeya Suguna Bodhini*, was launched in 1887. Initially it was shortlived, but was restarted in 1892. Since then, a large number of journals for women were published from different parts of the state. (Most of these journals did not give publishers as is the practice today. Copies, though not complete, are available at Sri Chitra Thirunal Library, Trivandrum.) Though they should not be seen from the perspective of 'radical' or 'feminist' journalism, they did contain many radical, forward-looking articles, despite the fact that it was a time when the royal house was important, caste/class feelings were strong and more men had taken to writing.

15. They were editors, publishers and writers.

16. Kannan Nair was a nationalist, government servant, teacher and activist in the Nair Service Society, but above all a fighter for patriarchal values. Without informing his first wife, he married another woman to save her from a *sambandham* with a Tamil Brahmin (Nair 1989: 107). Despite all this, he played the role of *karanavar*, brought up his sister's sons and married his daughter to one of them.

17. Ancient Hindu texts, among which the Manusmriti is treated by Brahmanical orthodoxy as *the* treatise on law, morality and ritual.

18. Classical Hindu texts.

19. Men were ranked on a scale beginning from no education, some level of education in Malayalam schools, some knowledge of English (even the ability to sign) and still higher up to B.A. level.

20. Jeffrey's observation (1992) that the ideology of patriliny was not intentionally propagated by the British government needs to be qualified with the view that the British presented their practices as superior and more civilised.

21. One unfortunate result of this is that women's vision is blurred towards the realities working against them. An example is the absence of strong organised protests by women against increasing atrocities against them. While the women of Kerala may be said to be better off than their counterparts elsewhere in India, they cannot be said to be 'free' of shackles.

22. *Dharma* in the ordinary sense means duty, but with the idea of the well-being or good of others as central. Philosophically, it is an elevated concept, the first of the *purushardhas*.

References

Aiya, N., 1906, *Travancore State Manual*. Trivandrum: Government Press.

Aiyar, D.S., 1922, *A Treatise on Malabar and Aliyasantana Law*. Madras: Madras Law Journal Office.

Arunima, G., 1992, 'Colonialism and the transformation of matriliny in Malabar, 1890–1940'. Unpublished Ph.D. dissertation, University of Cambridge.

Census of India, 1991, *Final Population Tables*. Delhi: Government Press.

Census of Travancore, 1875, 1881, 1891, 1911, 1931, Trivandrum: Government Press.

Fuller, C.J., 1976, *The Nayars Today*. Cambridge: Cambridge University Press.

Innes, C.A., 1908, *Madras District Gazetteers: Madras, Malabar, Anjengo*. Madras: Government Press.

Iyer, L.A. Ananthakrishna, 1909, 1912, *The Cochin Tribes and Castes, Vols. I and II*. Madras: Higginbothams.

Iyer, L.A. Krishna, 1937, *The Travancore Tribes and Castes*. Trivandrum: Government Press.

Jeffrey, R., 1992, *Politics, Women and Well being: How Kerala became a model*. Basingstoke: Macmillan.

Joseph, M.P., 1918, *The Principles of Marumakkathayam Law with a commentary on the Nair Regulation*. Kottayam: The Author.

Lakshmi Bai, 1908–20.

Logan, W., 1887/1951, *Malabar Manual*. Madras: Government Press.

———, 1882, *Report on the Special Commission on Malabar Land Tenures*. Madras: Government Press.

Mahila, 1908–1930.

Mayer, A.C., 1952, *Land and Society in Malabar*. Bombay: Oxford University Press.

Menon, A.S., 1979, *Kerala: Social and Cultural History*. New Delhi: Sterling.

Nair, K.K.A., 1989, *Atmakatha*. Kozhikode: Mathrubhumi.

Pillai, N.K. Krishna, 1945, 'Nayanmarude dhanastithi' (The Economic situation of the Nairs), *Service*. April 1945: 9–18.

Pillai, T.K. Velu, 1940, *Travancore State Manual*. Trivandrum: V.V. Press.

Rao, M.S.A., 1957, *Social Change in Malabar*. Bombay: Popular Book Depot.

Malabar Marriage Commission, Report of the, 1896. Madras: Government Press.

Travancore Marumakkathayam Committee, Report of the, 1908. Trivandrum: Superintendent of Government Press.

Sarada, 1908–1925.

Saradamoni, K., 1983, 'Changing land relations and women: A case study of Palghat', in V. Mazumdar (ed.), *Women and Rural Transformation*. New Delhi: ICSSR/Concept.

Service, 1920–1945.

Schneider, D.M. and K.E. Gough (eds.), 1961, *Matrilineal Kinship*. Berkeley: University of California Press.

Varghese, T.C., 1970, *Agrarian Change and Economic Consequences*. Calcutta: Allied.

Ward, Lt. and Lt. Conner, 1863, *Geographical and Statistical Memoir of the Survey of the Travancore and Cochin States*. Madras: Government Press.

II

Negotiating (In)security

6 Who Gains from Matriliny? Men, Women and Change on an Indian Island

Leela Dube

This chapter assesses the situation of women in a matrilineal Muslim society on the island of Lakshadweep, off the south-west coast of the Indian subcontinent. Kinship principles and relations, as providing the basis for the distribution and control of resources, group membership and perpetuation, the nature of entry into and exit from marriage, conjugal relations, rights over space and children, and the patterns of authority and power, are explored. The gendered dimensions of these aspects, as well as of the division of work, are elaborated. The manner in which matriliny and Islam have influenced and accommodated each other, and resulted in a flexible system, is made explicit. This has been through a social recognition of the father who, despite being a visiting husband, has special responsibilities towards his children, as well as the demarcation of the two kinds of property—matrilineal collective property and individual property governed by Islamic law. Well-known anthropological formulations regarding the inherent contradictions in matrilineal kinship organisation are questioned, by comparison with patrilineal principles and new findings on matrilineal societies. Stereotypes of

Islamic practice are implicitly challenged. Finally, some recent developments are outlined. Men's reactions to proposed changes in their matrilineal system are analysed, through their perceptions of the distribution of rights and responsibilities in the existing system and their Islamic identity.

This chapter attempts to assess the situation of women in a matrilineal Muslim society on one of the coral islands off the south-west coast of India. I focus on women's centrality in the perpetuation of groups, women and space, the organisation of production and the division of work, patterns of physical movement, rights over children, the nature and character of marriage, and matters relating to property, authority, and decision making. This is followed by a discussion of some controversial issues related to the general characteristics of matrilineal systems. Finally, I reflect on continuity and change in this island society. The main issue that needs to be explained is men's reactions to proposed changes in their matrilineal system.[1]

In the Islamic world, while adhering to the essential tenets of their religion, believers have tended to retain their social and cultural moorings (Utas 1983). This may be related to the Islamic distinction between *ibadat* (worship) and *muamlat* (worldly affairs).[2] In matters of personal or family law, where major adjustments have occurred based on local customs and practices and indigenous legal systems, Islam has evinced remarkable flexibility. In the operation of these laws, the most significant domain is that of kinship. Kinship provides the principles that govern the distribution and control of resources, the formation of groups and the placement of individuals in them, and the nature of group membership. Kinship is not a mere set of moral principles but something that is rooted in material conditions. The ideology of kinship cannot be separated from property and the production relations, which it governs.

While Islam took patriliny to be the natural form of social organisation and created a code of conduct and a system of law based on this assumption, the faith also spread among many societies that were rooted in kinship matrices of other kinds. Islam spread not only to several types of patrilineal social organisations, but also to Indonesia and Malaysia, where kinship was mostly bilateral, and to a number of communities in south and south-east Asia and Africa that lived by matrilineal principles of descent, inheritance, and succession and were rooted in matrilineal ideology. Lakshadweep, a group of islands in the Arabian Sea off the coast of Kerala, is a fascinating instance.

A Historical Background

The island of Kalpeni, which lies a little over 220km off Kozhikode (Calicut), is one of the four inhabited islands of the Laccadive group. The Laccadives, the Amindivi group and Minicoy together form the Union Territory of Lakshadweep. While the people of Minicoy are ethnically and culturally closer to the Maldivians, the inhabitants of the other islands are descendants of Hindu settlers from the Kerala coast. They speak a somewhat archaic and corrupted version of Malayalam, in which the influence of Arabic is distinct. According to historical and linguistic evidence, the major migrations probably took place in the 9th and 10th centuries AD. About four centuries later, owing to contact with Arab traders, the islanders, through a mass conversion, became Sunni Muslims following the Shafi'i school of law (Logan 1887). Hinduism was displaced by Islam, but the special form of matriliny which the original migrants had taken to the islands, and which had become entrenched there, survived; and in its essential features it persists until this day (Dube 1969, 1978; Ittaman 1976; Kutty 1972; Mannadiar 1977; Saigal 1990).

In this system, descent was traced through the mother—female links alone were recognised for membership in a matrilineal group and for a right to its resources. The exogamous matrilineal descent group known as the *taravad*—as in Kerala—was a group of individuals of both sexes who could trace their descent in the female line from a single ancestress. The depth of such a matrilineage might vary from three to six generations. A *taravad* might be a property group as well as a domestic group, a property and production group comprising more than one consumption unit, or it may have split into a number of property groups each of which is made up of one or more consumption units. The figures indicate some of the several possibilities.[3] Splits in a *taravad* or in lower-level matrilineal units tended to run on *tavazhi* or branch lines.[4] However, individuals derived their identities from their *taravads*.

The traditional pattern of marital residence was duolocal, a husband being a nightly visitor to his wife's home. Children lived with their mothers and their matrilineal kin. Thus, the elementary

Figure 6.1

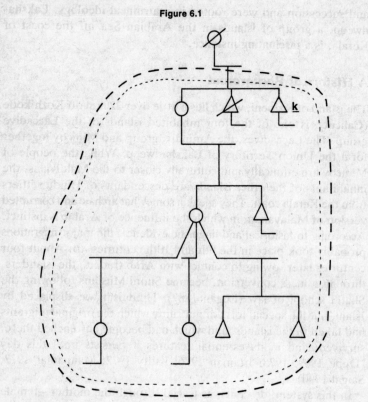

KEY

Figures 6.1 to 6.4

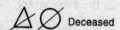

Visiting marriage

Man living with wife

k   Karnavar

Domestic group

Property group

Deceased

Figure 6.2

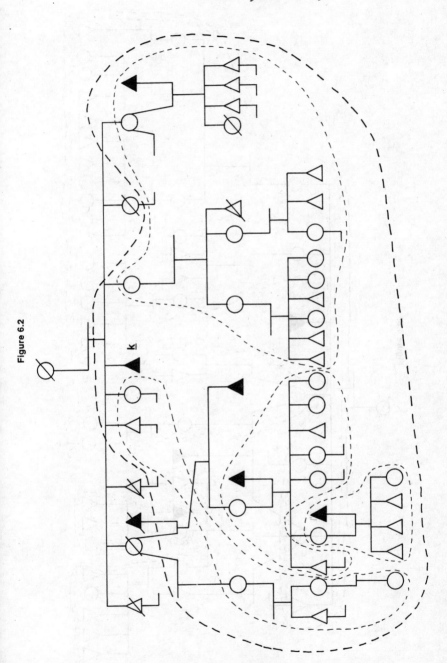

<u>k</u>

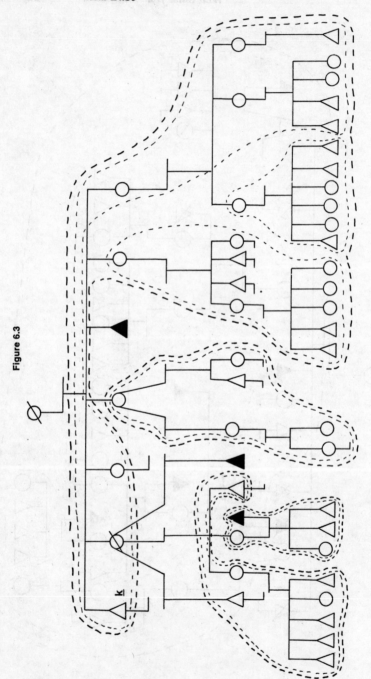

Figure 6.3

Figure 6.4

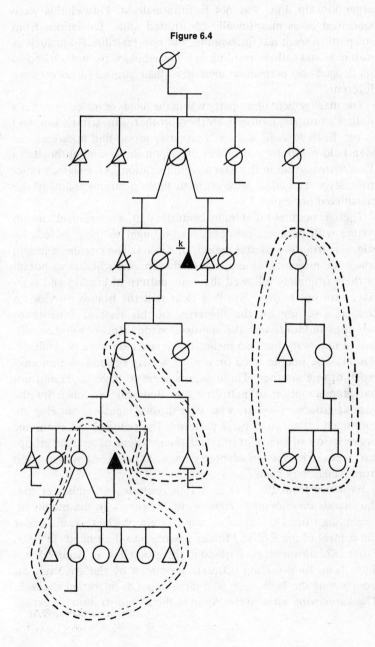

or nuclear family, either as an independent unit or embedded in a larger kinship unit, was not institutionalised. Households were conceived of as matrilineally constituted units. Deviations from this pattern were not uncommon, but non-matrilineal kin such as husbands and fathers residing in a household were not viewed as full-fledged and permanent members—their *taravad* identities were different.

The management of property was in the hands of males—mother's mother's brother, mother's brother, brother, son, sister's son, and so on. Each *taravad* and each property group had a *karanavar*.[5] Men held positions and offices of responsibility and authority in their *taravads* and in the island administration. All religious functionaries were males. Succession to these positions followed the matrilineal principle.

There is no doubt that many centuries ago, a matrilineal kinship system with duolocal residence was brought to these islands by migrants from the coastal regions of Kerala. The circumstances in which the migrants came to Lakshadweep, and whether or not all of them originally followed the same pattern of kinship and marriage, are not known. But it is clear that the islands provided a congenial setting for the flowering of this system. Subsistence activities and trade with the mainland made teamwork and coordination necessary but also meant that some men were periodically absent. The people lived on a narrow strip of land, within easy reach of one another. These factors seem to have facilitated not only the adoption of matriliny and duolocal residence by the various groups of settlers who were thrown together, but also the continued existence of these patterns. The political and economic organisation of the migrants and their system of graded groups also seem to have been adapted from what prevailed in the region from which they came.

Evidence from the 15th and 16th centuries AD indicates that the islands functioned as colonies of the rulers on the mainland. Beginning from 1857, the Laccadive group of islands came under the control of the British,[6] finally passing into their hands in 1905. From 1877 onwards, each island in the group had an Amin (custodian, head or presiding officer), appointed by the government, from among the *karanavars* who represented its important *taravads*. The *karanavars* assisted the Amin in the administration of justice.

The islands were attached to the district of Malabar. During their visits to the islands, the inspecting officers of the government heard and decided cases with the help of the elders. There was no written or codified law. The administrators were guided by the customary law of the islands which bore some features of Islamic law. The formation of the Union Territory of Lakshadweep in 1956 brought important changes in the administration and the judicial system and also increased the contact of the islanders with the outside world.

Over the centuries, the islanders had sustained themselves through trade with the mainland, using country sailing craft. Coconuts had been the basis of their economy. Their principal activities were the making and trading of copra, coir, jaggery and vinegar.[7] Besides coconuts and fish, some fruit, vegetables and coarse grain were also produced. The migrants depended on rice as a staple, which gave rise to regular trade with the mainland in which coconuts and their products were exchanged for rice and other necessaries.

One significant feature of these islands has been the presence of either three or four caste-like groups—interdependent, hierarchically graded, exclusive and exhaustive. Tradition traces their ancestry to various castes in Kerala.[8] Kalpeni's population was divided into three groups: the Koya, who were traditionally landlords and boat owners; the Malmi, traditionally navigators; and the Melacheri, coconut pluckers and toddy tappers. The Koya formed over half of the population and the Melacheri, over a third. The major economic relationship, one of the master-servant type, has been between the Koya and the Melacheri.[9]

Property and Authority in a *Taravad*

A child belonged to its mother's group, whose resources it shared. It derived its group identity through its mother and its rights to resources, shelter, nurturing and training through its mother's *taravad*. As the originators of *taravads* or *tavazhis*, women received special respect. The oldest woman in a matrilineal group had a position of honour and authority and an important role in decision-making. It was membership of a *taravad*, reckoned through female links starting with the mother, that gave an individual a right to a share in its property, which consisted principally of land, trees, boats, buildings, fishing channels, soaking pits and moveable goods.

The joint property of a matrilineal group could not be sold or given away without the consent of all its members. *Taravad* property was a kind of communal property and, theoretically, impartible. However, members could ask for their rightful shares for individual use, on the basis of a notional division.[10] Neither the men nor the women could dispose of their shares in *taravad* property, individually. On Kalpeni, the division was stirpital, that is, a mother's share was divided equally among all her children, irrespective of age or sex.[11]

Men and women had the same kind of right to *taravad* property, but the principle of inheritance in the female line ensured that while a woman's share devolved on her children, a man's share reverted to his close matrilineal kin on his death. During his lifetime, a man could join his share of his *taravad's* trees to his wife's share of her own *taravad's* trees and work on them, but this arrangement would end with his death. He could not give away his share of *taravad* property even to his own children, who were members of their mother's *taravad*. Another kind of property, *swontham-swottu*, one's own, was individually owned and disposable; its disposal was governed by Islamic law. As there were few avenues for independent earning, there was little property of this kind in the 1960s—only slightly over nine per cent of all the coconut trees on the island (Kutty 1972).

Besides matrilineal descent and inheritance, the mode of residence put women in a specially favourable situation. Just like a man, a woman too did not have to leave her natal home on marriage. A man spent the night at his wife's home and returned to his own in the morning. In the early 1960s, as many as 76.5 per cent of husbands in extant marriages were categorised as visiting husbands.[12] The predominant mode of residence, thus, was duolocal.[13] A woman was never estranged from her natal home and continued to live and work with her matrilineal kin, even after marriage.

Although the management of property and the organisation of work were the responsibility of the *karanavar*, a male, his authority could not normally be overbearing. The nature of property, which was communally owned but shares of which could be allotted to individual members for their use and over which no one had absolute rights, the organisation of work, in which women engaged

their natal homes. As a result, the women of Kalpeni seemed to enjoy a sense of security, self-respect, and autonomy. In this, they stood in sharp contrast to the women of the patrilineal Muslim communities of northern India, whose situation can be precarious. For the women of the patrilineal communities, marriage means the loss of membership of the natal group, transfer to the husband's home and a sense of insecurity inasmuch as acceptable behaviour seems to be a tacit condition for a woman's right to live in her husband's home. A wife could be asked to leave the house. Marriage contracts may contain clauses to prevent such an eventuality and it may not happen at all socioeconomic levels. But widespread violence and harassment do point to the contrast between the women of Kalpeni and those among the patrilineal Muslims (and Hindus) of northern India.

The houses of closely related female matrikin such as sisters, mother's sisters, daughters and sisters' daughters were often located close to one another, as matrilineal groups held contiguous lands. This was helpful in many ways, for example, in collective activities like coir making. Where *taravad* land was scattered, because of purchases, and where husbands built houses for wives and children, a few *tavazhis* might not have had houses close together.

The nature of property and the organisation of work are of relevance here. In the broad division of labour between the sexes, the major activities of men were copra making, cultivation, fishing, the construction of houses and boats, and periodic sailing for trade. Men of the lower group, the Melacheri, climbed trees to pluck coconuts and tap toddy, removed the husk from coconuts and helped in soaking the husk in pits. Besides household work and the rearing of children, which were primarily their responsibility, women engaged in coir making and in the processing of vinegar and jaggery. There were various stages in the making of coir and the organisation of this work was mainly in the hands of women. The division of work was thus gender-specific and led to a high degree of interdependence between the women and men of the matrilineal unit, which was the unit of production.

This division and interdependence did not lead, however, to any firm control over a woman by her male matrilineal kin; nor, of course, by her husband, even in uxorilocal residence or when he joined his share of *taravad* property to her household. Rights to property accrued through women and houses belonged to them, so there was no question of their being looked upon as helpless destitutes, as they are in many patrilineal societies. A woman could obtain help whenever necessary—from matrilineal kin or, in the event of divorce and remarriage, from another husband—to do the men's work on her property. Women were not ignorant of simple economic transactions and had the freedom to move about and actively participate in them.

In respect of segregation and seclusion, which are associated with Islamic populations and are thought to have religious sanction, the islanders provided a sharp contrast to mainland Muslims, especially to those of non-peninsular India. The practice of *purdah*, seclusion, was absent. A piece of cloth carried as an outer covering for the shoulders was often used for covering the head as well. It was customary for a bridegroom to present such a head-cloth to his bride at their wedding and on special occasions later. In a vague sort of way, it was thought to represent the Islamic notion of the seclusion or protection of females,[15] but it did not constrain women in any manner.

On some other islands, the wives of religious leaders were seen to use a proper veil, the *burqa*. Very recently, a cloak, of the kind that has become popular in Malaysia, seems to have made some impact on the women of these islands, as was apparent from a television report. The head-cloth has come to be more regularly used, even by little girls (Saigal 1990).

Women were not confined to domestic space. They moved freely about the island—working, buying and selling, visiting, attending religious discourses and participating in various functions and meetings, including the settlement of disputes and court proceedings. In the last, however, their participation was not as great as that of men, and they had to observe some gender-specific decorum. Often, they were represented by their matrikin or by the *mukhtiar*. They gathered in large numbers on the shore when boats departed or arrived. Neither at home nor outside was strict segregation visible. Women did not seem to hide themselves even from outsiders. However, the inside of the house was theirs, and whenever there was a *kootam* (a meeting to resolve a dispute), women who were asked questions or wanted to present their point of view generally stood behind the door of the inner room.

Few productive activities were carried out behind walls. For coir making, a collective activity, a space just outside the house was used. The 'fireplace' for making jaggery, also had to be outside the house. These spaces were ordinarily not enclosed in a manner that would render the women within them invisible. The places where men made copra were not out of bounds to women. When facilities for modern education were introduced, girls were not prevented from going to school.[16] The notion that the primary objective of education was the securing of jobs applied not only to boys, but also to girls, and some young women had begun to go to the mainland to be educated.

In general, however, the space beyond the island was not available to women. Deep water fishing was men's work. More importantly, only men went to the mainland for trade—women stayed behind and prayed for their safety. Many men also did not ever sail to the mainland, but this was because they did not have the resources. Women were taken to the mainland principally for medical treatment or on their way to Mecca. Away from the island and in the midst of strangers, they were seen as needing guidance and protection.

Rights and Responsibilities in Marriage and Divorce

Women's relative autonomy and their position of advantage were most clearly visible in marriage and divorce, an area in which women in patrilineal Muslim communities on the subcontinent are particularly vulnerable. Although marriage on Kalpeni was based on the Sharia and fulfilled the basic requirements laid down in the scriptures and in law, in reality its nature was radically different from what Islam visualised and emphasised in marriage.

Marriage involved very limited rights and obligations. In the traditional pattern of residence, marriage did not result in any reshuffling of the domestic units. In 1962–63, 76.5 per cent of married men were visiting husbands. A woman remained secure in her own home and was not viewed as 'transferable', 'a guest in the parental home', or 'a bird of passage', all common expressions for girls in the cultural idiom of both the Muslims and the Hindus in the subcontinent, where even intra-kin marriages do not do away with these notions. The role of the *wali* (marriage guardian) was a religious formality and the payment of *mahr* (bride-wealth) was only a formal compliance with religious prescription. The amount of the *mahr* was negligible[17] and it did not in any way establish a

172   *Leela Dube*

man's authority over his wife.[18] The Kazi's register of marriages showed that in many instances *mahr* had been given only in part or not at all.

Although lip service was paid to the Islamic conception of a husband's obligation to maintain his wife and children, in fact, marriage did not reflect the notion with any clarity. So long as a marriage lasted, the husband made the customary annual payment of two or three bags of rice and between 20 and 50 coconuts to his wife's household. He was also expected to give her gifts of clothes, cosmetics and so on. During pregnancy and childbirth, he was expected to provide special items like chicken. The cultural perception of this practice is somewhat unclear. We had earlier described it as gift-giving (Dube 1969; Kutty 1972), but the Malayalam-based term used for it on the island was *chilav*, meaning expense. Was it a kind of fee for sexual access to a woman or was it a nominal fulfilment of the obligation prescribed by Islam? Perhaps, it was a mixture of both. In practical terms, it could of course be interpreted as a contribution towards the expense that a wife's household incurred in providing the visiting husband's dinner, and often his breakfast as well.

There was nothing resembling the appropriation of a woman's labour or rights over her offspring by her husband or his kin group. Husbands and wives remained separate entities. Neither acquired a right to the other's productive labour. Conjugal relations had an entirely different tenor. A woman was not expected to defer to her husband and there was no trace of the notion that it is a wife's moral duty to render personal services to her husband.

Even when a woman flouted her husband's exclusive right of sexual access to her, he had neither the right nor the means to punish her physically or through the denial of necessities. Physical violence, which in some cultures is viewed as the 'natural' reaction of a man whose pride has been wounded by his wife's unfaithfulness and which also has sanction in the Quran, was unthinkable on the island.[19] Although it may not have been conceptualised in quite these terms, a married woman did not lose her rights over her person. A wronged husband could take recourse only to divorce, which often was what the women wanted, even though she might then have to forgo her dues.

A wife did not have an exclusive right of sexual access to her husbands, as he could, in theory, have as many as four wives at a time. Men did sometimes use this privilege, but women tended to react sharply to their husbands' other marriages or extramarital affairs and such situations could easily precipitate divorce. Bigamy was mostly short-lived and enduring polygyny was rare. In 1961–62, only six of the 670 currently married men had more than one wife (Kutty 1972). Given the pattern of residence, co-wives did not have to share a home or a cooking pot, but they did not seem to have taken kindly to sharing a sexual partner and a bringer of occasional gifts.

The *nikah* (wedding ceremony) established the paternity of the children, but in terms of lineage and social identity, access to resources, shelter and daily living, a child belonged to its mother and her matrilineal group. A father had little authority over his children and, traditionally, no legal responsibility for their maintenance. Depending on his capacity and the strength of his attachment to them, a man did spend on his children's education, clothes and their other necessities. With increasing contact with the mainland and with the larger Islamic world, the feeling was slowly growing that, perhaps, religion enjoined a man to bear responsibility towards his children; but this was still alien to the matrilineal ethos of the island. There was no question of a man's having to pay for the maintenance of his children by a divorced wife, nor of his having any claim to them.

The most important role of a father, recognised by the community, was the socioreligious. He had a definite part to play in the life-cycle ceremonies of his children and was expected to contribute substantially towards them. These were birth, the circumcision of sons, the ear-boring of daughters and marriage. A man's matrilineal group was actively involved in such ceremonies for his children. A father was expected to bring gifts for his children. There was no taboo on his demonstrating affection for his child. In their turn, children were expected to contribute and participate in the death ceremonies of their father.

The significantly different nature of marriage, and of the relationship between spouses, on the island becomes clearer when looking at the dissolution of marriage. Theoretically, Islam gives a man unbounded facility to divorce his wife at will, without having to give reasons, while it denies a woman the right to pronounce a divorce even in those rare instances where she is permitted to initiate proceedings. On the island, the facility of *talaq*, a divorce obtained without assigning reasons, was in effect available to both men and women. A man could resort to irrevocable *talaq* by pronouncing the formula 'I divorce you' three times in succession. A woman could not pronounce a divorce, but living in her own house she could make it known to her husband that she did not want his visits any longer. This left him with no option but to give her the divorce she wanted. He might delay the pronouncement or try to negotiate, in order to be absolved of paying his dues. In some instances, it was tantamount to the purchase by the wife of her freedom (*khula*).[20]

Divorce was fairly frequent. More than half the men and women on the island had married more than once and many had married several times. Marriage was brittle, divorce was easy. Men had a higher rate of remarriage—unlike women, they could remarry while a previous marriage was extant and did not have to wait out a three-month *iddat* period. There were many instances where divorced couples wished to remarry each other. The Islamic rule was followed, which allowed this only after the woman had married another man and been divorced by him.

I have argued elsewhere (Dube 1969) that since marriage did not entail the living together of spouses or their cooperation or interdependence in economic and social spheres or even a shared responsibility towards their children, its dissolution did not have much of a disruptive effect. Nor did it threaten the bond between mother and children, as it does in many patrilineal, including Muslim, societies. The socioreligious obligations of a father towards his children remained unaffected by his divorce from their mother. He could not be denied access to his children. The question of custody over children did not arise. The overall quality of a man's relationship with his children might change, particularly if he remarried, but dissolution of marriage between the parents did not lead to a lifelong estrangement.

I wish to emphasise that on Kalpeni, the continuation or dissolution of a marital bond was not an unilateral phenomenon. A woman, as we have seen, could use her initiative and take decisions in respect of *talaq*. In addition, in these matters, women did not suffer the kinds of constraints and risks likely to be faced by the patrilineal Muslim (and Hindu) women of the subcontinent— deprivation and homelessness, loss of children, stigmatisation and, sometimes, limited chances of remarriage.

Individual and Lineage Property

Transactions of property constituted an important activity on the island. A careful look at them is crucial to an understanding of the distinction between men's and women's situations and interests in this matrilineal society. Property was of two kinds—Friday or matrilineal, communal property; and Monday or *swontham*, one's own property. Both sexes had inalienable rights in matrilineal property which remained within the matrilineal groups. Men's rights reverted to their closest matrilineal kin, rather than their own children, while for women, their children were members of their own matrilineal group. Monday property, on the other hand, could be disposed of as its owner wished. Such property was acquired through one's own earnings or through gift deeds or inheritance from one's parents or non-matrilineal kin. An important method of acquiring Monday property, however was through the conversion of Friday property. This could be done only with the consent of all the adult members of the matrilineal group, whose property it was (Dube 1991).

While divisions and transactions of Friday property were regulated by custom and tradition, *parampara*, the disposal of Monday property was supposed to be regulated according to the Sharia. Intestate disposal was one possibility. It was also possible for an individual to gift away such property at any time or to prepare a will specifying the beneficiaries. Gifting away and making wills were both seen as having the sanction of Islamic law and, in the context of the island's social system, were perceived as a provision made by religion to enable a man to give some property to his children and wife. Since there were very few avenues of independent earning, attempts were constantly being made to convert parts of communal, matrilineal property into *swontham* property. This often involved bringing pressure on matrilineal kin, cajoling and manoeuvring.

Men were the main actors in cases relating to property and transactions in it, but they had to carry their female matrikin with them. Also, so far as matrilineal property was concerned, it was invariably argued that it was morally wrong to deprive women and helpless children of their legitimate rights. Some held that *taravad* property was a kind of *wakf* (religious trust) property, created for the benefit of the women and children of the matrilineage.

Women formed the links for the devolution of property to the next generation. Hence, they had to safeguard their children's rights along with their own. Theirs was the line that had continuity, and in all decisions that had to do with Friday property, their consent was essential. No appeal or deed was complete without the signatures of adult female members, particularly of those who were at that time the originators of branches.

Why were men the principal actors in transactions of property? This question has to be answered in the context of the roles of women and men, and their differential rights. Men were the principal actors in major economic transactions and they managed property. The Island Council that was in charge of administration and adjudication consisted of men and all religious functionaries were men. There was certainly greater motivation for men to be so involved. Men and women were in very different situations with regard to inheritance by their respective children. At the same time, by giving fathers a distinct recognition, Islam had brought a certain flexibility to the matrilineal principle. The category of *swontham* property gave legitimacy to, and fed religious sanction into, a man's desire to do something for his children.

However, those who fought against moves to convert Friday property into *swontham* property were also mainly men. The same actors, thus, could have opposite roles in different situations, depending on their interests. A father trying to bring some matrilineal property into his individual ownership and a *karanavar*, or other *taravad* member, defending the sanctity of the matrilineal heritage and protecting the rights of the innocent and helpless members of the group appear to be contradictory—but both roles might be played by the same man in different contexts, and both were a part of the island's culture.

Another interesting feature of these transactions was that at different points of time, a man might act by different norms and values in relation to the same unit of property. After he had succeeded in acquiring some *swontham* property, by the conversion of part of his *taravad's* joint matrilineal property, a man might proceed to give it to his wife's branch as joint *tavazhi-taravad* property rather than to his children and wife as property owned individually by them. This suggests a very firm faith in the matrilineal principle, even while taking advantage of other principles to deviate from it. There were several instances of such conversion and subsequent gifting (see Dube 1991).

Finally, it appears that what was viewed as being sanctioned by Islam was in a way rooted in the developmental cycle of property and matrilineal groups in the matrilineal system, and the male members' destiny in it. A man's desire to gift property to his children was considered both logical and appropriate. According to the cultural understanding, a man was sure to be well looked after, so long as his mother was alive. He would continue to receive attention, so long as his sisters, especially those of his age or older, were active. When his nieces and nephews took over, however, he would have to count more on his children and his wife. If he wished to be cared for by his children in his old age, the logic of the situation justified his inclination to gift some assets to their household. The intermeshing of materiality with the ideology of kinship, or their essential inseparability, was clearly demonstrated in these processes; and, to repeat, religion had imparted a certain legitimacy to the father-child bond. It is significant that this concession to men did not make women in any way dependent on them.

Matrilineal and Patrilineal Systems Compared

Thus, in terms of residence, the assurance of shelter, rights to space, property and sources of living, rights over children, and the exercise of choice in marriage and its dissolution, the situation of women on Kalpeni presented a contrast to that of Muslim women in the rest of the region. It seems that the kind of concentration of control over property, women's sexuality and reproductive power that a husband or other affinal male can achieve in a patrilineal, patri-virilocal system, often deriving justification from religion, is simply not available to a matrilineally related kinsman.

The proposition that an absence of co-ordination between lines of authority and descent—authority being a male function and group placement a female function—is characteristic of matriliny (Schneider 1961) and the idea of the 'matrilineal puzzle' (Richards 1950) need reconsideration.[21] Is authority always a male function? What are the connotations of authority? In matrilineal societies, authority is very often diffused. On Kalpeni too, we did not find evidence of the concentration of authority in a single individual or only in males, although males were the managers of property. Women, particularly those with respected kinship statuses such as mother's mother's mother, elder sister and mother's sister, had considerable importance and influence. Typically, a matrilineal male finds it difficult to establish complete control over his sister's children. He cannot have them under his thumb, as a father has his sons in a patrilineal system. The relationship between mother's brother and sister's son is not direct but mediated by a woman.

In a matrilineal system, women's sexuality is not under the oppressive control of either her matrikin or her husband and his group. Among matrilineal castes, such as the Nayar, concerned with boundary maintenance, an essential feature of caste, there were definite mechanisms to ensure that women chose their mates only from among accepted levels of caste. For this purpose, their sexuality had to be strictly controlled. Their freedom was circumscribed and they came under the authority of male matrikin (Dube 1988; Gough 1959, 1961). As a general proposition, however, it seems to be true that women in matrilineal societies are free of any intensive and oppressive control. The relationship between the wife and husband is, typically, not characterised by the authority and control of the man and the corresponding deference of the woman. Asymmetry and oppression are absent from it.

A patrilineal system too is beset with conflict and contradiction inasmuch as the biologically unrepudiable parent has nothing to do with the group placement of her children. At whose cost do patrilineal systems function and survive? Surely, at the cost of women. Women's peripheral membership of their natal groups, their transfer to their husbands' groups—where they remain outsiders and suspect for long—and their purely instrumental value as bearers of children for their affinal groups, all have certain definite implications. The absence of rights over property, over the means of living and over their children makes women vulnerable to oppression of different kinds. The opposition between outsider and insider, the tensions involved in the process of girls' socialisation which emphasises control over their sexuality, the asymmetry between brother and sister and between husband and wife, the internalisation of roles and of an ideology that circumscribes and devalues women—accompanied by many compensatory devices— the cultural association of women with witchcraft and the evil eye are pointers to the conflicts and contradictions in a strongly patrilineal system.

As for property, in patrilineal systems there are a number of sayings which point towards rivalry, competition and conflict over it among close kin—between patrilateral parallel cousins, father's brother and brother's son, and even father and son and among brothers. The disputes over property among patrikin recorded and analysed by anthropologists and historians in various patrilineal communities all over the world leave no doubt that they are a ubiquitous feature of social life. Patrilineal systems certainly do not function as smoothly as they are made out to, when contrasted with matrilineal systems.

There is, however, one difference which demands close examination. Rivalries and disputes over property and other resources among patrikin do not ordinarily disrupt the essence of the patrilineal principle. The descending generations, which are the main focus of interest, do after all, belong to the same lineage. Moreover, a woman, who has few rights in her husband's home, does not subvert the patrilineal principle in showing an interest in the future of her male children, who belong to her husband's line.

On the other hand, when it is expressed in a matrilineal system, a man's interest in his children can subvert the principle of descent and inheritance—for his children belong to their mother's group and have membership and property rights there, not in his own group. But does this always happen? As Elizabeth Colson (1980) has said, matrilineality need not be associated with a disregard for paternal claims; and the situation on Kalpeni corroborated this. Matrilineal systems are not all identical, so it is necessary to take a second look to locate a father's position in them, as well as the systemic safeguards that may be present.

Change and Continuity

I now turn to change and continuity in the matrilineal social system of Kalpeni after the Lakshadweep islands were made into a territory administered by the federal government in 1956. This marked a significant departure from the past. The territory sent a member to the national parliament, and the administrative and political set-up changed—in particular, the powers of the Amin and his council were curtailed. Steamer services, a post office and the telegraph gave the island improved communication with the mainland. Schools and medical facilities were provided. Higher education and technical training became available on other islands and on the mainland, for which scholarships were offered. A coir centre

was created, together with a fisheries department. Electricity and
the mass media arrived, many new employment opportunities
came into being and land reforms were introduced. Several development schemes, including new fishing technology and cottage
industries, were encouraged. The cooperative society created in
1962 brought under itself the sale of coconuts and copra and made
available rice and a variety of consumer goods. The small, un-
inhabited island of Bangaram was turned into a tourist resort.
Newly laid airstrips made some of the islands accessible by air.

All this resulted in a greater interaction with the outside world
through education, the mass media, involvement in national politics
and increased travel to the mainland and residence there. Muslim
and non-Muslim officials who were posted to the island adopted an
attitude of derision towards the islanders' ways. In the early 1960s,
some people were beginning to question their social structure and
raise their voice against features that were perceived as un-Islamic.
Some of those more exposed to the ways of the mainland insisted
that the Sharia be followed in regard to paternal property and
resented the turning of a man's *swontham* property into the collective *taravad-tavazhi* property of his children's group. Among them
were also those who would have gained if their fathers had followed
Islamic law in the disposal of their individual property. They also
expressed opposition to the people's 'casual' attitude towards
marriage and divorce and favoured the administration's efforts to
introduce legal measures to reduce the frequency of divorce. There
were not many such people, but it seemed that changes in the
economic sphere and exposure to pan-Islamic movements might
strengthen such thinking (see Dube 1969; Kutty 1972).

It appeared that land reforms, growing avenues for independent
earning through wages and jobs, changes in the methods of fishing
and the establishment of the cooperative society would make
individuals and individual households less dependent on larger
property groups and matrilineal groups. It also seemed possible
that these would give an impetus to an increase in the freedom of
endeavour for small units in traditional economic pursuits. Moreover, the new employment opportunities were likely to reduce
people's dependence on their traditional economy. Employment
outside the island would create conditions for the geographic
dispersion of at least some people, for whom duolocal residence
would not then be possible. All this would encourage the formation

of conjugal units consisting of husband, wife and children. The growing consciousness about the incompatibility of the island's social system and Islamic ideals and injunctions was likely to result in the development of apathy or opposition towards the age-old matrilineal system. It was anticipated that the already existing father-child bond, institutionalised and asserted by Islam, would help in the process.

Later developments showed that the changes we had visualised in Kalpeni's matrilineal system did not come about. The resolution passed in 1962, at a meeting presided over by the Administrator and attended by the Amin, the council of elders, and some other people, that a man who divorced his wife should be made to pay an annual fine that would go towards the maintenance of his wife and children, had not had any effect till 1969. According to Saigal (1990), who was Administrator in Lakshadweep during 1982–85, demands arose for change and reform on the lines of those adopted for the matrilineal communities of Kerala and Karnataka, but not from those who would be directly affected.

In 1971, the local administration appointed a committee of judicial officers to examine the feasibility of amending the system of inheritance. The committee studied the evolution of the system and interviewed 79 men. It turned out that the majority did not favour change. In Androth and Kalpeni, even the younger generation was opposed to any change. 'An overwhelming majority of people were anxious to retain the existing mode of enjoyment and inheritance of the *taravad* property' (Saigal 1990). The committee thought that it would be unreasonable not to pay any heed to the people's views. In 1982–83, when the proposed regulations to abolish the existing system were placed before citizens' councils for their views, most could not arrive at a decision, and as a result the regulations were shelved.

Society in Lakshadweep provided an instance of the resilience of matrilineality and its capacity to adapt to a religion with a pronounced patrilineal emphasis. Elsewhere, I have demonstrated the interaction between matriliny and Islam and the processes of accommodation and adjustment between the two (Dube 1969). I have argued that Islam imparted greater flexibility to the matrilineal system of Kalpeni and, thereby, helped to sustain it. All social systems are characterised by some conflict, although the kind and degree of conflict differs among them. Both kinds of unilineal kinship systems have conflict inherent in them. The argument that a few external influences or internal crises can throw a matrilineal system off balance is questionable. In many matrilineal societies, stability is associated with women, and Colson (1980) found that the Plateau Tonga have shown a remarkable capacity for adaptation in the face of economic and political changes. Another assumption that we have questioned is that authority is always vested in males, irrespective of the descent system, so that each unit of production or residence must have a male to wield authority. In trying to understand the unwillingness of the people of Kalpeni to opt for a transformation of their kinship system, we have first to disabuse ourselves of these commonly held assumptions about matriliny, authority and the like.

As Saigal (1990) has observed, no women were asked for their views on the *taravad* system and on the proposed changes to it. It was men, including the young, who expressed themselves in favour of the matrilineal system, as it functioned on the islands. We must re-examine the notion that in such a system women are the gainers, in every way, and men the losers; and its corollary, that at the slightest opportunity, men would wish to abandon matriliny.[22] On Kalpeni, men and women had essentially equivalent rights in matrilineal *taravad* property, the difference being that while a woman's rights were inherited by her children, a man's share reverted to his kin group on his death. Islam had tempered the system so that a man could give his individually owned property to his wife and children. With growing opportunities for independent employment and wage earning, men seemed to be in a better position. They had unquestioned rights in their matrilineal groups as well as a recognised right to keep their self-earned incomes–a right that had come to them when there was very little scope for such incomes.

In these circumstances, why would a man wish to give up the security he enjoyed as a member of a *taravad*? This security was both material and psychological in that he felt himself to have an identity and to be part of a larger grouping. There were also positions of importance to inherit. Men employed on the mainland asserted that they derived their identities from their *taravads*—they appeared to escape a feeling of rootlessness even here, by reference to their *taravad* identities.

A perusal of the nature of resources and property on the island is essential in order to understand the material basis of *taravad* identity and the people's unwillingness to abandon their system in favour of conjugal homes and Islamic law. The main form of strategic resource was the coconut tree, which in terms of longevity and divisibility had a character entirely different from that of land. A given number of trees could be divided and re-divided and exploited, separately or together with the trees either of one's matrilineal kin or of one's spouse and children. In many cases, individuals were given their shares. Such divisions did not pose a threat to the notion of collective matrilineal, *taravad* property. Because of the pliability of this basic resource, which could be moved notionally and aligned and realigned, divisions within a *taravad* did not pose a problem, neither did a man's going to live with his wife.[23]

Factors related to the possibility that more and more conjugal units may be formed with decreasing dependence on the cooperative activity of larger matrilineal units need to be examined. There are many societies which look at the beginning of married life as a kind of experimental phase. The notion that a husband will necessarily want to bear the entire burden of responsibility for his wife and children is related, in many societies, to notions of adulthood, the macho male and the dependent wife. On Kalpeni, there is no such cultural construction, which may explain the marked reluctance of men to break away from the security of their matrilineal homes. Nor should we assume that when both wife and husband have independent incomes, they will be eager to merge their resources and, moreover, that the husband will be the authority figure in the new arrangement. Pat Caplan (1984) has shown for the east coast of Africa that it is possible for the two to maintain separate income streams. Finally, geographical dispersion is unlikely to have any great effect. For one thing, men have not been going far from home for long periods. For another, even when conjugal units are formed away from the island, women do not wish to abandon their own and their children's rights in matrilineal property. A small number of instances are unlikely to lead to a structural disruption.

The tendency towards uxorilocality was greater among the older age groups. Accounts of property disputes and transactions from around the turn of the century also point to old men going to live with their wives and children. Uxorilocality, after a certain age, also seems to have had some cultural sanction. It is possible that in the changed circumstances, there may be a rise in *puthia swottu*, new and disposable property, and that this might encourage uxorilocality or neolocality. But even this is unlikely to make people stop converting individually owned property to collective matrilineal property—the danger of fragmentation of resources inherent in the Islamic mode of disposal is too clear to be missed and will almost certainly continue to be contrasted to the security of collective matrilineal property.

Concluding Remarks

Returning to the distinction in Islam between *ibadat* and *muamlat*, the Kalpeni islanders were rooted in *ibadat* and considered themselves true Muslims. In respect of birth, circumcision, marriage and death they followed the letter of the law. Where undisposable collective property was concerned, they likened it to *wakf* property. The distinction was often referred to in disputes and it could be argued that it helped matriliny to temper some of the relatively rigid prescriptions of Islam.

A crucial point is that in Islam there is no such thing as collectively owned ancestral property—all property is individually owned. Even the property of a married couple is theoretically separate and separable on divorce. The shares allotted by the Quran are to individuals standing in different kinship statuses. Children do not acquire any rights in property at birth. A man is free to do what he wishes with the property in his possession, even though many others may have contributed to it and may depend on it. All this is in sharp contrast to the Kalpeni islanders' notion of property as being in the collective interest of a kin group. A *karanavar* has authority, but he is really no more than a manager.

It is difficult to say that the islanders think in terms of such clear contrasts between Islam and their matrilineal system. They are attached to their tradition and also see themselves as faithful Muslims. But the contrasts between security and insecurity, collective interest and individual autocracy, inalienable rights at birth and total dependence on a father, all these are too glaring not to be noticed.

Notes

1. This paper is based on ethnographic data on Kalpeni, collected by A.R. Kutty and by me. Kutty did his field work in 1961–63, and I in 1969. I thank Mukul Dube for his assistance in editing and word processing. While essentially speaking of the situation of women in the 1960s, my analysis has taken into account later developments as well. In their basic features, the social structure and culture have not undergone much change.
2. Nikki Keddie (1987) deals with this subject in relation to the matrilineal Muslim Minangkabau. Islam is considered to consist, classically, of two parts: *ibadat* or worship, which includes the 'five pillars of Islam'; and *muamlat* or transactions, which covers the great majority of questions regarding the world, dealt with in law and jurisprudence.
3. The four figures represent four actual *taravads*. Figure 1 shows a *taravad* that was a property group and also a domestic group. The *taravad* in Figure 2 was a single property group made of several domestic groups. That in Figure 3 consisted of four property groups, each of which had in it one or more domestic groups. Figure 4 is of a *taravad* with three property groups that were also domestic groups.
4. The descendants of one woman were set off as a unit from those of her sisters, this unit being known as a *tavazhi* (This word is variously pronounced and sometimes transliterated as taivazhi, as in Saradamoni in this volume). Each woman of a *taravad* could thus have a *tavazhi* descending from her. It was a somewhat flexible term and was used to denote both intermediary and minimal segments of two-generation depth. According to a census taken in 1962, there were, on the island, 120 *taravads* comprising 359 households or domestic groups with varying kinds of composition. Forty-six *taravads* were simultaneously property, production and consumption units.
5. A *karanavar* managed property, organised production, assigned work to the male members of the group and dealt with the Melacheri labourers. He represented the group in its dealings with the administration. Theoretically, however, he did not have the right to act on his own in giving leases and in parting with any property of the *taravad*, including moveable property. The *karanavar* of a *taravad* which was divided into a number of property groups enjoyed special respect and was invited to act as head at ceremonies and rituals. A *karanavar* on the island was not, however, as powerful as a Nayar *karanavar* has been described to be (see also Saradamoni, in this volume). This point will be taken up when discussing the nature of property and of productive resources on the island.
6. In the period of the Arakkal rulers.
7. The monopoly in coir, introduced in 1764–65 during Arakkal rule, was the main source of government revenue. Tree tax was levied on *pandaram*, government land, during the British occupation. Coir depots were established on the islands around 1922, supplying rice in exchange for coir at rates of exchange fixed by the government from time to time.
8. The Nayar, Nambudiri, Mukuvan and Tiya.
9. This aspect is discussed in detail in my paper, 'Caste Analogues among the Laccadive (Lakshadweep) Muslims' (Dube 1978). Particular *taravads* or matrilineal property groups or households of the Melacheri were linked in service

relationships with particular Koya matrilineal units. Their matrilineal social organisation and the pattern of visiting husbands were similar to what obtained among the Koya. Collective production activity among closely related matrilineal units followed the same pattern. Many Melacheri had acquired land and trees, but even as *tandelan* (attached labour) they functioned as matrilineal units. With new avenues opening up, many may have started earning individual incomes and their service relationships may have weakened, moving towards cash payment in place of payment in kind and with fewer members of *taravads* working as *tandelan*.

10. This practice was not seen among the Nayars.

11. Division, according to stirpes or branches, was prevalent on the islands of Androth and Kalpeni. On all other islands, at the time of division, every individual got a share, irrespective of the generation. A similar system of per capita division prevailed on the mainland among the Nayar and other matrilineal castes and communities in Kerala, even where the *taravad* was divided into branches.

12. According to a household census conducted by A.R. Kutty. Of the 670 extant marriages, 124 (18.5 per cent) were uxorilocal; 23 (3.4 per cent) were neolocal; and only eight were virilocal. Uxorilocality was generally adopted only after a certain degree of marital stability had been attained.

13. The Nayars of central Kerala, mainly southern Malabar and Cochin, also followed duolocal residence. However, hypergamous marriage and the consequent constraints on women, which follow on the Nayars being part of the Hindu caste system, the system of land relations, the exposure of the community to the mainstream culture and European education render a comparison of the Nayars with the Kalpeni islanders problematic (Gough 1961).

14. In my assessment of the matrilineal kinship system of Kalpeni in relation to gender, implicitly and explicitly, I have compared it with views of the patrilineal Muslims of south Asia, particularly those of northern India and to an extent those of Bangladesh and Pakistan. Differences by class, rural or urban location, and pre-conversion beliefs and practices are present among the Muslim communities of this region. *Parda* (seclusion), for example, is observed by middle-class women and those in the older parts of cities, but not usually by women who engage in agricultural operations. In the later comparison of matriliny and patriliny, it is essentially south Asian patriliny that is considered, irrespective of religion. The matrilineal Mappilas of northern Kerala are not considered.

15. The use of the veil as symbolic shelter has been well brought out by Hanna Papanek (1982), particularly with reference to patrilineal Muslims in the Indian subcontinent. It is significant that women in south-east Asian Muslim communities that are rooted in matrilineal or bilateral kinship enjoy a considerable freedom of movement and participate in many economic and productive activities.

16. According to the provisional figures of the 1991 Census, the rate of literacy among females in Lakshadweep was 71 per cent. I did not observe any difficulty for girls in attending school. Early marriage and motherhood could, however, come in the way of girls who wished to continue their education beyond a certain age. Higher education and technical training are available only on other islands and on the mainland, and many more young men than women have benefited from the opportunities.

17. As is so in much of the subcontinent.
18. The Quran (S.IV: 34) says that woman is under the authority of man because God has made man superior to woman and because man pays for her or spends his wealth to maintain her. She is expected to obey him and submit to his will, and he has the right to inflict even physical punishment if she disobeys him. Man is the supporter of the household and must maintain and protect his wife. A look at the ethnographic evidence from Bangladesh (Aziz and Maloney 1985) will be interesting. Among the common people, a husband's authority over his wife is unquestioned and there is considerable violence against wives. As for a woman's right over her children, her husband may say: 'When you came to this house you were without a child. You got this child while eating my rice. So the child belongs to me.' All this is alien to the cultural ethos of Kalpeni.
19. It should be said here that physical violence of any kind was quite uncommon on the island. Disputes between groups did sometimes involve violence, but most accounts mention the peaceable nature of the islanders. Saigal (1990) has described a recent instance of a feud and murder between close matrilineal kin as most unusual. Lakshadweep has a rather high density of population: 1,258/sq km in 1981, which rose to 1,615 in 1991.
20. According to Islamic law, a woman also has the legal right to sever a marital bond through the pronouncement of dissolution of the marriage, by the Kazi under certain circumstances. This is known as *fasaq*. On Kalpeni, *fasaq* was resorted to only rarely, mostly when *talaq* was not obtainable owing to factors like the husband's lunacy or his absence from the island for an indefinite period. The other two forms of divorce permitted by Islam—*khula*, in which a wife purchases her freedom, and *lian*, when a husband pronounces an oath accusing his wife of adultery, resulting in an annulment of marriage—were not formally prevalent on Kalpeni.
21. It is argued that in all societies, males exercise authority. In the patrilineal system, the line of authority and the line of descent converge, going from father to son, but in a matrilineal system, the line of descent passes through females while the line of authority passes from maternal uncle to sister's son. The 'matrilineal puzzle' refers to this situation, in which conflict is assumed between a man's roles of father and mother's brother. Women and children have to submit to two kinds of authority: that of the husband/father and that of the matrilineal kin in the descent group. It becomes necessary to arrive at some kind of balance. As a consequence, the argument goes, matrilineal systems are unstable. Most analyses of matrilineal societies show the influence of the arguments of Richards (1950) and Schneider (1961). Recent feminist critiques include, among others, Poewe (1979), Schwede (1986, 1991), Tanner (1974) and Weiner (1976, 1979, 1980). For the resilience and adaptability of kinship systems, and of a matrilineal system in particular, see Colson (1980). Fresh researches by feminists show how, in many matrilineal societies, stability is associated with women, as it is they who live on and use the land, attend to rituals, safeguard knowledge, and nurture the next generation. Thomas (1980) contests the assumption that authority within the matrilineal descent group is predominantly vested in males and that there is a constant problem of striking a balance between a man's authority over his wife and children in the domestic group and the matrilineal kin's authority in the descent group.

22. Men are considered losers, and believed to be under considerable strain, because they are not able to do much for their children and have no permanent rights in matrilineal property, and because they must follow the values and norms which require nephews to be treated as heirs. Hence, despite wielding authority—which, in fact, very few men really do—they try to subvert the system when the opportunity arises.

23. Indeed, each unilineal system underplays the role of one parent and has to make a special effort to assert the continuity of the line of descent. At least to some degree, bilaterality eases the situation. Flexibility in the matrilineal system of Kalpeni certainly points towards this.

References

Aziz, K.M.A. and C. Maloney, 1985, *Life Stages: Gender and fertility in Bangladesh*. International Centre for Diarrhoeal Disease Research, Monograph No. 3. Dhaka: ICDDR.

Caplan, P., 1984, 'Cognatic descent, Islamic law and women's property on the East Africa Coast', in R. Hirschon (ed.), *Women and Property, Women as Property*. London: Croom Helm.

Colson, E., 1980, 'The resilience of matrilineality: Gwembe and Plateau Tonga adaptations', in L.S. Cordell and S. Beckerman (eds.), *The Versatility of Kinship*. New York: Academic Press.

Dube, L., 1969, *Matriliny and Islam: Religion and society in the Laccadives*. Delhi: National Publishing House.

———, 1978, 'Caste analogues among the Laccadive (Lakshadweep) Muslims', in I. Ahmad (ed.), *Caste and Social Stratification among Muslims in India*. Delhi: Manohar. Second edition.

———, 1988, 'The nature of bounded groups and the management of female sexuality: The Khasi and the Nayar'. Paper presented at the IUAES Conference, Zagreb. Mimeo.

———, 1991, 'In mother's line: Aspects of structure and change in Lakshadweep', Prepared for the Indian Council of Social Science Research. Mimeo.

———, 1993, 'Kinship and family in south and southeast Asia: A comparative view', Prepared for the United Nations University. Mimeo.

Gough, K., 1959, 'The Nayars and the Definition of Marriage'. *Journal of the Royal Anthropological Institute of Great Britain and Ireland* 89: 23–34.

———, 1961, 'Nayar: Central Kerala'; 'Nayar: North Kerala'; 'Mapilla: North Kerala', in D.M. Schneider and E.K. Gough (eds.), *Matrilineal Kinship*. Berkeley and Los Angeles: University of California Press.

Ittaman, K.P., 1976, *Amini Islanders*. New Delhi: Abhinav.

Keddie, N.R., 1987, 'Islam and society in Minangkabau and in the Middle East'. *Sojourn* 2 (1): 1–30.

Kutty, A.R., 1972, *Marriage and Kinship in an Island Society*. Delhi: National Publishing House.

Logan, W., 1887, *Malabar*. Madras: Government Press.

Mannadiar, N.S. (ed.), 1977, *Gazetteer of India: Lakshadweep*. Coimbatore: Government of India Press.

Papanek, H., 1982, 'Purdah: Separate worlds and symbolic shelter', in H. Papanek and G. Minault (eds.), *Separate Worlds: Studies of purdah in South Asia.* Delhi: Chanakya.

Poewe, K., ·1979, 'Women, horticulture and society in Sub-Saharan Africa: Some comments'. *American Anthropologist* 81 (1): 115–17.

Richards, A.I., 1950, 'Some types of family structure amongst the central Bantu', in A.R. Radcliffe-Brown and C.D. Forde (eds.), *African Systems of Kinship and Marriage.* London: Oxford University Press.

Saigal, O., 1990, *Lakshadweep.* New Delhi: National Book Trust.

Schneider, D.M., 1961, 'Introduction', in D.M. Schneider and E.K. Gough (eds.), *Matrilineal Kinship.* Berkeley and Los Angeles: University of California Press.

Schwede, L.K., 1986, 'Family strategies of labour allocation and decision-making in a matrilineal, Islamic Society: The Minangkabau of West Sumatra, Indonesia', Cornell University. Ph.D. thesis.

——, 1989, 'Male and female authority in Minangkabau', Paper for American Anthropological Association Annual Meetings.

——, 1991, 'Family sustenance strategies of husband-absent and husband-present families in west Sumatra, Indonesia', Unpublished.

Tanner, N., 1974, 'Matrifocality in Indonesia and Africa and among Black Americans', in M. Rosaldo and L. Lamphere (eds.), *Woman, Culture and Society.* Stanford: Stanford University Press.

Thomas, J.B., 1980, 'The Nemonuito solution to the 'matrilineal puzzle'. *American Ethnologist* 7 (1): 172–77.

Utas, B., (ed.), 1983, *Women in Islamic Societies: Social attitudes and historical perspectives.* Uppsala: Curzon.

Weiner, A.B., 1976, *Women of Value, Men of Renown: New perspectives on Trobriand exchange.* Austin: University of Texas Press.

——, 1979, 'Trobriand kinship from another view: The reproductive power of women and men'. *Man* 14 (2): 328–48.

——, 1980, 'Stability in banana leaves: Colonization and women in Kiriwina, Trobriand Islands', in M. Etienne and E. Leacock (eds.), *Women and Colonization: Anthropological perspectives.* New York: Praeger.

7   Negotiating Patriliny: Intra-household Consumption and Authority in Northwest India[1]

Rajni Palriwala

The subtle shifts and negotiations underlying intra-household consumption and authority patterns in a village in Rajasthan, India, are elaborated. The question as to why women foster kinship ties and values when these appear to be the immediate structures oppressing them is explored. Deepening economic inequalities, the growing need for non-agricultural employment and the search for economic security resuscitated networks of kinship, caste and clientage, and collective household strategies. Simultaneously, the individuation and objectification of property was evident and individual (male) earners were increasingly valued. Patriliny was being manipulated to exclude the extended kin group and women from property, while maintaining the extended group as a unit of social support and sanction. Authority over and rights in consumption were located in kinship links, in individual labour and income contribution, and in interpersonal relations. Given this context, male emigration had contradictory consequences for women's manoeuvrability and control in particular, and intra-household relations in general. The devaluation of girls was striking. There was an increasing dependence among women, on individual male kin and husbands. The latter guarded their circumscribed and competing authority pertaining to intra-household food distribution as ways through which to secure these increasingly fragile relationships. They reaffirmed family ideology as they attempted to reassert and widen their security base.

Feminists, in India and elsewhere, have highlighted and critiqued the family as an arena of gender-based oppression. Simultaneously, the fact that there can be no one 'family' has become a truism in anthropology and gender studies. Families are contextually specific relationships which people enter and remake. Two vexing and fundamental issues emerge, central to any understanding of gender relations and of feminist strategy. The first, concerned with the linking of domains historically, has been the impact of economic and political processes on 'traditional' kinship and gender relations.

The second issue is why women seem more concerned with maintaining their 'family', with fostering kinship ties and values, with negotiating their opportunities from within kinship relationships, when these evidently are the immediate structures constraining them. Limits on women's mobility and patterns of settlement, such that all their most intense and closest relations are with persons defined as 'kin', as also socialisation may be part of the answer, but not a sufficient explanation. This is especially so when, apparently, new opportunities, different values, interactions and relationships are emerging. Is there something in the very processes and directions of change which define women within kinship and foster women's 'family conservatism'?

Yanagisako and Collier's (1987) proposed strategy for a unified analysis of gender and kinship is a good starting point (though one may not agree entirely with the path they take). They argue for the analysis of social wholes, through the explication of cultural meanings, the dialectics between practices and ideas constituting social inequalities and the historical analysis of continuities and change.

This chapter attempts to answer in part the second question, by elaborating on the first. I outline the economic processes in the Shekhawati (Sikar) region in Rajasthan, a state in northwest India, and their impact on the social and economic strategies of households. These in turn are related to the practice of patriliny, in which the nature of property and residence are central in defining women's rights and women's space. The dynamics of intra-household consumption and financial management, of subtle shifts and women's manoeuvrings are analysed in this context. Underlying the discussion[2] are the distinctions between and mutual determinations of the household and family ideology and of intra-household and extra-household kinship.

The issues raised in this chapter are discussed in the context of Panchwas[3] village in Sikar district.[4] Panchwas lay about 12 Km from the district headquarters, along a dirt road. The sex ratio (female to 1,000 males), though above the district average, was biased against women. Work-related migration was overwhelmingly male.[5] The pattern of household composition indicated that complex or extended household living was of continued and stronger significance than in other parts of the country. Male agnatic kin[6] and their wives tended to live close to each other, even if in separate households. There were 14 Hindu and Muslim castes in the village, covering the range of the caste hierarchy.[7] Jats, a lower-middle level caste group, formed 53 per cent of the village population and the ex-Untouchables, consisting of Balais (Chamars) and Naiks, over 14 per cent. Muslims were nearly 15 per cent, Pathans being the most numerous amongst them. Much of the discussion in this chapter is based on the practices among these castes, particularly Jats.

Economic Processes, Household Strategies and the Valuation of Workers

Sikar Thikana was one of the largest, semi-autonomous, feudal estates within the principality of Jaipur. The Jat/peasant movements of the 1930s and 1940s, subsequent land reforms, the discontinuance of feudal cesses and the abolition of *jagirdari* (landed estate) in the '50s and early '60s changed the rural set up. Many ex-landlords lost control of vast tracts of land and of tenants, and faced drastic alterations in their way of life. Some were able to retain enough land which, combined with money compensations, loans and concessions, ensured them a renewed viability and on-going dominance in rural society. With the elimination of appropriations made by the landlords, there was an initial improvement in the economic situation for most other sections of the population.

The land reforms did not do away with severe differentiation in land-ownership. In 1980, 68 per cent of the households owned less than 46–55 unirrigated *kaccha bighas*, the minimum necessary for an average living for a household of five. The broad congruence between land distribution and caste ranking, especially at the lower levels, meant a continual sustenance to caste ideology and caste idioms. Though the largest landowners in Panchwas now were the earlier occupancy-tenants, the Jats, many of them, owned only medium and small holdings. Smaller ex-tenants and subtenants, including the Balais and most Muslims, gained little land with the reforms. Among them agriculture was crucial, but not a viable option. However, the value on land-ownership—both as an economic means and as a symbol of social, economic and political status—had intensified, even among traditionally non-agricultural households.

Semi-arid conditions prevail over a substantial part of the region. Many of the 'new' owner-cultivators sank wells on their holdings. With electrification in the 1970s, there was a dramatic increase in the number of tube-wells, the extent of irrigated land, and yield in the winter crop. Most landowners who sank tube-wells looked for 'safe' investment sources—a slowly accumulated agricultural surplus, savings from non-agricultural incomes, or loans through social ties. The enhanced outputs and possibilities in livestock production gave some stability to households with access to tube-wells. Official agricultural development programmes were also irrigation-dependent. The differential ownership of irrigation facilities magnified the differentiation in land-ownership.

There was a growth in the demand for female household labour in animal husbandry and agriculture, and male (households, tenant, hired) labour in cultivation. The use of hired labour, particularly by larger landowners and ex-landlords and their privileged tenants increased. Yet, the demand for hired workers remained less than the demand for agricultural labour, and did not keep pace with the supply. Exchange and gift labour were used and there was limited mechanisation. Most importantly, due to historical, social and technological factors, irrigated land tended to be cultivated in small holdings. There was a growth of short-term sharecropping arrangements, in which the tenants tended towards being labourers paid with a share in the crop. Landowner-tenant and landowner-labourer ties bore many carefully fostered extra-economic characteristics. Wage workers established ritual kinship[8] with large landowners, so as to secure work, and in the case of women, to disguise the fact of wage work.[9]

Agricultural growth in the region had been recent and its benefits remained uncertain and differentiated.[10] Some commercialisation of agriculture was witnessed, but land sales were few. Though agriculture remained central to the rural economy and society, an increasing percentage of workers were in non-agricultural sectors in 1981. Traditional artisans and service workers faced competition from machine-made goods and commercialised services. They maintained *jajmani* (patron-client) ties (cf. Beidelman 1959; Palriwala 1990; Pocock 1962; Wiser 1936), even as they increasingly worked for wages or sold their products in the market. Work-related emigration became widespread. The regional administration, the army and the police were major employers. In the 1970s, migration to the Gulf, the construction boom engendered by remittances, as also the growth of ancillary industries to, and services in, agriculture led to some expansion in labour opportunities.

The more remunerative, secure and prestigious non-agricultural jobs required education and contacts or money to pay recruitment agents. Large landowners, ex-landlords, and members of traditionally literate castes were able to take advantage of educational facilities and mobilised their caste and kinship networks to obtain such employment. At the same time, manual and skilled labour in the Gulf brought in high wages to the few illiterate land-poor men so employed.

As the absolute necessity for employment-related emigration and non-agricultural incomes spread, Panchwasis emphasised occupational multiplicity for individuals and for households. Unemployment and the search for subsistence reinforced traditional forms of security, even as new avenues were sought. Panchwasis fostered ritual kin relationships and patron-client ties with a view towards future loan, leasing and/or employment needs. Even for farmers whose subsistence was secure, these ties helped ensure hired, 'gift', and exchange labour at crucial times. New income sources not only depended on but also made possible the maintenance of social networks. A household's network was related to its ability to offer hospitality and the minimal prestations, particularly at rituals, which could in the immediacy cut into subsistence. Upward mobility, high status and symbolic capital (Bourdieu 1977)[11] in Panchwas were expressed through an extended social network. This entailed the acquisition of surplus to enable expanded gift exchange and hospitality. Thus, the overlapping and mutually supporting networks of kinship, caste and clientage were given a fresh life by the developmental processes. These networks provided the forms in which attempts to cultivate new links were shaped.

With the growth of a money economy and a shift away from the household as the unit of production and/or management, an important contrast emerged between village-based agricultural and traditional non-agricultural work on the one hand, and modern non-agricultural employment on the other. In the former, persons were engaged as household members in a household unit of production. Generally in the latter, persons worked as individuals, employed by other persons, households or institutions such as the government. The income earned in such employment is clearly earned by an individual, even when pooled in household income and though the initial motivation may be family responsibilities. Within Panchwas households, such persons were identified as individual earners bringing in known amounts of cash, as against family workers cooperating with other household workers and where cash may or may not be earned. Increasingly, individual earners were recognised and valued in a household's economic and social strategy. Not only were the earnings of the few women who were part of the category of earners very low, more and more households were dependent on individual male earners. In addition, agricultural developments had further devalued women's household labour.[12]

Social Networks and Patriliny

As discussed earlier, economic and social strategies of Panchwasis were connected to the maintenance and enhancement of their social networks. The most important segment of a household's social world were its *bag-vibhag walon*—kin, affines, neighbours, patrons and clients with whom interaction and gift exchange were most regular. The moral and ideological ethos integral to this world provided the prescriptive framework within which they operated. Maintenance or enhancement of a household's status, the accumulation of symbolic capital, entailed conformity to the social forms and values of its circle of interaction. These included gift relationships between kin and between affines, the normative division of gender roles and rules pertaining to women's behaviour, modesty and shame. Economic exigencies and new social pressures

were met with shifts, as from seclusion to veiling, and manipula-
tions, unmasking tensions which were often an exacerbation of
earlier stresses (See Palriwala 1990).[13]

Central to the ethos of their social world were notions and
practices of patriliny and patri-virilocal residence. Patriliny defined
both group membership and inheritance of property. The coparcenary unit, consisting of those men who by birth take an interest
in the joint property, for example, a person himself, his sons, sons'
sons and sons' sons' sons, was the core of the family. Group
membership and continuity were reaffirmed and marked, in conjunction with status, at rituals, particularly weddings, in the gather-
ing of the *kabeela*—the lineage of cooperation (Mayer 1960)—and
the kindred, and in public gift exchange among them. However,
processes of individuation, along with objectification of property,
had been fed by pauperisation, the increasing pressure on land,
and the growth of non-household production and work organisation
and individual incomes.

The logic of family interests, in terms of kinship structure and
economic necessity, required the separation of women from family
property (Palriwala 1990). At marriage, women were transferred
from their natal to their marital family. Defined as having dual
loyalties to both their natal and their marital groups, outmarried
or inmarried women had rights only to maintenance and to 'gifts',
but not to a share. Among Muslims, a daughter's Shariat right to a
half share was voiced as a residual right and, at the most, as a gift a
generous brother may give a destitute sister. The family and the
line was a patrilineal descent group with a core of male agnates;
female agnates and inmarried women being of varying and transient
significance. Where rights were contingent on group membership,
their transience was manipulated to weaken their own rights as
well as the claims made by 'avaricious' kinsman. Ambiguity in the
distinction between family and lineage was central to property
disputes among Hindus, hinging on reversionary rights of male
agnates to the property of a sonless lineage member versus the
right to 'appoint' daughters or their descendants to inherit the
property and the rights of widows. Family and settlement histories
indicate that such disputes have increased among the Jats and the
Charans. This has been simultaneous with the spread of information
regarding post-Independence legislation which gave daughters

limited rights in their fathers' property, and the increasing pressure on and demand for land.

Patriliny was being manipulated to exclude the extended kin group and women from property, while maintaining the extended group as a unit of social support and sanction. At the same time, the lack of economic alternatives for women, and their valuation in terms of dowry, meant their continuing dependence on family ties, even as the attempt was to restrict the scope of the latter when it came to responsibilities for women. A woman's rights in her 'family' were even earlier linked to the rights of her father/brother and/or husband. The focus of her rights had been narrowed and more firmly fixed on these individuals and explicitly accepted as contingent and dependent on her interpersonal relations. Her natal family's assertion of her contingent rights in her natal group and the transfer of her rights were fuelled, in part, by the shift in marriage prestations among most castes to dowry[14] and the intensification of post-wedding prestations, which were continually calling on those rights.

Patri-virilocal residence stressed male agnates as the core of the lineage and/or the family, making women junior and minimal participants in the life of their natal families/'lineages'. Women's residential practice continuously reiterated transience, ambiguous membership, and contingent rights (Palriwala 1990; 1991). For a fair length of time, new brides and young married women moved back and forth between their natal and conjugal homes (*aoni-jaoni*). It was perhaps the most difficult period of their life, when as young girls they had to make their home among strangers (cf. Karve 1958). Stays at the natal home meant some rest from the rigours and discipline of being a daughter-in-law. Over the course of the marriage, the period of stay in the marital home lengthened. While it is difficult to assess whether or not the duration of *aoni-jaoni* has changed, it would appear that back and forth visits have become more frequent, with visits to one's mother's natal home in the years before and just after marriage as well. This may be related to the continuing low age at marriage, the reduced distance between affinal villages, improved transport in terms of roads and bus services, the absence of migrant husbands, but particularly the increasing demand for unpaid family workers in agriculture. Thus, different segments of their 'family' and kin asserted their rights over young women, who moved between villages, working where and when required. However, this same phenomenon acted to minimise their rights, even of consumption, through obscuring and denying their labour contribution in each place of residence (Palriwala 1991).

Intra-household Authority and Control Over Consumption

Normatively, the household head was always the senior-most male adult. All members were expected to submit to the authority of the head in income pooling, cash expenditures and any actions seen as affecting the social and political relations of the household. He was the ultimate authority in labour allocation and distribution of consumption goods. He was expected to consult other household members, particularly men and senior women. However, nobody was expected to question the head once he had taken a decision. The presumption was that the head, having the most complete knowledge regarding household matters, would have taken the decision in the interest of the unit, for the family good.

The women of the household were under the triple authority of the head, their husbands and the senior woman—the wife or the mother of the male head of the household. Rules of avoidance and segregation led to the appearance of two separate, but interlocking, lines of authority. In practice, the authority of the male head depended on his age and the kinship composition of the household. Youth and very old age, widow(-er)hood or absence due to migration generally reduced the control of both the male head and the female manager. In the absence of adult household men, a woman manager was expected to be guided by male kin—her dead husband's and her own.

The management of various spheres of activities rested primarily on that household member who was seen as having the knowledge and responsibility of ensuring that the work was done. In many operations, there was no real decision to be taken or the decision was not in fact an intra-household one. Cultivation, carpentry and leather-work were primarily male responsibilities. The senior woman, as long as she was capable, was in charge of housework, day-to-day consumption and livestock production. If there was conflict in agricultural work it could be between men, between women, and/or between men and women. In 'work in the house', it would be between women. Conflict over work was usually expressed in terms of a perceived discrepancy between work performed and access to consumption goods.

The dynamics of food consumption and control were indicative, and a metaphor for intra-household distribution and authority, and are hence examined. Ideally, there was little interhousehold variation. In practice, caste and religion tied in with economic levels and migration to introduce distinctions. Together, they mediated intra-household tensions, division of labour and ideals of status and respectability, leading to modification in absolute levels of consumption, in household composition and formation, and the attainment of seniority and headship by women and men.

Generally, it was held that women controlled the household grain stocks. They took out the daily or weekly requirements, as needed. Most households had an estimate of per day and per annum grain requirements. While these tended to be on the high side, and could be upset by sudden and fluctuating changes in household composition or the number of guests, possibilities of manipulation were narrow. Control was limited for both women and men by the fact that 55 per cent of the households did not grow enough grain, let alone all food items, for their annual requirements (Palriwala 1990). In a situation of deficiency, any avenues of manipulation open to women were likely to be used to obtain items of daily consumption for household members, particularly children.

Women managed only that grain which was brought to the house, and even then could not deny men access to it. In a few households, the grain stock was kept under lock and key, or seal, by the male household head. However, this stated a lack of trust in the woman and could only happen in the absence of the mother. Men conducted and controlled the sale of agricultural products and could veto women's assessments on the quantity to be retained. Surplus households, and even others, were selling their produce in the Sikar wholesale market, and proscriptions on women's mobility prevented them from striking any major deals unknown to the men. Nor would other men deal with a woman unless they were certain that the transaction would not be questioned later. Despite the ideal of prior consultation, men did not always do so. A woman's options were few if a man insisted on his decision. There were incidents where a man sold grain to buy alcohol and the woman was beaten for resisting. If there was serious depletion of stocks, especially due to profligate spending, she could ask her kin to remonstrate with him, but at the risk of intra-household and affinal conflict and tension intensifying.

Commercialisation and a money economy were diversifying men's options but whittling away women's control. Increasingly, they were dependent on men's cash earnings, on men buying and stocking wheat or millet for household use from 'their' earnings. Earlier constraints on women's management were exacerbated, and their control diminished, both as normative right and in practice.

Serving food, deciding what and how much to serve whom, especially non-cereal items, was a responsibility/right women jealously guarded. A household did not eat together. The meal was served to each individual by the senior woman, or another to whom she delegated the task. Norms indicated that a person accept what they were served, and the server take into account the former's status in the household. Nobody, including the head, could serve himself, for reasons of purity maintenance and etiquette. The earner, the household head, however, could demand. Children protested any perceived favouritism or demanded any extras they knew of. A woman could face the situation, considered 'reprehensible' by villagers, where a young son physically forced her to give him *ghee* (clarified butter) or some other item.

The possibilities of manipulation and discrimination were largely limited to special foods and/or through a reduction of the woman's own consumption. It depended on the household's subsistence level, such that women in surplus agricultural households had more scope for exercising discretion. In situations of deficit, conflict over suspected discrimination was likely to increase. This was a factor leading to the larger percentage of simple households among poor peasants and labourers (of which Balais were a significant proportion) than among the middle and rich peasants.

As a result of their responsibility for serving food, the onus of providing the means of consumption fell on women in many households, reinforcing constraints on their control. Women faced the brunt of men's anger and children's cries if food was not provided, was not to taste, or was not ready on time. Their particular charge was to provide a dish (*lagan*) to eat the bread with. Barter and 'borrowings' from neighbours and friends were ways to ensure a *lagan* at least for the household head. Pathan women used their tie-and-dye income, to buy vegetables or tea leaves for household use, though these earnings mere meant for their personal expenses. Money from sales of butter, notionally women's individual income, was also so used by Jat women.

The nature and perception of work and control over day-to-day consumption is well illustrated by an incident in an agricultural, Jat household, consisting of a couple and their young children. The husband and wife were having an argument—part serious, part mock. They asked their daughter, Kamala, whom she would side with. At first, Kamala said her mother, because 'Who will feed me if she refuses to serve me?' A little later, she said 'But no, I should side with Father, for it is he who earns and brings the grain, and what if he refuses to do so?' Finally, in a quandary, Kamala refused to say anything.

A common saying was that a household was made or broken by the skill and thrift of its womenfolk in managing household stocks. If the latter wished, they could barter it away on fripperies for themselves, for their daughters, or to take back to their natal homes. Barter was one way in which households short of cash expected to acquire consumption articles. Women, particularly, had little or no direct access to cash. They obtained tea leaves and sugar from the village shop, or cloth, thread, combs and lace from itinerant traders in barter. These dealings were often secret from men, especially when there were differences over the items of expenditure (cf. Srinivas 1976). However, the generation and age hierarchy, which gave control of household stocks only to the senior woman, denied junior women even these possibilities.

Further, a range of women argued, 'There are few women who do not wish their marital households to prosper. Ultimately we do not gain by frittering away household stocks on only ourselves or on those who are not members of our households.' Women who could and did so were exceptions, few and far between. They continued to be economically and socially dependent on their homes for subsistence. Their personal status depended on their reputation as skilled housewives. However, while accepting the idea of family needs, they insisted that items classed as useless trifles were often essential in ritual exchange or prestations, necessary for both the daughters' well-being and the maintenance of the household's status vis-à-vis the affinal household. Men talked of them as wasteful, but would blame women if the household suffered 'face' because these gifts were not given.

Contradictions in norms and women's direct responsibility meant that tension over consumption was likely to get expressed in anger with or conflict between women. This was made more likely as day-to-day consumption was one of the few areas in which women exercised some authority. They used it to strengthen their situation in a social and economic context which defined them as ultimately dependent on men and their own influence over household members. This was magnified with the increased significance of individual male incomes in the household economy.

A woman's hope of achieving status in her marital home was through her sons (cf. Hershman 1981). The mother-son bond, viewed as especially tender (cf. Das 1976; Gore 1962; Madan 1965; Pocock 1972), was succoured by women as their one support and security. Women favoured young sons over older nieces and daughters-in-law and used their control over daily consumption to discipline young children and instil a feeling in them that their mothers exercised power (cf. Minturn and Hitchcock 1963). They used it to play one son off against another, or to give the emigrant special treatment on his return. 'He had been denied good home food, though he had been working hard to earn money for the household.' They also hoped to ensure that the emigrant was favourably disposed towards them. The women who gained most influence in their marital homes had been successful in these matters, able to contain possible tensions. Suspicions were strongest where the woman manager was the mother or the spouse of the emigrant, and brother's wife to the other men.

How are these manoeuvrings, these negotiations to be understood? Looking through Kolenda's framework (1967), connecting high and low incidences of the joint family to a wife's wish to escape that oppressive institution and her lesser or greater bargaining power to ensure partition, Sikar women have very little bargaining power. Kolenda linked variation in the last to certain systemic and relational features of kinship and marriage. In discussing descent systems, Leach (1962) argues that any system, if it is to be viable, must have areas open to individuals for manipulation to their own benefit. Intra-household day-to-day consumption was such an area for women, who in the course of their life-cycle hoped to control it. The knowledge and hope of future power, the apparent exercise of autonomy, gave women an interest in the system, adding to its strength. However, on examining women's authority, it can be clearly seen that the agenda and the options had been fixed before the actual decision-taking, as Lukes (1974) points out in his discussion of decision-making and power. Women (and men) operated from within a habitus, 'a community of disposi- tions . . . schemes of perception, appreciation and action, which are acquired through practice', allowing a 'conductorless, orches- trated improvisation' (Bourdieu 1977: 97).

The Discourse and Practice of Food Distribution

The distribution of food was governed by rules and values, witnessed and practised from infancy onwards. Kinship status, specifically agnation, contribution to household income and work, and the concrete context of social relationships were the determinants of intra-household access to consumption. These dimensions could either reinforce or contradict each other, resulting in variations in practice. Adult male agnates had first priority, but the male head of household and the person who 'earned' were first among equals, particularly in the case of delicacies and 'nutritive' items such as butter. The 'earner' was the person who ploughed the land, the main worker in the fields, the manager of household lands, the person who earned a regular non-agricultural income—always a man, except when there was no adult male in the household. Conflict in priority could emerge if the head and the main earner were two different persons, an increasingly possible phenomenon, if household income was low and, as with age, the head's authority became a formality.

The aged and children had a right to food as agnates and/or because of past labour and future labour respectively. Old men and women continued working on some task or the other, even after retiring from cultivation, rhetorically asking who would feed them otherwise. Children were scolded for playing rather than completing a task their mother had given them, and told not to expect to be fed if they did no work. Simultaneously, kinship and family solidarity dictated the support of agnates, the old, the sick and the young. The old had reared, supported and established the present generation, passing on the basis of livelihood, property and a way of life (cf. Parry 1979). The young, particularly sons, were the future support, the heirs, and represented familial continuity. For women, their children rather than their aged in-laws were the loved ones. Together, this meant that often the young were given priority over the aged.

Hence, with the old and the sick, there was often bitterness and suspicion on both sides; the old felt they were mistreated, the present generation resented the former's attempts to retain control. With women living longer than men, the older generation was often represented by an old widow. Thus, the conflict was part of the tension-ridden mother-in-law/daughter-in-law relationship. Even if it was poverty which led to insufficient food for all, or the household head or 'earner' decided that the old be given only the basics, it was the woman responsible for cooking and serving who was blamed. Mothers-in-law socialised new brides into their roles as household manager and food distributor. An oft-repeated saying was that an old woman mistreated by her daughter-in-law had so taught the latter by the example of her own behaviour with her aged mother-in-law. I know of only one case, a Balai family, regarding which it was openly said that the men for the last three generations had mistreated the old parents and by example had taught their wives and children to do the same.

Most people denied discriminating against female children. 'Children are children, whether male or female', they insisted, and 'cries of hunger from either are painful for the mother who brought them into the world.' Knowing that their daughters would be denied special foods in their marital homes, some women said that they made it a point to serve them what delicacies they could in the years before they left. Villagers asked, 'When as children, daughters are a greater help than sons, why should they be discriminated against? As goatherds, they earn for the household and their own right to consumption.' Goatherds were given a few extras to persuade them to spend the day in the sun. Many said that daughters cared more for their parents than sons did.

Yet, sons were the embodiment of the family's future, and were often favoured with the justification that they must quickly grow into young men and work for the whole family. Furthermore, since a large percentage of households were complex, the mother of the girl was in fact often not the person responsible for serving food. Other women in the household seemed to give in to the demands of nephews or grandsons more quickly than those of nieces and granddaughters. Also, as Madan (1965) pointed out, relations with their mother influenced the treatment of grandchildren by their grandmother.

Evidence contrary to the statements regarding lack of discrimination is overwhelming, in terms of the sex ratio of children in the under 10 age group. It was 884 in Panchwas. Sikar is among the districts in the country with the lowest ratio of young girls to young boys (Miller 1989), even though the overall sex ratio is above the all-India average. The higher overall sex ratio may be related to male emigration and the lower sex ratio in the under 10 age group to discrimination between baby girls and boys in food and medical care, as well as differences in the nutrition of mothers of sons and of daughters. Alternatively, these contrary sex ratios represent a new trend of devaluation of and bias against female children. Hypothetically, selective discrimination against later born female children rather than all female children, which Dasgupta (1987) found in the Punjab, would appear to hold.[15]

New mothers, pregnant women and all other men and women were said to follow in priority in the order listed. The person who cooked and the youngest daughter-in-law, usually the same person, ate last. This itself acted against her, even if there was no conscious discrimination. Thus, after feeding unexpected guests, the cook would prefer to do without food rather than cook again. In middle level peasant households, often there could be no vegetables or lentils left and she made do with a pepper paste. In a situation of deficit, she went hungry when other household members did not have to.

Normatively, new mothers were given special foods, classed as 'non-heatening' and milk-producing, for 40 days or so after childbirth. Not only was childbirth seen as debilitating, it was literally labour. Actual consumption depended on the economic status of the woman's marital and natal home, and the sex and the serial order of the child. The natal home was expected to provide some of the special diet the new mother would consume. This was often the only extra nutrition she obtained. The mother of a boy was fed special foods for longer than the mother of a girl. Her marital household took greater care of her and her natal family was expected to send more. People would exclaim, 'If a mother of a son is not fed, who will eat!'—one more articulation of patriliny, the status of mothers of sons being crucial in determining women's access to consumption.

The rights of women to consumption in different castes and classes were discussed in terms of the labour they provided the household. Pathan and Charan women, among whom norms of *purdah* and seclusion operated such that they were not to work in the fields, would say that Jat and Balai women had a right to eat because they worked, whereas if nobody gave them food they could not protest as they did not work or earn. However, as will be seen in the section that follows, Pathan women tended to have greater access to and control of cash income than Jat or Balai women.

Generally, female work was valued lower than male work and the requirements of women were presumed to be less than those of men. Dual residence was used to deny a daughter-in-law's labour contribution, with the statement, 'She works elsewhere (her natal home), and eats here.' Women rarely questioned the view that tasks such as ploughing and bunding, men's work, were heavier than women's agricultural work, or that non-agricultural workers were the earners. However, they did question the valuation of other tasks, as well as of their requirements relative to those of young non-working males or young emigrants who contributed minimally to household income. Daughters-in-law insisted that with the long hours they worked—grinding flour, fetching water, and cutting grass—they also needed extra nutrition. At the risk of furthering intra-household tensions, they could complain to the husband, to be told that this was for his mother to decide.

In these contexts, labour contribution as a demarcator of rights to the products of labour was overridden, though not without strain and conflict, by interpersonal relations, by income contribution and, crucially, the parameters of agnation and ownership of property. The last encapsulated the ideas of the male household head and the 'good of the family'. It was the core of the household, the coparceners, the male agnates and their representative, on whose wellbeing the good of the household depended, and who had the first rights to consumption. The women, whether inmarried or agnatic, had secondary rights, in congruence with their peripheral status in the coparcenary and residual rights in land, which were linked to their 'contribution' to the 'family'. The *dhanni* (owner) had the first right to the harvest from his land—part of his identity—

as against the worker. Similarly, the lineally ascendant male agnate, the *dhanni*, had prior claims to a child, though there was recognition of the 'labour' the mother contributed in bearing and rearing the child. The male child and the male agnate, the *dhanni*, were expressions of each other, not to be lightly separated.

Individuation of property and the significance of individual earnings were acting in concert to strengthen men's consumption rights as against women's. These processes stressed individual male control of property and resources, as against that of the 'family' in which women were perceived as necessary dependents, and were relatively devaluing their work. A woman's present dependence on husbands and sons and future dependence on the latter, as well as the normative rights of men, the *malik*, the *dhanni*, to all household products, and the possibility of the use of physical force limited women's access to and control over food allocation. The power women exercised was primarily over the work and consumption of daughters-in-law and daughters. It was the circumscribed power of an increasingly subordinate category.

Male Migration and Control of Household Finances

Ideally and in practice, men made the decisions regarding cash expenditures, whether on production or on consumption, and especially where large sums were involved. Control of household money wealth lay with the male head, with the proviso of consultations as mentioned earlier. This was especially true if it involved the taking of loans, selling or pawning household assets (particularly women's jewelry) and/or using the income from *ghee*. With the constraints on female mobility and the widely held belief that village women knew little beyond their kitchen and their animals, it was accepted that men 'knew best' and would decide on matters which took a person beyond the household and the village. Women were expected to ensure and remind men that kinship obligations in terms of prestations at life-cycle ceremonies and to visiting affines were fulfilled. Blame for default was placed, as much if not more, on women than on men, but the final decision lay with men and the household head.

It was expected that the earnings of any household member would enter the pool managed by the household head. Individual male earners, particularly those whose earnings were regular, substantial and entailed emigration, could keep a portion not only for living expenses, but also for other personal needs. Households which barely met their subsistence requirements or earned little cash income, had little money. While the head's control of the household pool hence had little meaning, conflicting demands on what there was could be intense.

Women's own wage earnings were part of this household pool, but ideally, income from the sale of *ghee*, tie-and-dye work and the earnings of daughters were in a different category. All three were classed as women's personal income, to be spent as they desired. However, especially where *ghee* money was concerned, women's responsibilities to serve and feed their households, and the ideology that women work for their families, were crucial. Often it appeared that women's control over their earnings implied that they spent it on those 'household' requirements for which they were responsible in terms of work. Further, it was only when the sales took place at their homes that women could keep control. Once money entered the household pool, its expenditure was decided as part of the pool, under the control of the household head. To this extent, junior men also had little say in the disposal of household income. Of course, in many households, there was no income from *ghee* or it was crucial to subsistence. Finally, households had rights to a daughter's labour, but not to her earnings. Only at the bare survival level were such earnings used for subsistence. However, they were often kept aside to be spent on the trousseau or prestations that daughters were expected to take with them to their marital home. Women saved their personal incomes for gifts to daughters.

As mentioned earlier, the processes of individuation and objectification of property, of manipulation and shifts in patriliny, of the simultaneous attempts to restrict the family and extend the hold of the family on women was strengthened by agricultural developments and the growth of non-household production and work and the significance of individual earners. Since many of these earners were absent male migrants and junior men, given the values and practices of intrahousehold authority and extended household formation, the emerging dynamics were complex. In particular, an increasing tension between an individual's control of his earnings and the control of household resources and income by the household head was manifest.

Three main types of male migration may be distinguished with differing implications for control of household finances. Migrants were (*i*) junior men; (*ii*) senior men who made periodic visits to the village, every one to three months; (*iii*) senior men who returned to the village on annual or biennial visits. Related to these modes of migration were the distance between the place of migration and Panchwas, the type of work and the mode of remittances.

In the first type, authority patterns were the same as broadly described earlier, but with an exacerbation of previous tensions, as will be discussed in the following section. Even if remittances were handed over, the emigrant expected to be given some importance in decision-making. Turning to the other two categories, if an emigrant was the head of a complex household, the next senior most man took charge and managed the household finances in consultation with the senior woman and other household members. However, the absent household head had to be informed and his approval obtained for any major expenses.

In the second mode of migration, the men continued to control household expenditure on a regular basis. They tended to bring their earnings when they returned to the village, rather than remit them in their absence. Usually, the entire household migrated where the emigrant was the head of a simple household and had regular work. Where there was no resident adult man and little land was owned, the emigrant ensured that there were enough stocks of grain, firewood and fodder bought and stored to last until his next visit. Clothes and other articles were similarly bought by him. If he returned with insufficient money, he took a loan, bought the basic necessities and left a small sum with his wife for petty expenses.

While he was away, his wife managed the day-to-day consumption as described earlier, under the guidance of her husband's closest agnates. Occasionally, she had to buy some goods on credit or borrow some money, to pay for medicines or for a gift to give a visiting affine or at a life-cycle ceremony. Decisions made on her own had to be approved by her husband, or his agnates if that was not possible, if he was to pay costs. She borrowed from close women friends, usually ritual kin, or from households with which her husband's family had long-standing ties of kinship, credit, patronage or employment.

These latter patterns were more marked where the emigrant visited the village only annually or biennially. A large portion of his earnings was dispatched by him during his absence. In the few cases where he was the one adult man in the household, including Balais, Minas and Pathans, the woman/women had to manage the land, if any. She arranged for storage or sale of agricultural produce, bought or transported grain, firewood and any other consumption articles, arranged for loans or returned loans, and ensured that the household's obligations to kin and affines were fulfilled, particularly at life-cycle ceremonies. Transactions were usually along established ties. Many decisions were communicated through letters by the husband, especially those involving major financial transactions. Often, a particular remittance was accompanied with instructions as to its use. It was common for major decisions to be put off until the emigrant could make a trip home.

However, particularly when emigrants were in the Gulf, women were taking decisions independently and, at times, in opposition to their husbands. These men, mostly Muslims, particularly Pathans, returned after long stretches, by which time the women hoped they would have forgotten the matter. Women argued that their absent husbands could not know all the complexities of a situation, and nor could they send details in a letter. Khatoon, for example, said that she was anyway a much better planner, with more sense than her husband, and he also silently recognised this. She used the gratuity he had received on leaving the army to build two brick and plaster rooms. He had left for the Gulf before the money arrived, but had opposed the idea saying that their debts must be repaid first. However, she decided that since their creditors were kin and would not press for the return of the loans, they should do something concrete which would otherwise never get done. Bismillah stayed in her natal home, though her husband had written that she should return to her in-laws, and she continued to receive remittances from him. Though her husband had advised her to sell it, Salaamat kept the fodder from their trees for her goats, which meant a hut had to be built for its storage. 'In the next letter, our husbands express anger at being crossed but it will fade by the time they return.'

The most marked variation in the control of finances was among Pathans, and between Pathans on the one hand and Jats and Charans on the other. The impression built up was that among the former, not only was the factor of Gulf migration important, the conjugal tie received more emphasis than among the latter castes, so that a woman was confident that she had only to persuade her husband and not contend with his entire family. This could be related to the lesser control of the family due to the lower level of household resources and of household enterprises (including agriculture); to women's independent tie-and-dye income; to their rights, however minimal, in their father's property; and also to patterns of cross cousin and parallel cousin marriage which affected the nature of relationships.

Shifts in household composition are reflective of changes in intra-household relations. Studies on the impact of an increasing dependence on non-household based occupations and income sources have put forward contradictory conclusions.[16] Some have stressed a tendency towards simple households, with sons separating from their parents soon after marriage. However, complex households have also been noted as being particularly adaptable to occupational multiplicity and temporary emigration.

Both these contradictory tendencies were noticed in Panchwas. Complex household living not only continued to be admired but was also much the practice, along with maintenance of extended ties. However, changes in the timing of division in terms of the phase in the household developmental process (Shah 1973, 1988) indicate earlier partitions. Of divisions which took place more than 10 years earlier, 25 per cent occurred when both parents were alive, 31 per cent after the father's death and 37 per cent after both parents' deaths. In the last 10 years, 46 per cent divisions took place while both parents were living, 40 per cent after the father's death and 12 per cent after both parents had died. Thus, there was a greater tendency in the last 10 years than previously, for sons to form independent households in the lifetime of both parents or after the father's death, rather than waiting till both parents died. Also indicated is the decline in the mother's ability to keep her sons together, once their father was dead. Crucially, if households were tending to divide sooner, it meant that in the domestic sphere, both junior men and junior women were gaining control of their respective spheres earlier than in the past.

Parry's discussion (1979) on the balance of advantage in remaining in a complex household or partitioning, for both the emigrant and the brothers who remain behind, is apposite. Temporary emigration which did not allow a man to return to the village whenever necessary, and where the land share was substantial, acted to keep the landholding joint. The emigrant's wife stayed in the complex household, under the authority of his parents and/or brothers. The emigrant and his wife thus ensured that his land was properly maintained, his interest in the land did not lapse, and economies of scale were practised, particularly since urban living was more expensive than rural. Parents and brothers of an emigrant desired that the latter remain in their household to ensure them access and rights to his cash income as well as to the produce from his land share.

On the other hand, the expansion of non-agricultural, non-village employment and income, increased the sources of tension in intra-household relations. Accepted patterns of consumption and food distribution were disturbed and lines of authority and control were being questioned. The special position given to emigrants in consumption and household decisions created resentment when seen as incommensurate with his and his wife's labour and/or money contribution. This was especially so in middle peasant households where agricultural and other village work provided a substantial portion of household subsistence and in deficit households. A Jat father complained that after having given life, education and a job to his son, now that the latter was earning he made no contribution to the household.

The emigrant, in reverse, could resent the lack of special treatment and non-consultation, although it was 'his' earnings which were being spent. He often developed new ideas and tastes regarding consumption and lifestyle, particularly for his children and wife, which he could not put into practice. This also led to division. If the landholding was small, the emigrant and his wife were likely to establish their own household, with either the woman managing on her own in the agricultural season, or leasing it out and joining her husband.

Sharma (1989) points out that the individual wage complicated the relationship between parents and son. However, it also complicated the relationship between junior women and other household members and between husband and wife. Often an emigrant brought his wife a small gift or left a small sum of money with her for personal expenses. Such junior women had more cash to spend as they pleased than women from households in a similar or even higher income bracket, where the income source was agriculture or a craft or traditional service or whose husband was not himself an emigrant. This could be true of such women in comparison to middle and poor peasant men as well. These gifts in kind and cash had to be kept secret from others in the household if tensions were to be avoided (cf. Parry 1979). Women used the money to buy articles like ribbons, medicine, an occasional food item, or gave it in small loans at interest.

On the other hand, the treatment of the wife of a junior emigrant in a complex household depended on his fulfilling his obligations, in particular, giving money to the household pool. The wife of a young emigrant found it more difficult to influence household decisions or even keep track of what was being planned in the absence of her husband, her main informant. In some cases, other household members felt that the emigrant's wife had become 'uppity', and there was nobody to mediate for her. Given norms of modesty and veiling, dependence on her own and/or her husband's male kin continued or increased, even in simple households. Furthermore, in a household dependant on village-based income sources, the woman had some independent knowledge of household income and how it was spent. Kin sanctions had operated more directly and easily to ensure that a man did not neglect his household or his wife and children.

Overall, the wife of an emigrant (whether head or junior male) had more cash to spend, but control over household consumption and expenditure depended on the pattern of migration and remittances, the level and sources of income, household composition and the presence of close kin of the husband. She was simultaneously more dependent on the individual man, her husband, on what he told her regarding his income and on what he sent or bought, on his being pleased and approving of her behaviour. This in itself reduced possibilities of autonomy and reinforced the link between her consumption levels and fulfilment of ascribed roles (cf. Maher 1981). Along with pressures of declining economic resources and the absence of husbands at times of crises, their personal income tended to be integrated into household income.

One common view which gained the status of a sociological truth, though contested (cf. Parry 1979; Shah 1973, 1988; Srinivas 1987), was that it was women's quarrels which led to household division. Many Panchwasis, while expressing the 'popular' view, presented a slightly different picture also: quarrels between women were often only the immediate and visible factor leading to division. Many of the women's quarrels about sharing of work or consumption were a reflection of conflict between agnates over budgeting, control over property, and household strategy.

Parry has argued that the most common sources of tension between brothers were their respective contributions to the household economy and their bearing on consumption (also see Shah 1973, 1988). This was inherent to the structure of the joint household, but may have been exacerbated by outside employment and a cash economy, where individual contribution could be precisely measured (Parry 1979). However, the tension between the individual and the household-collective were as much, if not more, the underlying factor as the tension between the fraternal and the conjugal bonds which Parry emphasised (also see Gore 1962, Madan 1965). His argument was based on the notion that the morality of kinship (Fortes 1969)—unreturned altruism—is strained by the last tension. However, in Shekhawati, even as the special claims of agnates were recognised, reciprocity was the basis of ties between brothers and unreturned altruism that of affinal ties (as in marriage prestations, especially dowry). The possible high cost of morality was measured against the likely results for long term security (cf. Bloch 1973). Implications of individual earnings for long term security and the balance between the individual and the household-collective (cf. Sharma 1989) seem to have intensified this. Lapses in reciprocity were quickly noted.

Working for the Family Good

Gender, age and kinship hierarchies of agnation, seniority and property were the parameters within which authority, consumption rights and the requirements of various members of a household were played out. Work and income contribution were further delineators, themselves based on a sexual division of labour moderated by caste, class, and source of income. The emergent patterns of consumption and authority were integral to definitions of household needs. Economic and employment trends were sharpening the disagreements over valuation of labour and income contribution and thence conflict over consumption, unmasking the true nature of intra-household 'sharing'. Junior men and junior women were interested in establishing households in which they would be in charge, escaping the constraints of age hierarchies. Differences over family strategies, the definitions of family well-being and the needs of various household members were magnifying.

The household, in family ideology, was the patriline. If a household and family were to survive and prosper, men and women,
young and old, were essential and had to give and receive their
due, which were inherently differential. Ultimately, family good
meant the maintenance and upward mobility of the male agnatic
core. Importantly, women were seen to have no legitimate needs
outside common household needs. However, as men mediated
between the world and the household, they had individual expenses
such as tobacco or a cup of tea in the market. As conflicts developed,
women saw these as wasteful rather than as status markers, while
men would describe as frivolous the prestations women viewed as
essential.

Central to the prosperity of the patriline was the fostering of its
social network. As outlined in the beginning of this chapter, the
bag-vibhag walon was oft-mobilised for economic and social security,
besides expressing status. Women were persons via whom social
networks were reaffirmed and expanded in marriage, dowry and
continuing affinal prestations. Obligations and rights of daughters
and sisters continued even after their marriage, to be balanced
against those which were part of their being daughters-in-law.
However, this very quality of women undermined their integration
into any one agnatic core.

Ideologically, the household as a concrete unit and expression of
family was an individual's primary responsibility, and not any
single person who was a member of the unit. It was accepted that
persons did develop greater commitment to some members, such
as their own children and spouses. However, women's ambiguous
membership made their strategies to attach individual men to
themselves suspect, especially as obligations to wife, sister, daughter
were increasingly cast as fulfilling an individual's needs.

Conflicting pulls over investment in one's social network and
fulfilment of obligations to kin versus restriction of the latter to
immediate household members or even oneself were continuous.
Dowry and gifts to a daughter lessened the immediate economic
viability and wealth of her natal household and its agnatic core.
The diffusion of dowry practices and the inflation in prestations,
both at the wedding and after, accentuated the contradiction
between retaining wealth and income in the household and giving
it away to affines. This was ever more a contradiction between
social gain and economic loss, a contradiction between gifts to and

desires for an individual's, a daughter's, 'happiness' and the long run economic advancement of the giver's household.

The daughter and sister were cast as liabilities rather than a strategic resource, even among the Jats where their labour was recognised, and dowry had been minimal. Similarly daughters-in-law were valued for the goods they brought in. Women's labour was seen to defray the expenses incurred in providing them with prestations rather than contributing to household subsistence, continuity and mobility. Thus, a vicious cycle was established—the devaluation of women's labour and significance for the 'family' and thence her rights to consumption, the justification of dowry in terms of a woman being an economic burden, and demands for prestations feeding into each other.

The shifts in land-ownership and the pattern of access to new economic opportunities had not seriously upset caste hierarchies or 'traditional' forms of symbolic capital. Behavioural norms for women as well as the normative gender division of labour were reinforced rather than questioned. Developmental processes and the paucity of employment, on the one hand were resuscitating the need for social networks, collective household strategies and occupational multiplicity. On the other hand, they were demarcating and valorising individual earners, almost entirely men, and individuating and objectifying patrilineal property, creating the basis for individual rights. This was reflected in the aspirations of younger men and conflict over the definition of the 'good of the family' and justified expenditure.

Women's economic dependence on husbands and kin had intensified, with crucial implications for their manoeuvrability and valuation and hence for their consumption rights, the form in which obligations to them were to be fulfilled and the readiness to do so. Critically, this would intensify the vulnerability of some categories of persons—the landless, widows, divorced and abandoned wives—as their links to networks of support were individualised and lost. As women became increasingly dependent on individual males, tensions between women—between mother-in-law and daughter-in-law or between sisters-in-law—and the control they exercised on each other were exacerbated.

Women's concern to ensure that obligations to daughters and sisters, to affines and other members of the household network were met, that 'family relationships' were kept alive, was central not only to household strategy and deeply embedded moralities, but also to their own personal strategies. Their 'family conservatism' and reassertion of kinship values and sanctions were fuelled by their need to widen their support base, their security net, to resocialise individualised ties, even if these meant a revitalisation of those very structures which controlled them.

Notes

1. I wish to thank Carla Risseeuw and Kumkum Sangari for their comments on earlier drafts of this chapter.
2. Which takes the form Geertz has termed 'thick description'.
3. A pseudonym.
4. This paper is based on material collected for my doctoral dissertation (Palriwala 1990) over 1980–81. Field work was undertaken during a year's residence in the village. Brief visits to other villages and secondary and historical sources provided additional material.
5. At the end of 1980, the population stood at 1,901 and the sex ratio at 991. If the 306 migrants who were absent from the village for six months or more in the year were excluded, the sex ratio was 1,071. There were 272 households in the village and around 38 per cent were simple (or elementary) in composition. Residential neighbourhoods were broadly caste and kinship based, but not exclusively so. As with many villages in the region, the settlement had shifted towards a semi-nucleated, semi-dispersed pattern over the last 40 years. For more on these aspects of the village and the region, see Palriwala (1990, 1991).
6. Agnates are kin, related through the father or in the male line.
7. Hindus are placed by birth into a hierarchical gradation of ritually pure and impure groups, which are endogamous, commensally restrictive, occupationally specialised and exhaustive. Caste-like groups are found among most other religious communities in the Indian subcontinent. Factors, such as the continuance of caste practices and the significance of caste ideology, despite the legal proscription of untouchability, are central to an understanding of contemporary Indian society.

    The Hindu castes in Panchwas were Gaur Brahmin (priest), Misar Brahmin (priest), Charan (the ex-landlords, traditionally also bards), Khati (carpenter), Sonar (goldsmith), Nai (barber), Daroga (retainer to Charan, Rajput), Jat (farmer), Mina (watchman), Balai (leather worker) and Naik (osier and midwife). The Muslim castes were Pathan (soldier, landlord, cultivator), Manihar (banglemaker) and Fakir/Kazi (mendicant/learned man). For a further discussion on caste in Shekhawati and the specific castes, see Palriwala 1990.
8. Various varieties of fictive kinship were established ritually and involved giftgiving, food exchange, and material and moral help. It was the idiom of friendship and gave an inmarried woman natal kin in her marital village (See Palriwala 1990).

9. As I have discussed elsewhere (Palriwala 1990, 1991), manual wage work by women was considered the most degrading and immediately implied low status. Various strategies were employed to disguise or make invisible such work.

10. Productivity levels were much below the national averages.

11. 'Symbolic capital, a transformed and thereby disguised form of physical "economic" capital, produces its proper effect inasmuch, and only inasmuch, as it conceals the fact that it originates in "material" forms of capital, which are also, in the last analysis, the source of its effects' (Bourdieu 1977: 183).

12. According to my assessment of contribution to household subsistence and income, women were 53 per cent of all earners, main or supplementary, but only 17 per cent of main earners, which was biased to cash income. Women were under 6 per cent of individual earners, excluding tie-and-dye workers, and 28 per cent including them. Whereas non-tie-and-dye women earners were labourers in construction and brick-making, all low wage areas, nearly 50 per cent of men earners, in addition to the high-earning Gulf migrants, were professionals, white collar employees, in government service, own-account workers or 'entrepreneurs'.

13. *Ghunghat* (veiling) and *purdah* (seclusion) were crucial to female modesty and behaviour, demarcating categories of social space and work which women of different castes could enter and of men they could interact with.

14. Life histories, random statements and the texture of the Kisan agitations in the 1930s, indicate that this shift began by the '40s and was most marked in the late '50s and '60s. While most Jats now practice dowry, among Balais bride-wealth and bride-price, given the garb of dowry, is still common.

15. Dasgupta (1987) argues that discrimination of female children is related to family-building strategies of parents. She found that rather than a uniform discrimination against girl children, discrimination was determined in particular by serial order. Most mothers wanted at least one daughter, particularly to help them in the house. She relates the discrimination to the differential economic and social value of sons and daughters.

16. For discussions of the problem-ridden debate on the decline or otherwise of the Indian joint family, see Shah 1973, Kessinger 1974, Madan 1976.

References

Beidelman, T.O., 1959, *A comparative analysis of the jajmani system*. Monographs of the Association for Asian Studies VIII. New York: J.J. Augustin.

Bloch, M., 1973, 'The long-term and the short-term: the economic and political significance of the morality of kinship', in J. Goody (ed.), *The character of kinship*. Cambridge: Cambridge University Press.

Bourdieu, P., 1977, *Outline of a Theory of Practice*. Cambridge: Cambridge University Press.

Das, V., 1976, 'Masks and faces: An essay on Punjabi Kinship', *Contributions to Indian Sociology* n.s. 10: 1–30.

Dasgupta, M., 1987, 'Selective Discrimination against female children in rural Punjab, India', *Population and Development Review, 13 (1)*: 77–100.

Fortes, M., 1969, *Kinship and the Social Order*. London: Routledge and Kegan Paul.

Gore, M.S., 1962, 'The husband-wife and mother-son relationship', *Sociological Bulletin* XI (1, 2): 91–102.

Hershman, P., 1981, *Punjabi Kinship and Marriage*. Edited by H. Standing. New Delhi: Hindustan.

Karve, I., 1958, *Kinship Organisation in India*. Bombay: Asia.

Kessinger, T.G., 1974, *Vilayatpur, 1848–1968: Social and economic change in a North Indian village*. Berkeley: University of California Press.

Kolenda, P., 1967, 'Regional differences in Indian family structure', in R.I. Crane (ed.), *Regions and regionalism in South Asian Studies: An Exploratory Study*. Duke University Monographs and Occasional Papers Series, No. 5.

Leach, E., 1962, 'On uncertain unconsidered aspects of double descent systems', *Man* 62 (214): 130–34.

Lukes, S., 1974, *Power: A radical view*. London: Macmillan.

Madan, T.N., 1965, *Family and Kinship: A Study of the Pandits of Rural Kashmir*. Bombay: Asia.

———, 1976, 'The Hindu Family and Development', *Journal of Social and Economic Studies* 4 (2): 211–31.

Maher, V., 1981, 'Work, consumption and authority within the household', in K. Young, C. Wolkowitz and R. McCullagh (eds.), *Of Marriage and the Market*. London: CSE Books.

Mayer, A., 1960, *Caste and Kinship in Central India: A village and its region*. London: Routledge and Kegan Paul.

Miller, B.D., 1989, 'Changing Patterns of juvenile sex ratios in rural India, 1961 to 1971'. *Economic and Political Weekly* XXIV (22): 1229–36.

Minturn, L., and J.T. Hitchcock, 1963, 'The Rajputs of Khalapur', in B.B. Whiting (ed.), *Six Cultures: Studies of Child Rearing*. New York: John Wiley and Sons.

Palriwala, R., 1990, Production, Reproduction and the Position of Women: A Case Study of a Rajasthan Village. Unpublished Ph.D. dissertation, University of Delhi.

———, 1991, 'Transitory Residence and Invisible Work: A Case Study of a Rajasthan Village', *Economic and Political Weekly* XXVI (48): 2763–72.

Parry, J.P., 1979, *Caste and Kinship in Kangra*. Delhi: Vikas.

Pocock, D., 1962, 'Notes on jajmani relationships', *Contributions to Indian Sociology* 4: 78–95.

Shah, A.M., 1973, *The Household Dimension of the Family in India*. Delhi: Orient Longman.

———, 1988, 'The phase of dispersal in the Indian family process', *Sociological Bulletin* 37 (1 & 2): 33–47.

Sharma, U., 1989, 'Studying the household: Individuation and values', in J.N. Gray and D.J. Mearns (eds.), *Society from the Inside Out: Anthropological perspectives on the South Asian household*. New Delhi: Sage.

Srinivas, M.N., 1976, *Remembered Village*. Delhi: Oxford University Press.

———, 1987, *The Dominant Caste and Other Essays*. Delhi: Oxford University Press.

Wiser, W.H., 1936, *Hindu Jajmani system: A socio-economic system interrelating members of a Hindu village community in services*. Lucknow: Lucknow Publishing House.

Yanagisako, S.J. and J.F. Collier, 1987, 'Toward a Unified Analysis of Gender and Kinship', in J.F. Collier and S.J. Yanagisako (eds.), *Gender and Kinship: Essays toward a Unified Analysis*. Stanford: Stanford University Press.

8   Women's Position and Fertility: The Case of the Asians in Kenya

Parveen Walji Moloo

The dramatic decline in fertility levels among Kenyan Asians may be understood through the interaction of macro sociopolitical factors and shifts in the kinship structure, family and women's roles. The particular social, political and economic conditions of an apparently privileged, immigrant minority engendered feelings of insecurity, uncertainty about their future in Kenya, multiple nationalities within families and an orientation to possible emigration to Europe or North America. These factors affected the ideals of 'family' and kinship behaviour, the meaning of children and strategies of reproduction based on smaller families. Internal variations in fertility between different communities (castes) among Asians in Nairobi were linked to differences in the roles and statuses of women. A number of indicators of women's status are used. Variations and shifts in women's multiple roles emerged with differentiated responses to their specific contexts, including concepts of self-identity and community, greater individualisation and narrowing of the family and its control over resources, the changed value of children, as well as the continuing economic dependence of women on husbands.

Introduction

Kenya is a developing country with a population of 25 million.[1] The estimated crude birth rate for the country is 50 per 1,000 population and, on the average, women give birth to between six and seven children (Kenya Demographic and Health Survey 1989). The high fertility rate, coupled with relatively low mortality, gives the country a population growth rate of 3.4 per cent per annum (Kenya Statistical Abstract 1991), which is considered to be one of the highest in the world. Although data from the Kenya Demographic and Health Survey 1989 provide the first evidence that fertility has started to decline, it still remains relatively high. In the midst of a pro-natalist African population, one finds a small, immigrant minority community of Asians,[2] which is unique in having undergone its demographic transition in a period of less than five decades. It exhibits demographic characteristics comparable to those of the more developed countries. It is therefore useful to know what factors have influenced the demographic behaviour of the Asians, whereby they are limiting the number of children they have to between two and three, through the extensive use of contraception.

This chapter examines at the micro level, the relationship between kinship structure, the position of women and fertility among the Asian community in Kenya. It also shows how specific macro-level social, economic and political factors have influenced the demographic behaviour of its members. Furthermore, the analysis presented is important for the present volume as it provides a link between the two continents by offering cultural insights into a community originally from South Asia, but now settled in Africa.

According to J. Caldwell (1976), fertility behaviour is rational only in so far as it is rational within a given social context. Thus, a discussion of this 'context is important in order to show why the Asians have behaved demographically so at variance with the rest of the Kenyan population. Since the Asian population of Kenya is a heterogeneous one, composed of diverse groups which differ on the basis of size, religion, language, caste, socioeconomic status, social structure and organisation, group-level data on four communities living in Nairobi were analysed (Nairobi has the largest concentration of Asians in Kenya). These include two Muslim communities, the Ismailis and the Luhars, and two Hindu communities, the Shahs[3] and the Suthars.

The Economic and Political Context for Asians in Kenya

The Ismailis belong to the Shia branch of Islam and are commonly known as the followers of the Aga Khan who is their 49th Imam or spiritual leader. He provides a focus for a worldwide community of approximately 20 million, of whom the Kenyan Ismailis form a small part. As Imam, he guides them in spiritual as well as temporal matters. Ismailis in Kenya have evolved an elaborate community organisation, and number approximately 8,000 today. Their population in Nairobi is estimated at 5,000 (Salvadori 1989). The Luhar Wadhas (referred to here as Luhars) are a small group of Kutchi Sunni Muslims numbering about 1,500. Originally, they were Hindus living in the state of Kutch in India and were converted to the Sunni branch of Islam in 12th century AD. Although they were traditionally carpenters and blacksmiths, they found it difficult to practice their trade in Kenya and most men are presently engaged in related manual occupations such as car and building repairs, furniture making and clerical jobs. Education levels for both men and women are low due to the emphasis on religious rather than secular education. The pattern of social behaviour of this group is very closely governed by religious law and tradition.

The Shahs or Jains are numerically and economically the most dominant of all the Asian communities in Kenya, numbering about 15,000 (Salvadori 1989). Although a large number of the men are professionals, the Shahs are predominantly a business community (their traditional occupation in India was farming). The success of the Shahs in business can be attributed both to their ethical doctrine, which emphasises simplicity and asceticism, as well as their strong kin and communal support. A large number of them are British citizens and are therefore likely to emigrate there eventually. The Gurjar Suthars are a small Hindu group of about 1,200 who originally came from the state of Gujarat. From their origins as carpenters, they have expanded into various trades and professions associated with the construction industry. However, economically they are relatively poor when compared to the Shahs. In common with many of the other groups, the Suthars are socially exclusive, with strong communal traditions and identity. As is the case with the Shahs, the majority of the Suthars have opted for British citizenship.

These four different, contrasting and internally homogeneous groupings were selected to enable generalisations on the Asian

community in Kenya. The data analysed in this chapter are based
on interviews conducted between 1977–78,[4] of a sample of 150
wives and 134 husbands, together with key informant interviews,
participant observation, and published and unpublished data. A
brief description of the economic and political context of Kenyan
Asians is provided in order to understand the background within
which their demographic behaviour has evolved.

Although contact between India and East Africa can be traced
back to many centuries as a result of long-established trading
activities between the two areas, the large-scale immigration of
Indians for the purpose of settlement in Kenya is a recent phenomenon which started during the 20th century. The first generation
of Indians in Kenya came mainly from the North-western Indian
states of Gujarat, Kutch, Punjab and from Goa (Bharati 1972;
Salvadori 1989). The majority of the Asians in Kenya today are
Gujaratis and Punjabis. According to the 1989 Census, the Kenyan
Asians number 52,968 and form 0.25 per cent of the total population. In fact, ever since their settlement in Kenya, and despite
their rapid rate of population growth before the 1960s, the Indians
have at no time been numerically a very strong group. Even during
their demographic peak in the early 1960s, the Asians numbered
1,76,613 or about 2 per cent of the country's population (Kenya
Population Census 1962: Vol. III).

Despite their very small numbers vis-à-vis the country's total
population, the Asians are a highly visible—though politically
weak—minority in Kenya's multiracial, pluralistic society. This
visibility can be attributed to their colour, culture, urban concentration and economic position, which appears to be out of proportion
to their numbers. The growth of the Indian settlement in Kenya
and their present position is closely tied up with, and largely
shaped by, the historical process of development in the country
which was influenced by the British colonial regime. The colonial
policy of dividing Kenyan society along racial principles, not only
on the social and cultural plane, but also in the economic and
political spheres, led the Asians to occupy an intermediate position
between the politically supreme Europeans at the apex and the
numerically preponderant Africans at the base.

The Indians had to face several restrictions on their economic
activities, imposed by the Europeans who perceived them as a
political and an economic threat. Thus in 1948, Government legislation restricted Indian immigration to Kenya, which in turn limited

their numerical expansion. Secondly, the Asians were precluded from acquiring land rights, since the best agricultural land was reserved for the Europeans while the rest belonged to Africans. This phenomenon, coupled with the fact that the Indians themselves did not show too much interest in agricultural pursuits (although many originated from rural backgrounds in India), resulted in confining their activities to wholesale and retail trade and employment as skilled artisans and clerks in private and public sectors. This employment pattern was further reinforced by administrative measures designed to keep the Europeans in the top executive and administrative jobs. Thirdly, a series of ordinances prevented Indian traders from conducting business outside specified townships and trading areas. This prevented them from gaining a foothold in the rural areas and resulted in their urban concentration, thereby further alienating them from the Africans. And yet, it was the Indian petty trader (*dukawallah*) who set up shops or *dukas* in local trading centres and also helped establish trade in the interior where none existed before. They extended the monetary economy into the subsistence areas and paved the way for the transition from a barter to a cash-based economy. In fact, the role of the Indian had become crucial for the economic life of the colony.

The response of the Asians to this set of restrictive policies established their status in Kenyan society. They organised themselves into economically independent and socially exclusive communities in the urban areas. Their isolation was further enhanced by the colonial policy of segregating residential, educational and other public facilities along racial lines. The strong religious, community and caste traditions of the Asians themselves reinforced this isolation so that they fell back on their own resources to provide basic services and amenities through the organisation of communal institutions.[5] Until Kenya attained independence in 1963, most Indian communities had their own schools, social and cultural halls, clubs, places of worship, burial places and even hospitals. Although the institutions were opened up to other communities then, they continue to exhibit communal orientations to this day.

The Kenyan Asians today present the picture of a self-sufficient, highly urbanised, educated and economically powerful group, engaged in trade, commerce and manufacturing, as well as middle and high level employment; an unpopular minority resented by the Africans mainly because of its economic success and dominance in certain fields. They have further incurred African hostility because of the inward looking organisation of their social structure, which is closed to outsiders so that Asian ways remain a mystery. The general racist attitude of the Asians also contributed to these negative attitudes. The younger, better educated generation of Indians is much more open and accommodating in its attitude towards, and interaction with, the Africans. As a result of this hostility, there is an underlying feeling of insecurity and apprehension among the Asians regarding their future in this country, although the majority of them consider Kenya rather than India as their home.

Social Organisation of Kenyan Asians

Having highlighted the demographic, economic and political position of the Asians in Kenya, we can briefly look at their social organisation. Although the Asians are treated as one large homogeneous entity within the Kenyan structure, they are in reality a heterogeneous group composed of diverse subcommunities differentiated on the basis of religion, language, caste and community, each with its own internal organisation, social structure and norms about boundary maintenance. In their efforts to accommodate themselves into a different social and economic structure stratified on the basis of race, the Kenyan Indians could no longer practice the caste system as they had known it in India. The caste concept adapted in a flexible fashion to new conditions. Of the five caste principles, namely, caste hierarchy, commensality, trade exclusiveness, ascription and endogamy, only the last two are still adhered to. Thus, the individual Indian's reference group and his reference point in terms of his values, traditions and customs is his community which, more often than not, is based on religion. His behaviour is determined less by the fact that he is an Asian and more by his communal membership, for example, whether he is an Ismaili, a Patel, a Sikh or a Shah.

Values and rules on marriage and the family are based on religious and community considerations. All the Kenyan Indian communities are patrilineal and patriarchal as a result of their origin from the patrilineal societies of India. The occurrence of marriage outside the community is rare and where it does occur, it is usually with other Asians. There are some instances of marriages to Europeans and very few cases of Asian–African marriages. Marriage customs and rituals, in general, are closely related to the Hindu marriage practices in India (Salvadori 1989). As in much of South Asia, marriage is a one-time event, in contrast to the African societies where it is a process spread over time. Hindu marriages involve the payment of dowry while the Muslims give *mahr*, a gift given or pledged by the groom to the bride. There is a close link between marriage, sexuality and procreation, as in patrilineal communities across South Asia. Thus, marriage as an ideal is upheld, virginity is highly valued, unwed mothers are rejected, infertility is not easily accepted and there is a stigma attached to divorce. In most communities, marriages are still arranged by the family, at times with the cooperation of the couple (ibid.) and the family plays a vital role in the individual's life. It is argued that a wide and closely-knit network of kin was a key factor for the successful establishment of businesses in some communities (Zarwan 1977). The extended or joint family is still widespread; even where households have split physically, the family still remains economically, socially and emotionally extended. The impact of education and 'Western' values in effecting change within the family structure can be seen in the desire expressed by the younger women to replace the extended family pattern by the nuclear form.

The status of women derives from cultural prescriptions about the sexual division of labour and gender inequalities in a patriarchal society. In most of the communities, the men generally control the resources and are in charge of decision-making. The traditional division of labour allocates all household work to the woman even when she is employed outside the home. Many women gave up employment after marriage because their husbands or in-laws expected them to. However, as a result of increased economic pressures created by a relative decline in income (due mainly to inflation and a decline in the economy), there is a trend towards increased labour force participation by women.[6] It can be argued that compared to their counterparts in India, the status of the Indian women in Kenya is relatively higher when measured by such indicators as sex ratios, female infant mortality rates, longevity, education and nutrition levels (Gurwitz 1988; Khan 1992).

The social organisation of the Asians reflects an interesting blend of 'Indian' and 'Western' values, with some African influence at a more superficial level. The Kenyan Indians have reconstructed a value system by transferring the religious ideology, values and customs from India in a modified manner, incorporating some aspects of what they perceive as 'a Western lifestyle' and making it relevant within the African urban context. With this adaptation, social relations and friendships continue to remain within the group and social networks are patterned along communal lines.

Women's Status and Fertility

Although the Demographic Transition Theory identified women's education and labour force participation at the macro level as factors affecting fertility, in recent years, the focus has shifted to the analysis of the status of women as a critical factor in explaining demographic phenomena (cf. Anker et. al. 1982). Women's status generally refers to the position they hold within the structure of a given social set up. The concept usually implies a hierarchical arrangement of positions, each involving a set of rights and obligations. It has been pointed out (Newman 1984; Oppong 1980; Whyte 1978) that women's status is a difficult concept to categorise and index because of the lack of a single measure. In this section, major aspects of women's status, which have been the focus of research in recent years, have been analysed to show how these differ by community and what impact they have on family size. The overall status measures discussed here are women's age at marriage and type of marriage, the preference for male children, education and occupation.

Age at Marriage and Type of Marriage: Women's age at marriage is used as an indicator of their status because of its implications for their education and their economic and domestic roles. It is also based on the notion that the greater the ability of women to control important life events like marriage and their age at marriage, the higher will be their status.

The mean age at marriage for Asian women in Kenya was estimated at 23.9 years (Khan 1992: 59). Our sample showed that almost 90 per cent of the women were married by the time they were 25 years old. There were, however, variations by community; almost half the Luhar and Suthar women were married before reaching age 20, whereas among the Shahs and Ismailis less than one-third of the women were married by that age. The pattern of early marriage among the Luhars and Suthars and several other groups can be explained by two factors: the first, arranged marriages and second, the relatively low education levels for girls. Girls usually left school around age 16 and stayed at home, where they were given training in good housekeeping and domestic science till their parents arranged their marriages. All the Luhar and most of the Suthar women stated that their marriages were arranged by their parents and their consent was rarely sought. A further indicator of the subordinate position of Luhar women is the persisting adherence to their religious law which does not permit a woman to marry out of the community, although it allows a man to do so (Muhammed 1974; Salvadori 1989: 192).

For the Ismailis, the situation was different. Except for the older women, most claimed to have themselves chosen their marriage partners. Also, the majority married after the age of 20. The relatively higher age at marriage and the trend away from arranged marriages was a reflection of the changing status of Ismaili women. This reflected the varied impact of education on these groups. These variations in the status of women appeared to have had an effect on their family size as is evident in Table 8.1.

Table 8.1   Number of Children by Community

Number of Children per Woman	Community				
	Total	Ismailis	Shahs	Suthars	Luhars
None	8.0	2.0	16.0	0.0	12.0
1–2	43.3	50.0	46.0	52.0	16.0
3–4	35.3	36.0	28.0	32.0	52.0
5 or more	13.3	12.0	10.0	16.0	20.0
Total	99.9	100.0	100.0	100.0	100.0
N	150				

It is clear from Table 8.1 that the Luhars tended to have more children than the other groups, the average number of children being 3.1, compared to a lower average for the other groups.

The Preference for Male Children: Evidence suggests that all contemporary societies are male dominated where women are excluded from certain crucial activities as well as rights and privileges, although there are cross-cultural variations in the degree of female subordination. One indicator of the relative subordination of females is the importance society places on male children (Das 1987). Preference for sons is a widespread phenomenon among patrilineal Asian societies. This is perhaps due to the fact that in these societies it is the sons who normally inherit family wealth, help run the family business, are a source of old age support, carry on the family name and perform certain rites, while daughters are married off and sent away. I argue that those societies where women's status is relatively higher will not put a higher premium on male children.

The respondents' preference for sons was revealed by answers to questions on whether or not a couple should have an extra child if (1) it had four girls and no boys, (2) it had four boys and no girls. Table 8.2 shows clearly that Asians put a higher premium on boys than on girls, but differences by community are very significant.

Table   8.2 Son Preference by Community

Community	Extra child if						
	4 sons only				4 daughters only		
	Yes	No	Total		Yes	No	Total
Ismailis	16.0	84.0	100.0		20.0	80.0	100.0
Shahs	8.0	92.0	100.0		32.0	68.0	100.0
Suthars	12.0	88.0	100.0		44.0	56.0	100.0
Luhars	48.0	52.0	100.0		80.0	20.0	100.0
	$X^2 = 19.4$ df = 3				$X^2 = 37.6$ df = 3		
	Significant at .001				Significant at .001		

The data show that for the Ismailis, son preference was not high. The figures reflect a significant change among the Ismailis as regards this traditional value. Among the Ismailis, the proportions who said that couples should not have an extra child were more or less the same in both cases. They felt that the sex of the child was not important. However, for the other groups, the proportions in favour of an extra child were much higher if there were no sons. Gurwitz (1988) in her study on the status of Sikh women in Nairobi, found that the preference for sons was high; 50 per cent of the women indicated that they would try another pregnancy in order to get a son. From Table 8.2, it appears that once again the Luhars were the most traditional, in so far as they attached a very high value to sons, followed by the Suthars and Shahs, respectively. The main reasons given were that sons could carry on the family name and support the parents in old age. The implications of this factor for fertility are obvious. Those couples with no sons will have little interest in controlling fertility. In fact, 75 per cent of the respondents with no sons indicated that they wanted more children.

Education: Women's education has been the focus of much attention as a major aspect of women's status. Education not only provides women with knowledge and skills and opportunity for employment, especially in high status occupations, but it also improves their access to social and family resources and facilitates their fuller participation in society.

The Kenyan Indians are a highly educated and literate community. The survey results showed that only 5 per cent of the women, all in the older ages, had not been to school while over 55 per cent had secondary school and higher education. The men have higher education levels than the women. Less than 2 per cent had no education while 75 per cent had secondary and higher education. Table 8.3 shows the significant differences in women's educational statuses between the different groups.

Table 8.3   Education Level of the Women by Community (Percentages)

Education level	All women	Community			
		Ismailis	Shahs	Suthars	Luhars
No education	5.0	4.0	2.0	0.0	16.0
Primary	39.0	28.0	38.0	48.0	56.0
Seconday	40.0	44.0	44.0	44.0	20.0
Higher	16.0	24.0	16.0	8.0	8.0
Total	100.0	100.0	100.0	100.0	100.0
(N)	(150)	(50)	(50)	(25)	(25)

The Luhars were the least educated; over 70 per cent had either no education or only primary education. This contrasted very clearly with the other communities, especially the Ismailis, whose education levels were relatively higher. About 70 per cent of the Ismailis, 60 per cent of the Shahs, and 52 per cent of the Suthars had secondary and higher education compared to only 28 per cent for the Luhars.

The relationship between education and fertility is a complex one, since education operates also through many other variables (Cochrane 1983). Further, when an inverse relationship between education and fertility is found to exist, it is not clear what particular characteristics of education are important since a variable like education represents 'overlapping penumbras of meaning' (Ryder 1959: 414).

For the Asians, education was negatively related to fertility (Table 8.4). However, it was found that education was significantly related to 'exposure'[7] and 'Westernisation'[8] levels and son preference, all factors which were found to have a relationship with the number of children women have. Thus, the effect of women's education on fertility may not be an independent one.

Table 8.4   Number of Children by Education (Percentages)

| Number of Children | Education Level | | |
	No education	Primary	Secondary and above
0	0.0	5.0	11.0
1–2	29.0	24.0	58.0
3–4	0.0	51.0	27.0
5 or more	71.0	20.0	4.0
Total	100.0	100.0	100.0

$X^2 = 45.8$ df = 6   Significant at .001

Occupational Status: Women's employment in the formal sector is the other major variable of interest in studies on women's status and fertility. It has usually been hypothesised that fertility and women's labour force participation are inversely related.

Asian women showed a relatively low level of participation in the labour force. Table 8.5 shows that 85 per cent of the sample women were housewives and only 15 per cent were employed, and yet, data on the professional training of the women showed that 45 per cent were trained in various professions as secretaries, dressmakers, teachers and managers. Once again, there were variations by community. The bulk of the employed women were Ismailis (75

per cent), whereas none of the Suthar and only one Luhar women
were employed.

Table 8.5   Occupation Status of the Women by Community
(Percentages)

Occupation	Total	Ismailis	Shahs	Suthars	Luhars
Housewife	85.0	66.0	90.0	100.0	96.0
Semi-skilled					
and Clerical	11.0	26.0	6.0	–	4.0
Professional	4.0	8.0	4.0	–	–
Total	100.0	100.0	100.0	100.0	100.0
(N)	(150)	(50)	(50)	(25)	(25)

Although the proportion in employment was highest for the Ismailis,
it was still rather low, considering that 60 per cent indicated that
they had been trained in various professions and also taking into
account the very high education levels within the community.
However, an upward trend among them is probable, as indicated
by an informal survey, conducted in 1992 by an Ismaili community
organisation, which showed that about 55 per cent of the women,
aged 20–60 years, were engaged in the labour force. The proportion
of women trained for a profession was lower for the other groups;
40 per cent for the Shahs, and 36 per cent for both the Suthars and
the Luhars.

It appears from the survey results that except for the Ismailis,
the married Asian women, although manifesting some changes in
their lifestyles attuned to potential migration to western countries,
had not taken to working outside the home. The majority of the
upper and middle class women were homemakers. In the poorer
families, many women combined housework with income-generating activities within the home such as cooking food for sale, selling
Indian condiments, keeping boarders and/or paying guests, sewing
and beauty treatment. As has been previously mentioned, prior to
their immigration to Kenya, the Indians were engaged in agriculture, trade or as artisans. The women performed duties related to
the farm and/or the home. The situation of the Kenyan Indian
women is not only different from that of the first generation
immigrants, but also from that in several of the western countries

to which they were aspiring. There, often a larger proportion of women are in employment.

Table 8.6 supports the employment-fertility hypothesis. Those women who were employed seemed to be having fewer children than the housewives. However, this relationship must be viewed with caution. Only 15 per cent of the women stated that they were employed, of whom the bulk were Ismailis. Since the Ismailis were also the most educated and 'Westernised' and had the highest exposure levels, it is difficult to know the real effect of employment on fertility.

Table 8.6   Women's Employment versus Number of Children

| Number of Children | Employment status | |
	Employed	Housewives
0	17.0	6.0
1–2	61.0	40.0
3–4	17.0	39.0
5 or more	4.0	15.0
Total	99.0	100.0
N	(23)	(127)
$X^2 = 9.04$ significant level = .05		

Standing (1978) has pointed out that the relationship between work and fertility is a complex one and depends on the type of work women do and the extent to which work and child care are incompatible. The case of the Asian women is interesting. For the working women the question of role incompatibility should not arise because of (1) relatively inexpensive domestic help; practically all the Ismaili women (98 per cent) had hired domestic help, either houseworkers or maids or both; (2) easy availability of kindergartens and places which facilitate child care outside the domestic unit. Yet, these women had few children. It could be argued that employment for these women entailed an alternative satisfaction to children (for example, companionship, recreation, stimulation, sense of freedom and independence) or it provided the monetary means to such satisfaction.

The fact that non-working women, especially the Shah and Ismaili, had a small family size is interesting. It has been shown that educated women who approve of non-domestic roles, even if they don't work, have a desire for fewer children. Studies show that the amount of time women devote to housework decreases with education, while time spent on leisure activities increases. This appeared to be the case with the Ismailis and Shahs. It entailed socialising with family and friends, entertaining, sporting activities, community social work and engaging in other activities of personal interest.

To summarise this section, there were significant differences in the status of women by community, with the Ismaili women having apparently much higher status than the Luhar women. It was also found that all the status variables discussed influenced family size among the Asians which, although relatively low, still varied by community.

Women's Roles

Taking role as the dynamic aspect of status, a woman's status can be seen as multidimensional due to the many roles she plays. It is therefore useful to examine these various roles. In doing so this chapter uses Oppong's framework (1980; also Oppong and Abu 1987). Her categorisation of seven roles of women is helpful in briefly sketching some of the roles of Indian women, highlighting their relative importance and salience, variations by community and their relation to fertility behaviour.

Maternal Role: Regardless of community affiliation, marriage and motherhood are ideals aspired to by all Indian women and very few remain single out of choice. Moreover, because of the stigma attached to unwed mothers, marriage is the only vehicle to motherhood. A few women in the sample, mainly Shah, who did not have any children expressed disappointment and concern over this. However, while it was important for Asian women to have children, it was not important to have many children. When asked if having a large number of children gave prestige to a woman, over 90 per cent replied in the negative saying that this was a traditional idea and, on the contrary, having many children brought about social disapproval. Three-quarters of the women considered that the ideal number of children should be three and under. The maternal role now revolved around raising 'quality' children, rather than on the number of children. Mothers were trying to give 'quality' socialisation by spending more time with their children and being actively interested and involved in all aspects of their children's lives, as well as giving them maximum exposure. Among the Ismailis and Shahs, the social organisation of parenting was changing so that younger generation men were becoming more actively involved with their children.

Domestic Role: The nature of the domestic role of the women varied by family composition and by community. The extended family system was dominant in the social organisation of the Asians, especially the Hindus. 65 per cent of the respondents were living with their in-laws. Gurwitz (1988) found that 80 per cent of Sikh women were living in extended families. The Ismailis differed significantly in that only 28 per cent lived with their in-laws, thus showing a trend towards nucleation. This implies substantial differences in the domestic roles of the women. The assumption is that those women living in the extended family tend to have relatively less independence and decision-making powers than those in nuclear families. Moreover, their domestic duties are under the control of the elder kin, especially the mother-in-law. These women are expected and tend to devote more time to cooking, keeping house and the general care of in-laws, as well as looking after and entertaining the husband's other relatives.

Participant observation data showed dissatisfaction on the part of many Shah women regarding their domestic role and resentment at having to live with their in-laws, especially where the mother-in-law exercised a great deal of control. However, in many cases, the sons were not willing to move out both because of the close relationship to their parents, particularly mothers, and also involvement in the joint family businesses. The wives, however, indicated a preference for nucleation. For the less educated Luhar and Suthar women, the domestic role appeared to be rather important.

Kin Role: For all the Asians, maintaining close ties with relatives was important. After marriage, women continued to maintain close links with their parents and siblings, as well as keeping close contact with the husband's relatives. There was frequent exchange of visits, especially between female relatives, as well as assistance on important social occasions. Financial support of relatives was prevalent among the Shahs and Suthars, most of whom lived in extended families. Slightly over 50 per cent of the Shahs and Suthars gave financial help to relatives, compared to 28 per cent of the Luhars and 32 per cent of the Ismailis.

It appears that close ties and frequent associations with close relatives were important and satisfying for the Asian woman. In fact, her main support networks consisted of her relatives, her husband's relatives, friends and, where existent, community institutions.

Community Role: The community played a very important part in the life of Ismaili women, who showed the highest participation in community activities. 74 per cent of them indicated that they held responsible positions in community institutions. In her study of the Ismailis in Tanzania, S. Walji (1974: 60) emphasised the active participation of women in community activities. The Shah women also showed high involvement in community activities (60 per cent), whereas the participation by the Suthar and Luhar women in similar activities was low, 16 per cent and 20 per cent, respectively. This difference could be attributed to the elaborate community organisation and the various institutions for managing community affairs among the Ismailis (and to a lesser extent the Shahs). These institutions operate mainly on a voluntary basis, which gives women a lot of opportunity to participate in community work.

For Muslims (and hence Ismailis), Islam is a 'way of life' for its followers and the dividing line between religious and social spheres is fine. In this context, mosque attendance has many dimensions such as participation in religious rites and ceremonies, spiritual satisfaction, social interaction/networking, as well as leisure (cf. Mawani 1975). Such activities in turn reinforce the Ismaili community identity and create a sense of belonging. Ismaili women devoted much time to and obtained satisfaction from visiting the mosque, almost 90 per cent of the women indicating that they went practically every day. The last implied spending almost one hour a day on this activity. This is a significant difference from Ismaili and Muslim practice in western India. Within the mosque precincts, Ismaili women participated in activities such as keeping the premises clean, serving water and maintaining discipline. Outside the mosque, opportunities for service arose in various community councils as well as the social and economic organisations of the Aga Khan Developmental Network. The women in the other communities indicated that they went to the mosque/temple only rarely; most prayed at home.

Occupational Role: The general situation of Asian women regarding employment has already been discussed. Participation in the labour force was low and was confined mainly to Ismaili women. Whereas 34 per cent of the Ismailis were employed mainly in semi-skilled, clerical and professional occupations, corresponding figures for the Shahs, and Luhars were 10 per cent and 4 per cent, respectively, and none among Suthars. Thus, going out to work was not a high priority role for married Asian women. This can partly be explained by the fact that many depended on their husbands for financial support and benefited from the husband's social and economic status. Those in the upper and middle classes are not expected to provide financial support for their children as has been found among Kenyan African women. Moreover, many women indicated that their husbands did not want them to work. Many Ismaili women were working, possibly because they found the work interesting and satisfying; they had few children and it gave them a sense of independence and perhaps security in the face of an uncertain future. It was unlikely that they felt role strain in terms of time in performing their occupational role, because of the availability of paid domestic help as well as kindergartens.

Individual Role: The Ismailis, far more than any other group, spent a lot of time on leisure activities like going to plays, variety shows, nightclubs, restaurants and vacationing at beach hotels or lodges. The Suthars and Luhars did not indulge in these costly activities. Their leisure pursuits mainly included visiting relatives, listening to Indian music and watching Indian movies. Moreover, the Ismailis, and to an extent the Shahs, spent material resources on enhancing personal status (travelling overseas, expensive houses, cars, modern gadgets, clothes). Thus, the emphasis on individual material security, self-gratification and advancement was highest among the Ismailis, who also extended less financial help to their kin and whose family size was also the lowest, and lowest among the Luhar women, who had the highest number of children.

Thus, the individual and community roles had become very important for the Ismaili, and to a lesser extent Shah, women from which they derived great satisfaction. This was less so for the Luhar and Suthar for whom the intermediate arẹna of kinship retained its priority along with domestic and maternal roles.

Specific Contextual Factors

Thus, far, I have discussed the position of women in the Asian community and I have noted significant internal differentiations. I have also found differences in ideal and actual family size by status of women; the Ismaili women with relatively higher status and more emphasis on the individual and community roles, desired and had fewer children than the Luhar women whose status, by all indicators, was much lower and who emphasised the more traditional maternal and domestic roles.

However, although differences in family size and preference exist internally in the Asian community, in general the Asian population exhibits fertility levels far lower than the national norm. Evidence from various Kenyan censuses (from 1931 up to 1979) indicates a marked and rapid decline in Asian fertility since the late 1950s: from a crude birth rate of 40–45 per 1,000 population and a total fertility rate of 6 around 1950, to a crude birth rate of 20–25 and a total fertility rate of 2.8 in 1979 (Khan 1992). These rates stand in marked contrast to those of the indigenous African population which had a crude birth rate of 55 and a total fertility rate of 8.1 in 1979 (Osiemo 1986).

What has made the Asian community respond in this unique way as regards its demographic characteristics? Based on Caldwell's (1976) arguments that fertility behaviour is rational only in so far as it is rational within a given social context, we argue that certain specific contextual factors have influenced the demographic behaviour of the Asians in Kenya. They include the existing socio-economic context of the Asians in Kenyan society; their perceptions of insecurity because of their minority status; the existence of multinationality and split families whereby members of the same family belong to different nationalities resulting in the physical separation of such families, which makes them potentially mobile; the possibility of eventual migration mainly to North American (Canada) and west European countries (Great Britain); orientation to upward social mobility and related aspirations to 'Western' lifestyles and the high premium on children's education and quality children.

Since a detailed discussion of all the factors mentioned is not possible here, I highlight only the salient points.

The Socioeconomic Context: As already discussed, the historical, economic and political developments in the country have led to the existing socioeconomic context of the Asians. A summary of this context is the high degree of urbanisation, the extremely high exposure to education vis-à-vis the African population and, by implication, high levels of aspiration to 'Western' lifestyles, high wage or self-employed incomes, high standards of living and an orientation to upward social mobility. The Asian community can therefore be seen as a highly privileged minority group within the country, visible because of its conspicuous lifestyle which actively reinforces its privileged position. This is done through the increased value for education and social mobility.

A high premium is put on education; the data show that not only were the parents highly educated but they also indicated very high aspirations regarding their children's education. Many of them (those who could afford to do so) sent their children to very expensive private schools and then to universities in English-speaking countries because of the assumed higher education standards. It was clear that the major expenditure on children was schooling; parents concentrated more concern and expenditure on fewer children in order to be able to take advantage of new and different economic opportunities, so as to be more socially mobile. There were clear distinctions between the different groups, so that the Luhars were both the least educated and appeared to put lower emphasis on their children's education than did the other groups.

According to Caldwell (1976; 1982), when the direction of the intergenerational flow of wealth is from the older to the younger generation, the rational choice for parents is to have fewer children. For the Asians, children had become a drain on resources, both in time and money, rather than an economic benefit. There was no economic benefit to be derived from having a large number of children, even when the parents were old. Slightly over 40 per cent of the respondents expected to live with their married sons although there were significant variations by community; the two Hindu groups showed a higher preference for the extended family system. According to Gurwitz (1988), over 50 per cent of the Sikhs did not want to live with their married sons. In addition, the majority of the respondents felt that, compared to the past, married sons were less willing either to live with or support their parents in old age. Thus, the benefits derived from children were more social and psychological. The costs of children were related to the emphasis on the quality of children (cf. Leibenstein 1957). Thus, the main reason given for not wanting large families was that 'quality' children nowadays are too expensive and demanding.

The Asian's visibility as a privileged minority group is reinforced through high levels of conspicuous consumption. The data on income and living levels show that the Asians, some groups more so than others, indulge in consumption patterns which are extremely conspicuous, for example, driving expensive cars, living in high status areas, dressing expensively and ornately, owning modern gadgets like television and video sets, washing machines and even swimming pools, frequenting restaurants and movie theatres, having holidays at beach hotels or paying weekend visits to game lodges. This type of consumption pattern is also in evidence among the emerging urban African élite. Nevertheless, it stands out more markedly among a small, highly visible and racially different minority group when compared to the general African population which has much lower income and living standards.

As regards the influence of these factors on fertility, the Economic Theory of Fertility is relevant here (Leibenstein 1975). The theory holds that fertility is inversely related to the quality of children. The Kenyan Asians wanted 'quality children' who would get the best education and acquire a certain given style of life. This requires not only a lot of parent time. care and attention, but also money. The latter is also necessary for the active leisure pursuits and conspicuous consumption patterns indulged in by the Asians. This appears to be a major factor in determining why they wanted and had small families.

Perceptions of Insecurity, Multinationalities, and Potential Mobility: Another important contextual factor specific to the Asians is the existence of multinationality and split families, which makes the entire Asian population potentially mobile. Thus, while the husband might be Kenyan, the wife might be British, the parents Indian and the children any of these. Also, the majority of the respondents indicated that they had very close family members who had emigrated already and resettled, mainly in the United Kingdom and Canada.

This factor raises the whole question of the meaning of possessing Kenyan nationality for this minority group. It was hypothesised in our study that the non-citizen Asians would tend to be more mobile and perceive themselves socially and economically more insecure than the citizen Asians. This potential mobility would result in fewer children initially, because they would be more conscious of the problems and costs of immigration. Almost 90 per cent of the respondents felt that a large number of children would make it difficult to settle in a new place. They felt that it was problematic and expensive enough to settle down, even with only a few children. Secondly, their mobility was geared to countries like Britain, the United States and Canada, which emphasise the costs of children and therefore advocate small families. Over 70 per cent of the respondents indicated that if they had to, they would immigrate to these countries.

Possession of Kenyan nationality did not seem to significantly influence attitudes relevant to mobility and insecurity. A number of factors can be seen to enhance the perception of insecurity, namely:

- the Government's emphasis on accelerating Africanisation of commerce and industry;
- periodic anti-Asian speeches by politicians, or anti-Asian sentiments in letters to the editors in the local dailies;
- hostility shown towards them during the attempted coup in 1982, during which many Asian businesses and homes were looted, and
- the fear that the 1972 Ugandan strategy of mass expulsion of Asians could be a political possibility in Kenya.

These factors reactivated the conventional belief that all Asians in Kenya are a highly mobile, unstable group, which was further reinforced by multinationalities within very many families. A comparison of the 1969 and 1979 Census figures shows that the population of both the citizen and non-citizen Asians declined significantly due to emigration. In 1969, the Asians formed 1.3 per cent of the total Kenyan population. Of these, 44 per cent were Kenyan citizens and 56 per cent non-citizens (Kenya Population Census 1969). In 1979, the Asians comprised less than 0.5 per cent of the country's population and that proportion has declined even more. The percentage change for the citizens and non-citizens was −46 per cent and −41 per cent, respectively (Kenya Population Census 1979). Regardless of citizenship status, the Asians have been a highly mobile group. The social perception of the Asians as being 'paper' citizens appears to create feelings of economic and political insecurity amongst them as a whole.

Concluding Remarks

I have highlighted the specific factors at the macro level which have interacted to influence the unique reactions of the Asian minority with regard to fertility behaviour. The majority of the Kenyan population has not been responding in a similar manner despite the existence of an official national population policy in the country (Kenya Sessional Paper No. 4, 1984). While the African urban élite is controlling its family size, it is not responding as dramatically as the Asians, although there are similarities in income, education and 'Westernisation' levels (Agbasi 1977; cf. also Anker and Knowles 1982).

The societal level fertility of the Indians can be explained by special social, political and economic conditions affecting a minority immigrant group. The feelings of insecurity, the uncertainty about their future in Kenya and the possibility of eventual emigration to western countries, not only for the non-citizens but also for citizen Asians, have led them to limit their family sizes to what were perceived as manageable and acceptable in the 'West'. At the same time, internal group variations in fertility are definitely linked to differences in the roles and statuses of women, as these developed in differentiated responses to specific contexts and with distinct perspectives on and possibilities for mobility.

Notes

1. The Daily Nation, 12 March 1994.
2. In this chapter, the term Kenyan Asians refers to persons of Indian or Pakistani origin. Sometimes, the Kenyan Asians are referred to as Indians. Therefore here the terms Asians and Indian are used interchangeably.
3. Although technically the Shahs are not Hindus since they follow Jainism and not Hinduism, they have been selected here to represent the Hindus. Within the Kenyan context, they are culturally and linguistically very close to the Hindus. In fact, most Asians do not make a distinction between them and the

other Hindus. Zarwan (1977), Bharati (1972), and Salvadori (1989), all agree that even among the Shahs themselves there is little understanding of Jainism and many consider themselves Hindus and are treated as such.

4. It must be pointed out that although the information was collected some time ago, it is still useful in reflecting a relatively accurate picture of the Asian socioeconomic and demographic situation due to the fact that since the 1989 Census in the country, there is no national data available on the Asians. Nor has any recent detailed socioeconomic study of this group been conducted (see Khan 1992 and Salvadori 1989).

5. Right from their settlement in Kenya, the Ismailis have had a support system for its marginalised members in the areas of shelter, health, education, employment and maintenance. In recent years, this social care has been institutionalised through the creation of the Aga Khan Social Welfare Board. The mandate of the latter is to improve the standard of living and raise the quality of life of the disadvantaged members of the community and its scope includes, among the activities already listed, care of geriatrics.

6. In her study of Sikh women in Nairobi, Gurwitz (1988) found 40 per cent of the women working mainly in pink-collar jobs like teaching, nursing and secretarial positions. Personal observations of some communities by the author also indicate an increase in the number of working women.

7. The level of exposure was measured through the construction of an index using various media measures such as reading of newspapers, listening to radio, TV watching, etc., as well as overseas trips. Once total scores were computed, respondents were divided into categories of low, medium or high level of exposure.

8. The level of 'Westernisation' was measured through an index computed by scoring respondents on different activities, perceived in Kenya as western-oriented behaviour patterns, for example, mode of dressing, attending western plays/movies, visiting night clubs and restaurants, going dancing and staying at tourist hotels/lodges. Apart from such indicators incorporated in the question-naire, other factors taken into account were:

- the shift away from the 'traditional' Indian extended family towards the nuclear family, particularly in the 1960s and '70s;
- the increase in higher educational and professional opportunities for women. There was an enlargement of scale pertaining to women attending the universities and going out to work. This was part of the colonial system which offered such opportunities which were considered equivalent to modernisation or westernisation.
- increasing use of the English language in the home in preference to the Indian vernacular. In many Asian households (particularly Ismaili ones), children do not know their mother tongue and parents even encourage the use of English. It is common to find English incorporated into the vernacular in the course of day-to-day conversation.
- a move away from arranged marriages to Western-style dating and choice of spouse by individuals.

What has emerged is an incorporation of these patterns into an earlier way of life, so that the 'traditional' and more 'western' exist side by side.

References

Agbasi, G.O., 1977, 'Differential fertility in urban Kenya', New York: Fordham University, Unpublished Ph.D. thesis.

Anker, R., M. Buvinic and **N. Youssef** (eds.), 1982, *Women's Roles and Population Trends in the Third World*. London: Croom Helm.

Anker, R. and **J.C. Knowles**, 1982, *Fertility Determinants in Developing Countries: A Case Study of Kenya*. Liege: ILO, Ordina Editions.

Bharati, A., 1972, *The Asians in East Africa, Jayhind and Uhuru*. Chicago: Nelson-Hall.

Caldwell, J.C., 1976, 'Towards a restatement of the demographic transition theory'. *Population and Development Review* 2(3, 4): 209–31.

———, 1982, *Theory of Fertility Decline*. London: Academic Press.

Cochrane, S.H., 1983, 'Effects of education and urbanization on fertility', in R.A. Bulatao and R.D. Lee (eds.), *Determinants of Fertility in Developing Countries Vol. 2*. New York: Academic Press.

Daily Nation, 1994, 'Kenya population passes 25m mark'. *Daily Nation*, 12.3.1994, Nairobi.

Das, N., 1987, 'Sex preferences and fertility behaviour', *Demography* 24 (4): 517–30.

Dow, T.F., Jr., 1967, 'Attitudes toward family size and family planning in Nairobi'. *Demography* 4 (2): 780–97.

Gurwitz, H., 1988, 'The status of Sikh women in Nairobi', Nairobi: University of Nairobi, Unpublished M.A. thesis.

Kenya Sessional Paper, No. 4.—Population Policy Guidelines, 1984. Ministry for Home Affairs and National Heritage, Nairobi: Office of the Vice President.

Kenya Demographic and Health Survey, 1989, National Council for Population and Development and Institute for Resource Development, Columbia, Md.: Institute for Resource Development/Macro Systems.

Kenya Population Census Vol. 2, 1979, Nairobi: Statistics Division, Ministry of Finance and Planning.

———, *Vol. 3*, 1962, Nairobi: Statistics Division, Ministry of Economic Planning and Development.

———, *Vol. 4*, 1969, Nairobi: Statistics Division, Ministry of Finance and Economic Planning.

Kenya Statistical Abstract, 1991, Nairobi: Government Press.

Khan, A.E., 1992, 'An estimation of levels and differentials of fertility and mortality: A case study of the Asian community in Kenya'. Unpublished M.A. thesis. Nairobi: University of Nairobi.

Leibenstein, H., 1957, *Economic Backwardness and Economic Growth*. New York: Wiley.

———, 1975, 'The economic theory of fertility decline'. *Quarterly Journal of Economics 89*: 1–13.

Mangat, J.S., 1969, *A history of the Asians in East Africa, 1886–1945*. London: Oxford University Press.

Mawani, P., 1975, 'The Jamat Khana as a source of cohesiveness in the Ismaili community in Kenya'. Nairobi: University of Nairobi, Unpublished M.A. Thesis.

Muhammed, A., 1974, *Marriage, Divorce and Sex*. Lahore.

Newman, J.S., 1984, *Women of the World: Sub-Saharan Africa*. Washington, D.C.: U.S. Department of Commerce, Bureau of Census.

Oppong, C., 1980, *A Synopsis of Seven Roles and Status of Women: An outline of a conceptual and methodological approach*. Geneva: ILO, World Employment Programme Research Working Paper, mimeo.

Oppong, C. and K. Abu, 1987, *Seven Roles of Women: Impact of education, migration and employment on Ghanaian mothers*. ILO, Women Work and Development Series No. 3. Geneva: ILO.

Osiemo, J.A.O., 1986, 'Estimation of fertility levels and differentials in Kenya: Application of Coale–Trussel and Gompertz relational models', Nairobi: University of Nairobi, Unpublished M.Sc. Thesis.

Ryder, N.B., 1959, 'Fertility', in P.M. Hauser and O.D. Duncan (eds.), *The Study of Population: An inventory and appraisal*. Chicago: University of Chicago Press.

Salvadori, C., 1989, *Through Open Doors: A view of Asian cultures in Kenya*. Nairobi: Kenway.

Standing, G., 1978, *Labour Force Participation and Development*. Geneva: ILO.

Walji, P., 1980, 'The relationship between socio-economic conditions and fertility behaviour among selected Asian groups in Nairobi'. Nairobi: University of Nairobi, Unpublished Ph.D. thesis.

Walji, S., 1974, 'A history of the Ismaili community in Tanzania', Madison, Wisconsin: University of Wisconsin, Unpublished Ph.D. thesis.

Whyte, M.K., 1978, *The Status of Women in Pre-Industrial Societies*. Princeton: Princeton University Press.

Zarwan, J., 1977, 'Indian businessmen in Kenya during the 20th century: A case study'. Unpublished Ph.D. thesis. New Haven: Yale University.

III

The Articulation of Legal Systems
and the Family

9 Family Rights in Kenya: A Preliminary Examination of the Legal Framework

Kivutha Kibwana

This chapter examines the legal framework for family rights in Kenya and in the process, develops a framework to examine family rights and law. The predominant, patriarchal family in Kenya is described briefly, covering the various forms and types of marriage and family found. Though the emphasis in the concept of family rights may appear to be on group rights, here, the notion is developed as a summary of individual rights. The starting point is the right to a family and family life—an umbrella right on which other rights are premised. Problematic areas elaborated include women's rights, economic rights, children's rights and rights of those on the 'periphery of the core family'. Changing societal conditions necessitate reform in a gamut of laws and policies, including those which apparently do not pertain directly to family and marriage. Among the issues highlighted are women's rights to matrimonial property and the links with the non-recognition of women's labour.

Introduction

The existence of family rights, especially from moral and social standpoints, is usually assumed. Since the family is commonly perceived as the core micro unit of the larger society responsible for fulfilling the individual's basic emotional, security and economic needs, it is believed that family rights will naturally exist to support these needs. Domestic laws and international instruments concentrate on individual and, more recently, non-family group rights, to the exclusion of family rights. As a consequence, due to legal indifference or legal and societal paternalism, legal surveillance is lacking and tyranny, neglect and abuse do stalk the family.

This chapter examines the legal context for family rights in Kenya. In this background, I develop a framework for examining family rights and the law. Such a task, if achieved even at a modest level, can expand a rights discourse and further, lay the basis for the nurturing of a stronger and more stable family and society. I will argue that, although policy documents and political ideology emphasise the centrality of the family in Kenyan society, the legal articulation of family rights is routinely marginalised; lacunae and rhetoric predominate in the family rights sphere. Further, an attempt will be made to suggest the reasons for the neglect of family rights and the remedial action necessary to rehabilitate them within the legal corpus and societal practice.

Although the group character of the family is generally emphasised, especially in African societies,[1] we are interested in highlighting family rights as individual rights, first and foremost. Men, women and children possess individual rights in and through the family and outside the family. In the family as well as other collectives, individual rights, which usually give identity and dignity to the individual, are often sacrificed and lost in group rights discourse. However, family rights will also be discussed as group rights, for example, rights to proper moral development, security, protection, sustenance etc., where these enhance family individual rights. I shall return to this point later. I need to place a threshold caveat: this chapter presents preliminary thinking and secondary research findings on the subject.

Family and Family Rights Defined

In this chapter, the family is taken to be a microbiological, sociocultural and economic unit of society responsible, therefore, for biological, sociocultural, economic, political and class reproduction of human beings.[2] The individual, friendship and neighbours constitute three other basic institutions of society offering competition to and supplementing the family.

Historically, there have been multiple forms and types of marriage and family (cf. Engels 1972). In Kenya (and Africa) today, the monogamous and the polygynous family types coexist and are recognised by the four existing marriage and family law systems[3]— Christian/statutory, Hindu, Islamic and African customary.[4] Some specific norms, such as constitutional, succession and land laws, also define the family in terms of monogamy or polygyny. However, under Kenya's legal regime, the monogamous family is given superior recognition and status, despite the numerical superiority of the polygynous population.[5] This situation can engender tension in realising individual rights within the larger unit.

The family can also be described as patriarchical or matriarchical (including intermediate forms of these two systems); nuclear or extended; single parent or two parents' based; etc. Further, the family is a reference point for defining an individual's *relatives* and therefore the social and kinship network, the *social family*.

Although the modern family is said to be principally associated with the dictates of emotional/conjugal support and the need to ensure a stable upbringing of offspring, its economic *raison d'être*, in many respects, becomes controlling. The patriarchical family[6] creates for the man, an environment conducive to the exploitation of the labour of his wife/wives, concubine(s)/mistress(es), children and male relatives for accumulation purposes. For these latter categories, the family then serves to socialise them from an early age to accept and live with asymmetrical relations, subjugation and exploitation.

The form and type of a family, including emphases on certain characteristics or features, largely determine the nature and quantity of family rights to be enjoyed by individual family members. Ideally, a family would be defined as a collective of spouses, usually with children, in a situation where family rights and values recognise equality of status between the spouses and a self-identity and reasonable autonomy in relation to offspring. The internal regulation of such a family, taken as a core basic unit of society in which extended kin may have expectations, mirrors and, in turn, defines the identity and regulation of the larger society. For example, if the democratic ideal is not recognised in the family and other micro sites, its realisation in the larger society tends to be problematic.

The definition of the patriarchical family, the prevalent type in Kenya, may be summarised diagrammatically as in Figure 9.1. The figure reveals:

- The family is man-centred. In an ideal scenario, a single woman, together with the man, would occupy the centre as the foundational core in the family unit.
- Often, the man may place a higher premium on 'his' children than on the wife/wives.
- A man can be married to more than one wife; a woman cannot, usually, be married to more than one husband.
- The man considers 'his' children equally, whether they are born within or without marriage. The controlling principle is undisputed paternity. In Kenya, this principle has been legally recognised by including 'illegitimate' children as heirs (Contrast with Goonesekere in this volume).
- An ambivalence exists and is encouraged by the male dominated society regarding the relationship and rights *inter se* wives and near-wives and with the man.
- A man and a woman could enter into and maintain a 'marriage' without legal capacity.
- Relatives, especially under customary law and in present day Africa, are still important family members.
- Domestic servants—especially live-in household help—become important social and economic members of the family. For example, 'housemaids' in Kenya, practically bring up the children of many urban middle class families. Young children will call them 'mummy', older children 'auntie'.

Societies differ in the emphasis they have given to group rights and individual rights. Historically, liberal democracy and market oriented economies have stressed the primacy of individual rights. The individual is seen as the fitting repository of legal rights and duties. Only recently have group or community rights been recognised (especially by international law) as second and third generation human rights. These terms cover economic, social and cultural rights, and those rights benefiting entire countries or the persons populating an entire country or region. Third generation rights, for example, are the rights to development, peace, self-determination and a healthy environment.

Family rights could be viewed as a species of group rights, as an intermediate category between individual and group rights, or as individual rights in the strict sense. Family rights may be defined as consisting of specific, enumerable and enforceable rights that an individual possesses because he or she belongs to a family. Further, family rights consist of rights that all members, including children, have by virtue of belonging to the family. Even when a family right is a derivative of group membership, it is ultimately an individual right attached to and enforceable by or on behalf of a family member. This point deserves to be emphasised because individual rights are often submerged through politically and culturally inspired manipulative designs or other reasons under non-focused group rights nomenclature.

Individual and Family Rights in Kenya

Before discussing the problematique of family rights in the Kenyan context, it is important to point out that two broad types of families exist: the polygynous family under customary and Islamic law and the monogamous family under state, Hindu, and even customary and Islamic laws (many marriages are monogamous, though potentially polygynous). Within monogamous marriages, the two spouses are relatively independent of the extended family in terms of control and expectation of joint economic activity. In such marriages, personal and individual rights are recognised more than in polygynous marriages, where the spouses are ordinarily subjected to extended family and often clan control. Within customary law, several types and forms of marriages exist, for example, wife inheritance (levirate union), woman-to-woman marriage, etc. One of the greatest challenges facing legal reformers in Africa is to secure uniformity of the marriage form so as to better protect women's rights within the marriage institution.[7]

In discussing family rights in Kenya, I start from an umbrella right upon which other family rights may be premised. This is: *The Right to a Family and Family Life (and other Family Rights Incidental thereto)*. Kenya's domestic family laws do not explicitly

Figure 9.1
The Prevalent Family Type in Kenya

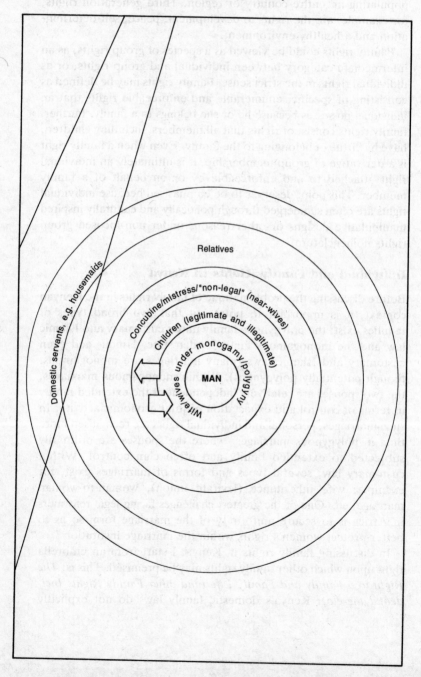

provide for such a right, though they do imply it. These laws, like other family laws worldwide, describe how individuals enter into, stay in, and leave marriage and the family.

Kenya is a party to two international covenants wherein the rights to family life are specifically and emphatically provided for. The first is the *Convention on the Elimination of all Forms of Discrimination against Women (CEDAW)*. This convention was adopted and opened for signature, ratification and ascension by the UN General Assembly Resolution 34/180 of 18 December 1979, and came into force on 3 September 1981. Article 16 of CEDAW very comprehensively describes the right to a family and family life and its constitutive elements, especially in relation to spouses within a family. It provides for, *inter alia*:

- Equal rights and responsibilities of spouses in marriage and family relations
- The right to freely enter into marriage and choose a spouse
- Equality of spouses during marriage and at its dissolution
- The right to choose freely the number and spacing of children, access to information, education and the means to make that choice
- The same personal rights *inter se* spouses, right to choose family name, profession or occupation
- Equal rights and responsibilities regarding ownership, management and disposition of property

The second international covenant is the *African Charter on Human and Peoples' Rights*. This Charter was adopted in June 1981 by the 18th Assembly of Heads of State and Government of the Organisation of African Unity and came into force on 21 October 1986. Article 18 provides that:

1) The family shall be the natural unit and basis of society. It shall be protected by the state, which shall take care of its physical and moral health.
2) The state shall have the duty to assist the family, which is the custodian of morals and traditional values recognised by the community.
3) The state shall ensure the elimination of every discrimination against women and also ensure the protection of the rights of

the woman and the child, as stipulated in international declarations and conventions.

Further, Article 29(1) of this Charter reinforces the right to a family and family life by providing that:

'The individual shall . . . have the duty: (1) To preserve the harmonious development of the family and to work for the cohesion and respect of the family; to respect his parents at all times, to maintain them in case of need . . .'

CEDAW perceives family rights as the individual rights of women (and men) within the family, based on a concept of individual dignity and human rights. The African Charter seems to subscribe to dual concepts of protecting the family as a group and also the individual rights of women and children within the family needing special protection. On the surface, these two approaches would seem to belie a tension. However, the aspects cf group rights recognised by the African Charter are intended to and must be supportive of family rights as individual rights.

From the above, we see that the existence of the broad right to a family and family life is not only implied in Kenya's domestic law, but is also provided for by the two international instruments described earlier, which are ratified by Kenya. Nevertheless, legal reforms are needed to incorporate these conventions into Kenya's domestic law, especially in relation to the pending marriage law reform.

The current umbrella right to a family and family life encompasses many other family rights. Some key points are:

- Freedom to choose a marriage partner
- Right to choose a marriage and family law system
- Right to enter into marriage as an equal partner to the other spouse
- Right to spousal equality in marriage relations
- Right to enter into a nuptial agreement
- Right to make own decisions regarding sexual behaviour
- Freedom from spousal and other domestic violence
- Right to alimony and maintenance
- Right to terminate an unsuccessful marriage

The Rights of Women/Wives Within the Family

As, in practice, these rights are not realised, they are in need of further discussion. I will do so in relation to women/wives, in terms of economic family rights, in relation to children and in relation to peripheral family members. In the course of the discussion, I pinpoint areas of concern, where legal reform is of urgent need.

As a first point, one may note the fact that the age at marriage differs by community. Under customary and Islamic law, non-consenting girls under 18 years of age can be married off by their parents or guardians.[8] Under some Kenyan customary laws, an infant girl (even an unconceived prospective child) can be promised by her would-be parents in marriage. Arranged marriages for male minors are also prevalent in Kenya. The age of consent under the Marriage Act[9] is 21 (and 18–21 with parental consent).[10] Harmonisation of marital age of consent on the lines of the Marriage Act is long overdue. If achieved, it will contribute to marriage entrants possessing the mental, emotional and physical capacities to enter into free marriages. Further, it is advisable that the law seeks to postpone the onset of lawful sexual behaviour in this era of the HIV/AIDS epidemic,[11] because individuals are better placed to understand the consequences and take decisions on sexual behaviour after attaining majority age (Kibwana 1992b: 20).

The realisation of the family rights listed earlier is hampered also by the present multiplicity of family laws. An individual may lack the freedom to marry under a preferred system which guarantees the maximum quantum of family rights possible. The four existing family law systems give individuals unequal marriage rights. (See Mbeo and Ooko-Ombaka 1989). Muslims rarely marry outside Islamic law. In most cases, élite African men prefer to marry under the customary law system which provides for a subordinate position for women. The argument that individuals are free to choose any of the four systems, depending on their religious, cultural and social backgrounds, fails to acknowledge that the four systems give unequal rights to the parties in marriage. Marriage law reform should harmonise the quantity and quality of family rights available to any citizen, irrespective of cultural and religious background.

Dowry, bride-price, bride-wealth or *mahr*, whatever their cultural origin, have been used to justify a subordinate role for the woman in a marriage. Marriage law reform should outlaw any one-sided payments in the marriage contract, so that individuals have the right to enter into marriage as equal partners.

Kenyan law does not clearly provide for the right to enter into a nuptial agreement. Where such agreements are entered into and their judicial enforcement is sought, the courts are likely to invoke contract doctrine to justify the agreements' enforcement. Nuptial agreements have the distinct advantage of introducing a bargaining element in marriage; they can be creatively used to ensure that the spouses set out an inventory of the critical rights, which will be observed during and upon dissolution of a marriage. Kenyan law should emphatically recognise the nuptial agreement.

Men continue to make the key decisions regarding women's sexual behaviour. As a consequence:

- No law enables married women to control their own fertility. Family planning decisions are usually taken by men. Many family planning agencies have realised that family planning services targetting women are doomed to failure.
- The law as well as cultural, religious and social practices forbid girls—even those who are sexually active and can become mothers—access to contraceptives and (for both girls and boys) sex education.
- Lawful abortion is restricted to situations where the health of the expectant mother is threatened. A broader abortion right should confer on women the right to terminate an unwanted pregnancy when it is medically safe to do so.
- Rape law should include spousal rape, especially due to the prevalence of HIV/AIDS.

Domestic violence is equated to and therefore treated as common assault under Kenyan law. An earlier law reform proposal which sought to define domestic violence as a special category of violence and therefore impose custodial sentence for such violence was defeated even at the prompting of women's organisations' leaders. (Asiyo 1989: 41, 47). Imprisoning a husband, it was argued, constituted depriving a household of the breadwinner and was, thus, unacceptable. Kenyan law must still seriously readdress the issue of domestic violence outside the narrow common assault criminal law parameter.

The specific right to spousal equality in marriage does not exist under Kenya's laws. Such a right should be provided for in a harmonised marriage law system or even within the Constitution. It could, alongside the right to family and family life, provide the jurisprudential framework for equality of spouses in marriage. Both these rights could be used to criticise any marriage and family law, as well as act as the basis for rights within the family.

The Matrimonial Causes Act (Cap. 152), the Subordinate Courts (Separation and Maintenance) Act (Cap. 153) and the Maintenance Orders Enforcement Act (Cap. 154) provide a substantial regime of matrimonial reliefs. Alimony and maintenance comprise part of such reliefs. For example, Section 11 of Cap. 153 authorises imprisonment of any person who does not fulfil maintenance obligations. However, maintenance orders are routinely flouted. Marriage law reform must therefore target the area of enforcement of maintenance orders to ensure that maintenance becomes a reality.

Kenyan law is yet to allow divorce upon irretrievable breakdown of marriage. No-fault divorce ensures that individuals avoid a marriage where constructive divorce has occurred. Freedom to enter into and stay within a marriage includes freedom to dissolve a non-viable marriage. However, the law would have to provide a reasonable period within which the non-viability of the marriage can be ascertained by both parties to the marriage. The law must shun 'quickie' divorces.

Divorce under customary law and Islamic law in Kenya can be relatively easy to obtain. Currently, such divorce can lawfully be extra-judicial. Marriage law reform needs to bring customary law and Islamic law divorce under court supervision, especially to ensure that women's rights after divorce are adequately protected. Marriage law reform would also have to enhance the rights of women consequent on customary law and Islamic law divorce.

In an earlier article (Kibwana 1992a), I showed how individual rights guaranteed by the Fundamental Rights and Freedoms chapter (V) of the Constitution[12] could also specifically apply to and be enjoyed by women. Viewed from this perspective, individual rights would not merely apply to the universal individual, but could become a gender specific category. Indeed, family rights can be defined in terms of and/or buttressed by the constitutional individual rights and liberties. Within the family environment, the right to personal liberty, freedom of conscience, freedom of expression, freedom of movement, and freedom of assembly and association, if enjoyed by female spouse(s) and children, can further secure family rights. Hence, specific civil and political rights can also be understood in a family rights context and can serve as a basis for the creation of further family rights. Obviously, if family rights are predicated on a constitutional or individual rights basis, they are better secured within the legal system since the Constitution is the fundamental law of the land.

Economic Family Rights

An important area of specific concern in terms of the need for legal reform may be termed economic family rights and discussed in relation to women.

Kenyan law—and generally family and property laws in patri-archical society—avoid(s) regulating the manner in which property generated within the family should be enjoyed or distributed among family members. The onus falls on the male household head to share such property, as he deems fair. When unfairness attends distribution—and it regularly does—the women and children of the family usually have no legal recourse, being at the mercy of male magnanimity. Moreover, Kenya's current law does not assist any family member, especially a woman, who wishes to enforce the principle of equal work within the family. For example, in rural areas, the bulk of agricultural work as well as the bulk of domestic work is performed by women.

This situation persists in spite of the fact that Kenya's law allows married women to own property. Section (1) of the English Married Women's Property Act, 1882, a statute received into Kenya's law, provides:

A married woman shall, in accordance with the provisions of this Act, be capable of acquiring, holding, and disposing, by will or otherwise, of any real or personal property as her separate property, in the same manner as if she were a *femme sole*, without intervention of any trustee.

By virtue of Section 1(2) of the same Act,

A married woman shall be capable of entering into and render-ing herself liable in respect of and to the extent of her separate property on any contract, and of suing and being sued, either in contract or in tort, or otherwise . . . and her husband need not be joined with her as plaintiff or defendant . . . .

Thus, although the law allows married women to own property and be able to enjoy family property rights, in practice, family property is registered as the husband's property. Further, the man will often dispose of it without his wife's consent.[13] The majority of women usually enter marriage without property of their own. Under customary law, women do not own land; they have usufructuary rights.

According to Kenyan law, income and property acquired by both parties during marriage is deemed joint income and property. Also, any improvements made by both parties to property acquired before marriage, or acquired by one spouse during marriage, will be accredited to both spouses (Muigai 1989). Such income and property should be disposed only upon agreement by both parties; the income and proceeds from the property's disposition should be enjoyed equally by both parties. Further, in the event of divorce, the law requires that such income and property be divided equally.

Despite the provisions already mentioned, one of the most problematic areas in family property relations in Kenya concerns the legal principle that domestic work by a spouse does not constitute half a contribution to the acquisition of family property. A woman's domestic work cannot, therefore, be equated to salaried or entrepreneurial work. If the man pursues salaried or entrepreneurial work, while the wife concentrates on the domestic front, her work will not, legally, form half a contribution to any investment the man makes. Such a woman will ordinarily depend on the magnanimity of the man to secure a share of the investment. Indeed, in the event of divorce, the woman will not be entitled to a half share of the investment. Even if some of the property is registered in the woman's name, the man could in court, successfully, show that she was registered merely as a trustee and that the property solely belongs to him.

The recent Court of Appeal case of *Mary Anne Mutanu Kivuitu vs Samuel Mutua Kivuitu* (1991 Kenya Appeal Reports 241) allowed, *obiter*, that a woman's domestic work be recognised as a contribution to the creation of family property in the form of investments. However, in *Mary Anne Mutanu*, the wife had made direct financial contributions towards the purchase of the property and served as manager of the property during her husband's absence from Kenya. In this case, the husband was still granted the major share of the property by the court.

To adequately make provision for family rights, especially for married women, the law should ensure:

- Spousal and sibling sharing of domestic work
- The quantification and ascribing of monetary value to domestic work
- Domestic work be recognised as a direct contribution to the earning of income and acquisition of property during marriage; income and property acquired during marriage by either or both spouse(s) becomes joint income and property
- Family land is automatically registered in the names of spouses, whether it was acquired before or after marriage
- Equitable distribution of income and property acquired during marriage
- The matrimonial home is equally owned by the spouses. In the event of divorce, the matrimonial home should revert to the party likely to experience most hardship in getting alternative accommodation and especially the party who will have custody of the child/children. Reasonable compensation should be availed to the disadvantaged spouse[14]
- Where a married couple lives in rented premises, tenancy law should ensure that the party likely to experience most hardship in identifying alternative rented premises upon divorce continues with the lease, especially if it is the party who has custody of the child/children[15]

Rights of Children Within the Family

In her article entitled 'Child Law in Kenya: An Analysis', Janet W. Kabeberi (1989: 21) surveys and criticises Kenyan law on children. From her analysis, she establishes that child law in Kenya is fragmented; it is contained in diverse acts whose concern with children is often tangential. These are, for example, the Age of Majority Act (Cap. 33), the Children and Young Persons Act (Cap. 141), the Penal Code (Cap. 63), the Education Act (Cap. 226), the Industrial Training Act (Cap. 237), the marriage acts,[16] the Liquor Licensing Act (Cap. 121), the Traditional Liquor Act

(Cap. 122), the Guardianship of Infants Act (Cap. 144), the Evidence Act (Cap. 80), the Adoption Act (Cap. 143) and the Law of Succession Act (Cap. 160).

Some of the important family rights guaranteed to children under Kenyan law are:

- Protection from domestic violence. Section 23(1) of the Children and Young Persons Act protects children from abuse, violence and neglect by parents and guardians. It imposes a penal sanction for failure to accord children the said protection
- Provision of necessities of life. Section 216 of the Penal Code imposes a penal sanction on a parent or guardian who does not provide the necessities of life to his/her child
- Right to education
- Adoption rights
- Custody rights based on the best interests of the child
- Succession rights for adopted, legitimate and illegitimate children, provided the latter are recognised by the male parent

Kenya's child law generally, and in the family context in particular, is still vastly undeveloped.[17] The multiple pieces of legislation in which it is articulated do not sharply focus on children's rights, especially on the same lines as the emerging international law on the child. For example, it constitutes bad policy to premise important children's rights on the criminal law regime; in practice, criminal law fails to redress many infringements of such rights.

Currently, the Law Reform Commission is involved in an important project of harmonising and unifying child law in a single statute as well as introducing new appropriate children's rights as a consequence to reform of existing law. Some areas of concern for this new law should include:

- Harmonisation of marriage age law and the proscription of marriage of minors
- Reviving affiliation rights[18]
- Right of a child to know his/her parent
- Extension of succession rights to any child for whom paternity is established

- Outlawing child labour especially within the home and in family income generating activities
- Right to play and leisure
- More comprehensive coverage of abuse, violence and neglect of children by parents, guardians, relatives and any other persons who have charge over them, for example, teachers
- Right to societal protection and to a stable life for street children and other marginalised children, such as, AIDS orphans
- Right to appropriate information, such as, in relation to family life education
- Right of the child to be heard in any matter affecting the child
- Freedom of expression, thought, conscience, religion and association
- Protection of privacy

Some of the rights enumerated here are expressed in the United Nation's Convention of the Rights of the Child, adopted by the General Assembly in 1989 and in force since September 1990. Kenya's new comprehensive child law should seek to domesticate the UN Convention. Obviously, the legal creation of children's rights will not *ipso facto* guarantee children their rights in Kenya. The socioeconomic and cultural context for the creation and sustainability of children's rights must exist. Political will and initiative are likely to play a pivotal role in the recognition and provision of children's rights within and outside the home.

Rights of those on the Periphery of the Family

I define those on the fringes of the family to include:

- close relatives of spouses
- live-in domestic employees
- concubine/mistress
- the non-traditionally married woman, for example, the wife in a 'woman to woman' marriage and other similar customary law marriages
- parties in a trial marriage scenario
- parties who think or believe they are married and yet have, *ab initio*, no legal capacity to contract a valid marriage

The rights of relatives, especially under customary law, will diminish as marriages increasingly assume a nuclear character. However, tension will continue to exist between relatives' rights[19] within the family and the rights of the core family. However, the nuclear family is fast emerging as the victor in this contest.

For all intents and purposes, live-in domestic employees, such as housemaids, are treated by the core family as family. However, they are often exposed to considerable exploitation while being expected not to complain, as they are deemed to be part of the family. Kenyan law must address the issues of sexual abuse and violence, as well as poor employment conditions for such persons, as in long hours of work and dismally low remuneration.

Kenya's law has yet to squarely address the question of the rights of a concubine/mistress and those living in a trial marriage. In the United Kingdom, the doctrines of *resulting and constructive trusts* have been employed to guarantee property rights to a cohabitant who contributed to the purchase of property (Muigai 1989: 113, 120). Also, a cohabitant may claim entitlement 'to a *contractual licence* to remain in premises acquired by the other cohabitant, i.e., she/he has the defence of a licence against the man's/woman's claim for possession' (ibid.). Under Nigerian law, where a cohabitant has invested money on the other, for example, on education, the latter cohabitant has a legal duty to maintain the former (ibid.). Kenyan courts could emulate the practice of UK and Nigerian courts described here.

Customary law marriages, which are not of the traditional vari-ant, create special problems in a modern legal system. In my view, law reform should gradually proscribe such marriages, as also future polygyny. However, in the short term, researchers must identify the exact rights guaranteed to the 'wife'. Subsequently, administrators and courts should ensure that the 'wife' enjoys the biggest possible content of such rights compatible with her human dignity. Legal education in rural areas should target such women and demonstrate to them the inability of their marriages to provide reasonable family rights.

Perhaps, the most problematic category of 'near marriages' is that of a 'spouse' who thinks he/she is married, while no legal marriage exists. The parties may have lived together without having contracted a marriage under any of the four marriage law systems; or the parties may have fulfilled some, but not all, of the conditions of a valid marriage, such as, under customary law; or the parties could have conducted a 'marriage' under one of the four systems while a previous marriage exists which is incompatible with the second or subsequent 'marriage'. Sections 42, 48, 49 and 50 of the Marriage Act seek to penalise those who knowingly purport to get married under the Marriage Act when they lack legal capacity. Section 8 of the Hindu Marriage and Divorce Act seeks to prevent such marriages among Hindus. The Penal Code criminalises bigamy.

In a scenario where all the conditions of a customary marriage have not been fulfilled, the courts have acted to save the marriage by acknowledging the few conditions fulfilled as sufficient. In my view, if a single customary law condition is fulfilled and the parties thereafter live as man and wife, a customary law marriage should be held to exist. After all, the conditions of a valid customary marriage do change with time; the conditions valid in antiquity should not be held to be constant and controlling today.

Where parties fail to comply with all the conditions of a valid marriage, and are attempting their first marriage or a subsequent marriage under a polygynous marriage law, but have lived together for a considerable period, or where the parties have lived together as man and wife for a considerable period without contracting a marriage under any of the four marriage law systems, the law should recognise the existence of a common law marriage, i.e., a marriage by habit and repute. Currently, there is conflicting authority in Kenya regarding the notion of common law marriage. In both *Hortensiah Wanjiku Yawe vs. Public Trustee*[20] and *Mbithi Mulu vs. Mitwa Mutunga*[21], it was held that Kenya's law recognises the concept of presumption of marriage. In *Mary Njoki V. John Kinyanjui Mutheru and Others*,[22] the majority held that the notion of a common law marriage was inapplicable in Kenya.

In my view, the Court of Appeal should harmonise presumption of marriage law in line with *Yawe* and *Mbithi Mulu*. The declaration of a common law marriage enables the parties to exercise family rights since their lives have been lived in conformity to marital status; the law should follow social practice in this matter.

Where parties purport to enter into a 'marriage' when an existing marriage inconsistent with the new 'marriage' still subsists, obviously, a valid marriage cannot be contracted. The law should still protect the children of the union as well as the 'spouse', who unknowingly entered into such a marriage. Marriage law reform needs, perhaps, to treat the couple as tantamount to having 'divorced', consequent to the declaration of the 'marriage' as invalid so that both 'spouses' can enjoy the rights guaranteed upon divorce. At any rate, the law needs to adequately protect the interests of the party or parties who live in an illegal relationship inadvertently.

Conclusion

An attempt has been made in this chapter to describe family rights and to pinpoint lacunae in relation to the rights of the individual within the family rights sphere of Kenya's legal system. I have suggested, mainly by way of example, how marriage and family law reform in Kenya can develop a more comprehensive family rights regime. I have also endeavoured to develop a framework for the examination of family rights from a legal perspective as well as popularise the notion of family rights in legal discourse.

I have argued that the patriachical system—whether in its traditional or modern forms—is the major agent for the diminution of family rights in Kenya. This is in opposition to the common expectation that the family—and especially women and children—are held so dear by men that men will uphold family rights even without their legal articulation.

My main thesis is that family rights are not adequately protected under Kenyan law and that marriage and family law reform needs to further guarantee the protection of family rights, especially by achieving the domestication of international family rights standards. In such reform, family rights should be recognised as individual rights of family members first and foremost.

Notes

1. In an important unpublished work, the Kenyan writer, David G. Maillu, identifies seven pillars of Africans' existence. These are *myself, my family, my neighbour, my clan, my tribe, my other tribes and my creator*. Maillu's discussion on the pre-eminence of collectives in African communalism refreshingly shows that there was/is indeed space for 'self'. See Maillu, n.d.: 76–107.
2. Frederick Engels in defining the family wrote, *inter alia*, 'The original meaning of the word "family" (*familia*) is not that compound of sentimentality and domestic strife which forms the idea of the present-day philistine; among the Romans it did not at first even refer to the married pair and their children but only to slaves. *Famulus* means domestic slave, and *familia* is the total number

of slaves belonging to one man . . . . The term [family] was invented by the Romans to denote a new social organism whose head ruled over wife and children and a number of slaves, and invested under Roman paternal power with rights of life and death over them all.' (1972: 121).

3. The key legislations on marriage and family do not define these terms explicitly. The legislations are the Marriage Act (Cap. 150), the African Christian Marriage and Divorce Act (Cap. 151), the Matrimonial Causes Act (Cap. 152), the Subordinate Courts (Separation and Maintenance) Act (Cap. 153), the Maintenance Orders Enforcement Act (Cap. 154) and the Mohammedan Marriage and Divorce Registration Act (Cap. 155). The Hindu Marriage and Divorce Act (Cap. 157), in Section 2, provides a *technical* definition of marriage under the Act.

4. Several forms of marriage exist under Kenya's multiple customary laws. See Cotran 1968.

5. African customary and Islamic marriages can be converted into English type monogamous marriages, but not vice-versa. A recent Marriage Bill which *inter alia* sought the above conversion is still in cold storage.

6. The patriarchical family is described by Maria Mies as 'a combination of co-residence and blood relationship based on the patriarchical principle' (1984: 104).

7. For recent contributions to this debate see Shem Ong'Ondo (1994) and Kivutha Kibwana (1994).

8. See *The Standard*, 25 March *1993*, 'The Child Brides and Society'. Under Section 3(1)(c) and (d) of the Hindu Marriage and Divorce Act, both bridegroom and bride must be 16 years old to be eligible for marriage. However, parental or guardian consent is required for a bride who is between 16 and 18 years. The general age of majority in Kenya is 18.

9. Section 11(1)(b).

10. Section 19.

11. *The Daily Nation*, 9 April 1993: 4, reported that 1.68 million Kenyans are HIV positive, i.e., 7 per cent of the population.

12. Section 70–86 of the Constitution of Kenya.

13. Under the Land Control Act (Cap 302), there is no requirement that a spouse must obtain the consent of family members before transacting in his/her family property. However, as an administrative practice, such consent is usually required.

14. In polygynous families, this principle could be modified so that a wife is given adequate compensation by her former husband on her leaving the matrimonial home upon divorce.

15. The relevant law to be amended would be the Rent Restriction Act, (Cap 296).

16. See *Supra*, note 3.

17. For an exposition of a comprehensive children's rights regime, especially as it exists in the international law area, see Veerman (1992).

18. The Law Reform Commission is currently working on a draft law in relation to affiliation rights. On other country experiences on this issue see Molokomme in this volume, and Goonesekere in this volume.

19. Examples of such rights are the rights to support and succession rights. A man's relatives expect to enjoy these from the man. See Tsikata in this volume, on the experience of Ghana.

20. Civil Appeal Case No. 13 of 1976.
21. Civil Appeal Case No. 17 of 1983.
22. (1982–88) 1 Kenyan Appeal Reports 711.

References

Asiyo, P.M., 1989, 'Gender issues and the legislative process in Kenya', in M.A. Mbeo and O. Ooko-Ombaka (eds.), *Women and Law in Kenya*. Nairobi: Public Law Institute.

Cotran, E., 1968, *Restatement of African Law, Kenya: Vol. 1 The law of marriage and divorce*. London: Sweet and Maxwell.

Engels, F., 1972, *The Origin of the Family, Private Property and the State*. Edited by E. B. Leacock. New York: International. First published in 1884.

Kabeberi, J.W., 1989, 'Child law in Kenya: Analysis'. *The Law Journal 1 UNLJ*: 21–24.

Kibwana, K., 1992a, 'Women and the Constitution in Kenya', *Verfassung Und Recht In Ubersee 25 (1)*: 6–20.

———, 1992b, *HIV/AIDS and the law in Kenya: Preliminary observations*. Institute for Development Studies Working Paper No. 484. Nairobi: Institute for Development Studies, University of Nairobi.

———, 1994, 'Marriage in Equality and Dignity: The status of Family and Marriage Law Reform in Kenya'. Paper presented to the Centre for Law and Research International (CLARION) Workshop on Women, Autonomy and Law held in Nairobi, 29 January 1994.

Maillu, D.G., n.d., African Communalism: Africa's indigenous political ideology. Nairobi: Unpublished manuscript.

Mbeo, M.A. and O. Ooko-Ombaka (eds.), 1989, *Women and Law in Kenya*. Nairobi: Public Law Institute.

Mies, M., 1986, *Patriarchy and Accumulation on a World Scale*. London: Zed Books.

Muigai, G., 1989, 'Women and property rights in Kenya', in M.A. Mbeo and O. Ooko-Ombaka (eds.) *Women and Law in Kenya*. Nairobi: Public Law Institute.

Ong'Ondo, S., 1994, 'Marriage Laws in Kenya: A Case For Reform'. Paper presented to the Centre for Law and Research International (CLARION) Workshop on Women, Autonomy and Law held in Nairobi, 29 January 1994.

Veerman, P.E., 1992, *The Rights of the Child and the Changing Image of Childhood*. Dordrecht: Martinus Nijhoff.

10 State Intervention in the Family: A Case-study of the Child Maintenance Law in Botswana

Athaliah Molokomme

A particular case of state intervention in the family through legislation is explored. The focus is on the response of the traditional legal system of the Bangwaketse (southern Botswana) to the emergence of unmarried motherhood and the operation and impact of the state-initiated 1970 Affiliation Proceedings Act. This legislation entailed a conceptual shift from seduction compensation owed to the father on the first pregnancy of an unmarried woman to the latter's rights to maintenance from the father of her children. Neither system of remedies was found to be effective currently. Transformed social and economic conditions, including changed settlement patterns and kinship and support networks, had weakened customary methods of securing compliance, while state-sanctioned methods were not used. Being flexible, the indigenous model of dispute settlement was adapted by expanding the number of persons and fora involved in dispute resolution. A section of the populace was thereby brought under the gamut of state law in concrete practice. However, strategic adaptations were not available equally to all. This was a result, particularly of the disconnection between state legal procedure and the life-conditions of people, especially women, the lack of know-ledge regarding new laws, and attitudes of adjudicators and law implementors. Conclusions regarding the necessity and design of legal reform are drawn out.

Introduction

The socioeconomic changes which have taken place in African societies and their impact on the family have been the subject of research and writing for some time now. Much of the research and literature is concerned with the social disruption which has occurred as a result of colonialism, industrialisation and urbanisation. In the case of southern Africa, the theme of labour migration has been dominant and identified as a major contributing factor. In Botswana, male absenteeism was found to affect household structure and viability, as well as marital patterns (Gulbrandsen 1986; Kocken and Uhlenbeck 1980; Molenaar 1980). To mention only a few examples, the increase in *de facto* and *de jure* female-headed households, reproduction outside marriage and the undermining of kin-based support systems have attracted the attention of researchers and policymakers alike.

Response to these trends has come from different sources, which include the state, non-governmental organisations and local communities. A common response on the part of African states has been to introduce law reform programmes aimed at effecting social change, depending upon their ideology (See Allott 1980; Griffiths 1990; von Benda-Beckmann 1989). Statutes have been imported, and sometimes transplanted, from the former colonial power into the legal systems of African countries with the idea of 'modernising' the legal system or the society at large. These statutory provisions were superimposed upon already existing traditional legal systems, based upon precolonial social and political arrangements. This resulted in the creation of a dual or plural legal system, with the so-called customary law existing side by side with the colonial and post-independence state laws. Pluralism also exists at a local level, where, especially in the rural areas there are a variety of methods and fora for resolving disputes between people (von Benda-Beckmann and von Benda-Beckmann 1991).

In Botswana, the process of state intervention through legislation in the area of family law began in the 1970s, shortly after independence from Britain in 1966. Family law statutes transplanted from

English law were passed by the Botswana parliament, aimed at filling gaps created by socioeconomic changes. These included the Affiliation Proceedings Act of 1970, which was meant to enforce support obligations owed by men to their extra-marital children; the Married Persons Property Act of 1971, which created new options for property arrangements during marriage; and the Matrimonial Causes Act of 1973, which sought to bring the divorce law in line with the universal move away from fault-based divorce.[1]

Based on research which was carried out among the Bangwaketse[2] ethnic group in Kanye, a large village in southern Botswana, this chapter presents an experience of legislative intervention in the support of children of unmarried women. The first section provides some background information on the development and increase in unmarried motherhood in Botswana (See van Driel in this volume). Section two discusses the response of the traditional legal system to this development, by looking at the laws of the Bangwaketse dealing with pregnancy outside marriage. Section three looks at the nature of state intervention through legislation in this area. Section four assesses the operation and impact of state law in the rural context of Kanye village, especially the response of unmarried mothers to the new legislative options. The final section contains general conclusions on the impact of state intervention in family matters and policy lessons to be learnt in this respect.

The Trend Towards Extra-marital Reproduction

Ideally, most communities in Botswana say that their family is based on marriage and that reproduction is only permissible within marriage. Many elders lament the dying of this ideal, being of the view that 'nowadays' young people have gone out of control, engaging freely in extramarital sex and having children outside marriage. It is certainly the case that at a national level, reproduction outside marriage has become common. Between 1971 and 1981, the number of unmarried mothers rose from 48 per cent of all mothers to 57 per cent (Botswana Government 1981). Births to girls between the ages of 15 and 19 years went up by 43 per cent during the same period (Botswana Government 1985). Alexander (1991) estimates that teenagers who are mothers rose from 10 per cent in 1981 to 24 per cent in 1988.

Several reasons have been advanced to explain this trend towards unmarried motherhood (See van Driel in this volume). First,

there has been the loosening of traditional practices such as initiation, and the weakening of control formerly exercised by elders
over young people due to the latter's absence from home to be at
school or at work. This is the reason most often cited by elderly
informants, who consider 'today's youth' loose and indisciplined.

Second, under pressure from socioeconomic change, marital
strategies are said to have changed, and there is a tendency towards
late marriage on the part of men. Schapera had observed that
among the Bakgatla, before the turn of the 19th century, the
practice was for girls to be married soon after initiation. Boys, on
the other hand, had to wait between four and seven years after
initiation and were expected to marry girls in the age set formed
after their own. With many young men migrating to the towns to
work or attend school, girls (some of whom also attended school)
had to wait longer after puberty and initiation for marriage. By the
turn of the century, the average age of marriage for men had
become 25–30 years, and 19–26 years for women, whereas previously it was 18–20 years for boys and even younger for girls
(Schapera 1933: 86). As a result, many women ended up not
marrying at all.

This trend towards late marriage, the apparent reduction in the
number of marriages and the increase in reproduction outside
marriage has also been noted by more recent studies (Comaroff
and Roberts 1977; Gulbrandsen 1986; Kocken and Uhlenbeck
1980). Some have reasoned that early marriage is no longer a
priority for young men because, with their access to wages and
economic independence, marriage is no longer essential for the
attainment of adulthood and the acquisition of property (Kochen
and Uhlenbeck 1980: 53; Kuper 1987).

This postponement of marriage by men creates a large pool of
unmarried women of marriageable age, who sooner or later become
pregnant and have children without being married. In the words of
one of my female informants, 'While there is a shortage of husbands
these days, there is certainly no shortage of men to give us children'.
Women, in Kanye, considered children as some kind of 'old age
insurance policy' and were not prepared to wait for marriage
before they had children, lest it came too late or not at all (Molokomme 1991). Finally, the processual nature of the traditional
Tswana marriage, under pressure from socioeconomic change,
may have contributed towards the increase in unmarried mothers.

One of the features which distinguishes Tswana marriage from western concepts of marriage is that, as opposed to being a single event, it is a process (Roberts 1977). The Tswana marriage involves a chain of events which may stretch over a long period of time: from the families' agreement that the couple will marry, to the exchange of gifts and other rituals and ceremonies, the delivery of *bogadi* or bride-wealth, the celebration of the marriage and the removal of the woman to the man's home. *Bogadi* does not have to be paid immediately. It may be delayed for years, but still the couple is considered by their families to be married. This has raised questions about when exactly a Tswana marriage comes into existence (Comaroff and Roberts 1981; Molokomme 1991).

Certain customs related to this marriage process, in new socio-economic conditions, may have also contributed to this trend. The first was *go ralala*, where, once the two families had agreed on marriage, the man could visit the woman at her parents' home before she finally moved to the man's home. The second custom, *kadimo* (borrowing), was where, following an agreement to marry, the woman moved to the man's home before *bogadi* was produced. In both cases, children could be born before completion of the marriage process and as long as the proper provisions had been made, premarital pregnancy was quite acceptable. What was apparently unacceptable was for pregnancy to take place without any arrangements between the families concerned.

It must be noted, however, that more research needs to be done in order to find out whether the 'traditional', or pre-1971, situation has not been mystified. In other words, it is entirely possible that the trend of premarital pregnancies began much earlier than elderly informants are prepared to accept. A related question for further research is how women who conceived outside marriage arrangements managed in more 'traditional' times, beyond the usual claim that they were ostracised and their children labelled 'bastards'? (Schapera 1933).

Today, however, there is no doubt that the earlier negative attitudes towards extra-marital birth have changed to the extent that it is now largely accepted. Several reasons may be suggested as the factors which lie behind this sudden shift. First, it may indeed be the case that the traditional situation has been mystified, and that attitudes were never really that strict. Second, the decline in the incidence of marriage, the high premium that Tswana society attaches to children and the status women derive from childbearing might have contributed to this change. In other words, with the decline in polygamy, society may have realised that not all women could be married at the 'right' time or at all. In such a situation, the norm encouraging women to have children may have overtaken that of marriage and social attitudes altered as a result.

Third and final, is the value of children as a source of labour and economic security. Traditionally, households were dependent on their young and productive members for farming and cattle herding. Under today's changed conditions, many households depend on their younger employed members for a living. Thus, while children remain an important source of economic security, it may no longer matter whether they are born within marriage arrangements or outside them. Be that as it may, the Bangwaketse continue to apply certain ideal norms and have certain expectations regarding extra-marital pregnancy. A discussion of some of these norms follows.

Bangwaketse Approaches to Extra-marital Pregnancy

Ideal Bangwaketse Norms

When an unmarried woman became pregnant, Bangwaketse law required the man to either marry the woman or pay compensation in cattle to her father or other male guardian. The reason compensation was payable to the woman's guardian is because the man was taken to have committed a wrong against her father. The wrong was known as *tshenyo*, literally spoiling, referring to the spoiling of the woman's marriage prospects by the pregnancy.

Under normal circumstances, the two families concerned should come together and find a solution to the problem. Should their negotiations fail, mediation by third parties was the next accepted step. Should mediation fail, adjudication by the headman and finally the chief could take place. The ideal compensation for a woman's first pregnancy among Bangwaketse was six heads of cattle, a seventh being added in cases where the man failed to provide nourishment for the woman during pregnancy and confinement. Since cash became the common medium of exchange, most compensation for pregnancy was paid in cash, especially today when cattle are scarce.[3]

Another important norm is that compensation is payable for a first pregnancy only; subsequent pregnancies are not compensated because, according to Bangwaketse reasoning, the woman has already been seduced. Some families have, however, been able to negotiate reduced compensation for subsequent pregnancies and this seems to happen more outside the formal courts (Molokomme 1991). Once compensation has been paid, the woman's guardian is responsible for the child's guardianship and is affiliated to his lineage.

Discussions with informants and a perusal of records from the chief's court at Kanye indicate that these ideal norms are by and large followed in dealing with extra-marital pregnancy. As is the case in other societies, however, the social practice is often varied and a close look at actual disputes reveals a much more complex picture. Two main features characterise this mosaic. First, norms are used by both litigants and third parties in different ways to achieve different goals and are not always applied in the same way to apparently similar cases. Second, litigants often move back and forth between the three avenues of negotiation, mediation and adjudication, in a manner which is not in strict accordance with ideal procedures. Third parties, such as chiefs and headmen, also collude in this process, insisting upon the application of ideal norms and procedures in some cases and ignoring them in others (cf. von Benda-Beckmann 1984: 117.

Other variations in the management of extramarital pregnancy include arrangements between the families for the child to be maintained by the father at the mother's home without the two marrying. When the child comes of age, the man's family may pay a number of cattle as *bogadi* and be allowed to take the child. Thus, there is a plurality of arrangements that can be made among the Bangwaketse, in response to the impregnation of an unmarried woman, as long as the two families are able to agree. Only when there is disagreement do they resort to dispute settlement agencies such as headmen and chiefs' courts.[4]

The Use and Effectiveness of Bangwaketse Remedies

A question which arises is the extent to which these tradition-based remedies are still in use and how effective they are in today's changed conditions. In a survey of 178 unmarried women in Kanye, it emerged that these procedures were commonly used (Molo-komme 1991). In the case of 40 per cent of the women in our sample, their families had entered into negotiations with the man's family. Our findings show that this avenue is not so effective: more than half (56 per cent) of the women who used it did not reap any positive results. Most said either that negotiations had dragged on for many years until they gave up or that the promises of mainte-nance or compensation by the man's family had not been fulfilled. In other words, most of these women and their families eventually abandoned any further attempts to get compensation or mainte-nance from their children's fathers. Only in 33 per cent of the cases, had negotiations been decidedly successful in the sense that com-pensation had been paid or support was forthcoming regularly. In the remainder of the cases, the outcome of negotiations was still pending.

The effectiveness of the orders of the chief's court was far from impressive. Full compliance with the court's decisions was rare, accounting for only 10 per cent of the cases brought before the court in a 10 year period (Molokomme 1991). Even when the cases in which the men complied substantially with the orders were added to this category, the figure remained very low, at 20 per cent of the total. The most common trend was for men to pay only part of the award, but thereafter delay payment of the balance. In the few remaining cases, there had been no compliance at all with the orders of the court. Out of the 50 awards for compensation made by the court during the period 1978–88, 19 (38 per cent) were still owing in 1989. The total amounts owed under these orders were as high as 43 per cent of the total amount awarded, with half of these owing for periods of five to ten years.

In the area of enforcement of the orders of the chief's court, traditional methods of securing compliance with the chief's court's judgements through social pressure do not work. This is a result of changing social and economic circumstances, where many younger people no longer permanently live in their natal homes, and do not feel a sense of shame if they fail to live up to their social obligations.

Moreover, the court rarely resorted to the enforcement mechan-isms made available to them by the state law, which involved the sale of defaulters' property to satisfy their judgements. Rather, the court merely threatened to use these statutory methods of enforce-ment against defaulters in the hope that this would induce them to pay. The usual practice was for the relevant court papers to be sent, warning the defaulter that his property would be sold in satisfaction of the judgement if he did not pay. Despite the fact that such men continued to default, we did not come across a single seduction case in which this threat was actually carried out in 10 year period. It was, therefore, not surprising that the court's 'threatening strategy' did not work in the majority of these cases.

State Law Remedies for Extra-marital Pregnancy

The Colonial Legacy: Roman–Dutch Law Provisions

State law consists of the Roman–Dutch common law, originating from the Cape during the colonial period, and statutes passed by the Parliament of Botswana after Independence. Like customary law, Roman–Dutch law regarded extra-marital pregnancy and birth as an irregularity and provided similar remedies. Thus, Roman–Dutch law provided the man with a choice either to marry the woman or pay damages for seduction.

The Roman–Dutch law approach was, however, different from that of the Tswana customary law in at least three respects. First of all, the right to proceed against the seducer and any damages awarded under Roman–Dutch law belonged to the woman herself, unless she was a minor. Second, the action for seduction was available even if pregnancy did not result, as long as the woman could prove that she had been a virgin before the seduction. Third, the action for seduction in Roman–Dutch law was separate from that for the recovery of maintenance and other financial claims relating to a child resulting from the seduction. A woman who bore a child as a result of the seduction could sue the man for the lying in expenses she incurred during confinement, as well as for maintenance of the child.

Because Roman–Dutch law, during the colonial period, applied mainly to non-Africans, these laws did not affect the majority of the local population, who continued to live according to their own traditional laws. Although this is still largely the case, a combination of socioeconomic change and post-independence legislation has brought some local people within the sphere of state law, as discussed in the following section.

Statutory Intervention: The Affiliation Proceedings Act

It was against the foregoing background that statutory intervention in the area of extramarital pregnancy and maintenance was justified. Presenting the *Affiliation Proceedings Bill* to Parliament in 1969, the Attorney General indicated that it was 'a major exercise in law reform, which to a large extent cuts through the whole of customary law' (Botswana Government 1970: 68). The main aim of the bill, explained the Attorney General, was to provide a more appropriate machinery for unmarried women all over the country to themselves sue the fathers of their children for maintenance.

He explained that the customary law approach had become more and more difficult to enforce, because of the mobility of people in search of jobs. On the other hand, the Roman–Dutch law remedies were unknown to most people, as they had only recently been made available to Africans. The bill was, however, not intended to replace these two sources of law, but rather to provide a more straightforward machinery for the making of orders relating to 'illegitimate' children.

The Affiliation Proceedings Bill became an Act of Parliament a month later on 25 November 1970. Like other family law statutes of its time, it was based upon the English Affiliation Proceedings Act of 1957, with only a few alterations. Also, as with other family reform statutes of the time in Botswana, there was no strong local lobby for its introduction. It appears to have been pushed personally by the Attorney General from his own concern and knowledge of similar statutes elsewhere. A perusal of parliamentary debates reveals that the bill had a double purpose: first, to protect women and children and second, to discourage illegitimacy by making men pay maintenance. This Act was therefore an attempt at directing behavioural change through law reform, the 'instrumentalist' perspective Griffiths (1990: 4) refers to. The success or failures of this attempt are dealt with in subsequent sections. Here, some of the Act's major provisions are discussed.

A single woman (who is defined to include a widow and a married woman who is separated or living apart from her husband) who is pregnant, or who has delivered a child, may make a written complaint on oath to a magistrate for a summons to be served on the man she alleges to be the father of her child. No court fees are payable, process being served free of charge by a member of the Botswana Police. The general rule is that a woman should bring her case within 12 months of the child's birth. This provision has led to conflicting interpretations in the courts, the dominant judicial attitude favouring a strict application of the 12-month rule.[5] This attitude produces great hardships for unmarried mothers, who are mostly unaware of the time limitation. It is also insensitive to the social reality that most women attempt a solution under the customary system first and only where this fails, resort to the statute. Our research in Kanye found that 40 per cent of the women in the survey had used this avenue and that negotiations under the customary system can take a much longer time than one year (Molokomme 1991: 109).

There are two exceptions to this general rule, under which women may bring cases later than one year after the birth of the child. The first situation is where the father is absent from Botswana during the first 12 months following the child's birth. In such cases, the woman may make a complaint within 12 months of his return. Second, the man alleged to be the father must have done or said something with the dishonest intention of inducing the woman from not making a complaint during the 12 months following the child's birth. This provision has turned out to be more of a hindrance because in practice, many men give support for a short period and then stop. In such a situation, it is difficult for the woman to establish that by supporting her the man intended to induce her not to take him to court. This provision is so notoriously difficult to apply that judges have appealed to the legislature to clarify it.[6] In the meantime, cases brought after the stipulated 12 months continue to be returned and children go without maintenance. The following passage from a magistrate's judgement reflects the hard judicial attitudes displayed towards these women.

Plaintiff alleges defendant did support but does not say if this influenced her not to report. Even if this influenced her not to report can it be said that (1) defendant intended to influence her not to complain and (2) in so doing there is reasonable ground to believe that he was being dishonest? I do not think plaintiff has been able to discharge and establish as to why her complaint should be entertained and accordingly I dismiss the application (Case 47 of 1987, Kanye magistrate's court).

Even where women registered their cases within the stipulated 12 month period, they were confronted by other problems. These included inordinate delays in the issuing of summonses and setting of dates for hearing of maintenance cases. Our research found that it took an average of eight months before summonses for maintenance cases had been served (Molokomme 1991: 173). Thereafter, the setting of a hearing date could take longer, as such a date had to be suitable to all parties concerned. The hearing itself was conducted in English, which although translated, inhibited many women from participating freely.

The maximum magistrates were allowed to award was fixed at 40 Pula[7] per month and had not been revised since 1979, despite high rates of inflation. The most problematic area was found to be the enforcement of maintenance orders, despite the provision that a *gharnishee* order may be issued against a defaulter's future earnings. Further, the enforcement provisions are contained in a separate statute, the Maintenance Orders Enforcement Act.[8] This statute makes failure to comply with a maintenance order a criminal offence punishable by up to one year's imprisonment.

As was the case at the Kanye chief's court, these enforcement procedures were only very rarely resorted to by the Kanye magistrate's court, despite the fact that 61 per cent of the men were in arrears of maintenance payments. Also, like the chief's court, it was more common for the court to threaten defaulters with prosecution, rather than actually prosecuting them. Prosecutions for failure to comply with maintenance orders were found to be rare; thus, although 22 out of the 36 men in the magistrate's court survey were in arrears for between four months and five years, only four of them had been prosecuted. Generally, we found that the police did not show as much zeal in prosecuting these cases as they did in other criminal matters. About a third of the men were acquitted or discharged on the basis of insufficient evidence, while charges against others were withdrawn for various reasons. The majority of those convicted received prison sentences averaging three months, which were wholly suspended for an average of two years, on the condition that they pay their arrears within that period. This practice was based on the reasoning that sending the defaulter to prison would be tantamount to 'killing the goose that lays the golden eggs'.

We came across only two cases in which defaulters were actually committed to prison. Thus, it was not surprising that men continued to default even following prosecution for failure to comply; as long as they remained within the period of suspension, they knew they were 'safe'. We also found that the central administration of justice did not consider maintenance cases as 'real cases' and were unwilling to invest additional resources in districts where there was a long backlog of these. In response, men prosecuted for failure to comply with maintenance orders in Kanye have taken advantage of this and devised further dilatory strategies.

This reflects a general tendency in the legal system and the administration of justice to marginalise women by treating their cases as unimportant. It also shows that the world of lawyers, magistrates and judges is far removed from the problems of ordinary people in places such as Kanye.

Reasons for Limited Compliance with Court Orders

A combination of factors were found to contribute to the very low record of compliance with the orders of both courts. Inability to pay was one, but it was not a principal factor because even those who could afford to pay defaulted. Moreover, total inability to pay was an acceptable defence under both customary and state laws. A major factor which explained low compliance with the orders of the courts was the attitudes of men towards their extra-marital children. Socially, they did not consider themselves the 'real' fathers of these children, as they did not live with them in the same household; rather, they said that they felt more affinity to the children of their unmarried sisters.[9] This may be encouraged by the cultural norm that extra-marital children were affiliated to their mother's lineage, which was primarily responsible for them. Hence, some families may refrain from pursuing men against whom seduction orders are made, which may in turn encourage further non-compliance.

Although the reasons for failure to comply with orders were found to be fairly similar for both courts, there were some differences. Total inability to pay was found to have been even less likely at the magistrate's court, because almost all the men included in the survey were in formal employment and earned monthly wages. Moreover, the amounts they were required to pay per month were quite low and were not adjusted to inflation with the passage of time. In addition to the lack of sociocultural affiliation to their extra-marital children, another factor seemed to lie at the basis of their failure to comply with state law maintenance orders. This was their commonly expressed resistance to the state law of maintenance, especially its provision for the payment of monthly instalments over a number of years. Men resented this because it encouraged a link with the woman, which they considered a source of instability in their current marriages or relationships. Hence their preference was for paying 'once and for all' in cattle or a lump sum in accordance with customary law. As noted earlier, this is understandable in view of the savings men make when they pay the cash equivalent of six cattle. That even customary awards are generally not complied with in any of the cases shows that this is more of a strategy to avoid payment on the part of men. The strategies of men and women confronted with a choice between customary and state law remedies are now discussed.

Strategic Manipulation of the Law

It should by now be obvious that the existence of a dual system of remedies for the same problem poses uncertainties and contradictions in the operation of the legal system. A question that naturally arises is whether women and their families are free to pursue the remedies under both systems. The answer to this question is not entirely clear; the policy of the state law is that someone should not be brought to court twice for the same case. Thus, the Affiliation Proceedings Act provides that a case may not be brought under it if proceedings for 'substantially the same relief' have been brought before a customary court in relation to the same child. It does not, however, elaborate on the meaning of 'substantially the same relief', and the courts have not provided sufficient guidance on the matter.

It is clearly unrealistic, however, for the state to expect people not to use both systems for the same case, in view of the fact that the two types of remedies address different needs and go to different people. It will be remembered that under customary law, the cattle are paid to the woman's father, who has responsibility for raising the child. Under state law on the other hand, the right of action belongs to the woman herself and she receives cash as future maintenance for the child. Especially in cases where the woman no larger lives at her natal home and where her father does not in fact raise her child, it may be unfair to preclude her from claiming maintenance under the Act simply because her father has claimed seduction damages. At the same time, village elders consider it their traditional legal right to continue to claim cattle for the seduction of their daughters.[10]

Faced with these options, contradictions and difficulties of enforcement under both legal systems, men and women have responded by formulating strategies to manipulate the law to their own advantage. These strategies may broadly be classified into two categories: 'bargaining in the shadow of the law' (Gallanter 1981), and 'forum shopping', a term originating from international private law and which has also been applied to the study of legal pluralism (see among others van Rouveroy van Nieuwaal 1977; von Benda-Beckmann 1984). These strategies are not mutually exclusive; they often overlap and sometimes represent different stages in the dispute settlement process.[11]

Bargaining in the Shadow of the Law

When men are unwilling to negotiate or delay negotiations or compensation, women have adopted a strategy where they threaten to register the matter with the magistrate's court. This may or may not be put into practice; in some cases the women are simply 'bluffing' the men into believing that they will do this. Because the magistrate's court and its remedies are so unpopular among men, the women hope that the mere threat to take them to court will induce the men to negotiate seriously and compensate them for the pregnancy. In some cases, this strategy is successful and the men and their families negotiate and eventually compensate the women for the pregnancy in accordance with Ngwaketse norms.

Should a man and his family not take heed, a woman may proceed to register the complaint without necessarily intending to have it heard. Her goal is to continue to apply pressure on the other side to negotiate and compensate her for the pregnancy and having the case registered may help. It is also a fall-back strategy in case negotiations do not produce the desired results.

This shows that in practice, litigants do not use the two legal systems in an either/or fashion; rather, they combine them in a way that they think will best serve their interests. In particular, it indicates that by initially choosing the procedures of one system, women are not necessarily making a choice in favour of the remedies of that system. This conclusion is especially important because the state law of maintenance is based upon the assumption that a woman who registers a complaint at the magistrate's court thereby expresses her wish to have her dispute resolved there, under state law.[12] In other words, it is sometimes wrongly assumed that the choice of forum goes hand in hand with the choice of law or remedy.

Some women may indeed desire state law remedies, such as an order for monthly cash installments. However, others do not, as they believe that monthly installments are unreliable and sometimes encourage men to feel they are justified in interfering in their lives. Such women may instead aim for a lump sum compensation for pregnancy, under Ngwaketse ideals. But because they have been unable to obtain this through negotiations, they use the magistrate's court to pressurise the men into compensating them. This strategy is vividly illustrated by the case summarised here.

Case One: The Woman Who Threatened to Sue:[13] A woman from Sengwaketse ward in Kanye had a child in 1983 by a man from the same village, who was employed in the South African mines. Although her parents informed his parents in the traditional manner, the latter did nothing and the man completely failed to support the child. When the child was five months old, the woman registered a complaint with the Kanye magistrate's court, where they were called for a hearing after another five months. Summons had to be issued three times and it took altogether one year before the defendant could be brought before the court. The proceedings are reproduced verbatim here, so as to give an idea of the strategy pursued by the woman.

12/6/85: Present: Magistrate, both parties in person before the court.

Mag.: What is the position?

Man states: I admit paternity but apply that the matter be referred to parents for settlement.

Woman states: I am opposed to the matter being referred to parents unless I am given an undertaking to return to the magistrate's court should no settlement be reached.

Mag.: The court adjourns the application for hearing on 24/6/85 at 8.30 am. Both parties advised to enter into negotiations with parents and to report progress in the matter by 24/6/85.

On 24/6/85: Present: as before; court resumes sitting; both parties before the court.

Mag.: What is the position?

Woman states: The matter has been resolved customarily. The defendant has been ordered to pay five heads of cattle as damages for pregnancy and maintenance for the child.

Mag. to def: What comments do you have on the matter?

Man states: I confirm that the matter has been resolved. I propose to pay or deliver the cattle to the plaintiff's people within two months from date.

Mag.: Are you aware that failure to effect the delivery of the cattle may cause the plaintiff to revive the maintenance claim in respect of the support of the child?

Man states: I am fully aware.

Mag.: By consent of both parties, the application for maintenance is withdrawn on condition that the five heads of cattle are paid as support of the child.

Discussion of Case One: The woman in this case initially sought compensation for her pregnancy through the established Ngwaketse procedure of parental negotiations, but the man and his people failed to respond. Then, she registered her case with the magistrate's court and there the man requested that negotiations between the parents be given a chance. Based on her previous experience with the man and his family, the woman, however, did not trust them. Thus, she demanded an assurance from the magistrate that she could return and revive the claim, should negotiations not produce results. The fact that the magistrate agreed to her demand shows that he was willing to assist her in carrying out her strategy, and the case was withdrawn on that condition.

However, this strategy is not successful in all cases, because men have developed counter strategies or tactics in response. These include persuading women to withdraw their cases by promising to compensate them. Having succeeded in this, the men delay payment indefinitely, until the woman tires of pursuing the matter and abandons it. Others keep delaying or provide irregular support until the child is one year old, the stipulated time-bar on an application. Yet others pay some part of the agreed compensation and delay payment of the rest indefinitely or until the woman takes serious steps to enforce the promise. The latter strategy was also observed with respect to men's compliance with the orders of both the chief's and magistrate's courts. The realisation that the enforcement procedures of both courts are rarely invoked and are ineffective may in turn encourage this strategy. The idea here is to 'buy time' by showing one's willingness to pay at least part of the compensation, and keep the women hoping to receive the rest. Hence the men's common offer to have the matter referred back to the parents, rather than have it heard under state law.

In a variation of the strategy discussed earlier, women use the magistrate's court not only to pressure men into compensating them, but also to actually bargain on the nature of the remedy itself. This may happen where, for example, the two sides fail to agree on the nature of the remedy. The woman then registers the case and the magistrate is used as a mediator who facilitates bargaining in court between the parties. Unlike case one, where the application for maintenance is then withdrawn, in other such cases, a court order may be made, usually for the payment of a number of cattle or a lump sum within a certain period. The case discussed next is an illustration of the working of this strategy.

Case Two: The Hard Bargainer:[14] She had a child in 1984 by a man who showed no interest in entering into negotiations for compensation and did not support the child. When the child was eight months old, the woman approached the District Commissioner (DC), who twice summoned the man to appear before him, but without success. Subsequently, she registered a complaint at the Kanye magistrate's court, which was eventually heard nine months later and summons had to be issued more than once.

In court, the man admitted paternity and the magistrate invited the woman to prove her case under the Affiliation Proceedings Act. The woman related the story of their relationship and her failed attempts to obtain maintenance from the defendant. The woman then made the following claim:

I am applying that the defendant be ordered to contribute monthly towards maintenance and support of our child. I am requesting that he be made to pay P40 per month until the child is 13 years of age . . . . I further apply that payments be effected through the clerk of the court, Kanye.

In case that did not succeed, she made an alternative claim:

If the defendant is prepared to pay in bulk, he may pay 12 heads of cattle.

Asked what the equivalent of 12 cattle in cash was, she replied that she did not know, but said that she had spent P648 on her confinement and transport costs, which bill she tendered to the court.

The following exchange then takes place between the parties during cross examination:

Man: I am not working and I don't think I can manage to pay P40 per month.
Woman: If you cannot pay P40 per month, you should then pay 12 heads of cattle.
Man: I put it to you that it is our tradition to pay six heads of cattle and that I am prepared to pay six heads of cattle.
Woman: It would not be sufficient.

After the man gave evidence repeating his offer of six cattle, the magistrate summarised the evidence and ordered that the man pay eight cattle within two months 'as maintenance and support of the child'. Such payment was to be proved to the clerk of the court by the plaintiff, who should confirm in writing that the cattle had been delivered.

Discussion of Case Two: The strategy pursued by the woman in this case differed from that of the woman in the previous case: she meant to and did have the case heard under state law. Clearly well informed about state law remedies, she made an unequivocal claim for the maximum permissible under statute.[15] In the alternative, she claimed double the number of cattle available under Ngwaketse ideals and insisted upon this. *Like the man in the previous case, the man in this case responded to the woman's claim by referring to the ideal Ngwaketse award.* It is not surprising that he expressed his willingness to pay this because, as noted earlier, this is much cheaper than the total amount he would have had to pay under a maintenance order. In the end, the magistrate played a mediatory role by deciding on a compromise between their respective claims.

Thus, magistrates are used by litigants to act as mediators or adjudicators in the manner of headmen under the customary system. Although not exactly authorised to do so under state law, most Kanye magistrates have been willing to be recruited in this way, reflecting their sensitivity to the social context in which they operate. Magistrates have not, however, been willing to be used in this way in cases where litigants are engaged in the second set of strategies: 'forum shopping', to which we now turn.

Forum Shopping

Although the two strategies are not mutually exclusive, this category is treated separately because the women who pursue it do more than invoke a combination of customary and state laws to serve their interests. Unlike the women in the previous cases, who used only one court as a 'shadow' under which to bargain, the forum shoppers *actually pursue this strategy in various courts*. In other words, the forum shoppers go to both the magistrate's and the customary courts, in an attempt to obtain a remedy under either systems. These categories may, however, overlap and a woman whose behaviour is classified under the bargaining strategy may later become a forum shopper, depending on whether or not she succeeds in the first forum. If she succeeds in her bargaining, she is likely to remain in that forum, whereas if she fails, she may move to the second one. The following case is illustrative of the behaviour of a forum shopper in this sense.

Case Three: The Successful Forum Shopper: [16] In 1981, a 17 year old schoolgirl from the village of Moshupa within the Ngwaketse area was impregnated by a 20 year old boy, who worked in the mining town of Jwaneng, some 80 km from Kanye. Because the man originally came from Tobane, a village more than 300 km away in the Central District, the girl's parents first approached the boy personally. He accepted paternity of the child, but indicated that he would not marry the girl. The girl's parents obtained the boy's parents' address and wrote them a letter explaining the situation, but they never responded. In the meantime, the girl made demands upon the boy to provide her with money in order to buy cloths for the child she was expecting. Her demands met with some success shortly before her confinement when the boy gave her P80 for the child's clothing and following the child's birth he irregularly gave her sums of money whenever she requested it for the child's milk.

Having observed that support was irregular and the boy was not visiting the mother and child, the girl's father summoned the boy to his home for negotiations, where he turned up with two relatives. The boy and his relatives took the position that he was too young to support a child and that the girl's father should support the child just as he had raised his own daughter. Alternatively, they suggested that the child be handed over to the boy's mother to look after. The girl's father was extremely annoyed by the first suggestion and rejected the second, but did not do anything to follow the matter up himself.

The girl herself then approached the customary court at Jwaneng, which refused to entertain her plea, apparently because she was not assisted by a male guardian. She then proceeded to the District Commissioner, who called the boy and made an order for P50 per month as maintenance of the child. The boy rejected the order and failed to comply with it, whereupon the girl and her parents took the matter to the Chief's Court at Kanye.

The case came before the deputy chief and three other members of the chief's court on 5 May 1984. The girl began by presenting the events leading to the dispute, alleging mainly that the boy had failed to support the child. For his part, the boy accepted paternity, but disagreed with the girl on the amounts of money he had given her.

Having established that the boy earned P250 per month, the deputy chief made his decision:

> There is a law meant for the protection of children which should be used . . . . I order you to pay P50 every month as mainte-nance, until the child reaches 18 years of age. It is up to the girl's parents to follow up the matter of seduction with the boy's parents.

Discussion of Case Three: The sequence of resolution of this dispute shows that the woman and her father initially followed the ideal

Ngwaketse procedure which begins with negotiation, to deal with her pregnancy. In what is today a common variation of ideal procedures, negotiations first took place between the young people themselves. When this failed, negotiations were attempted between the woman's father, the man and relatives other than his parents, as the latter were too far away. When these did not bear fruit, the father lost interest, but the woman continued to press the matter at the Jwaneng customary court. Upon being denied a hearing by the Jwaneng customary court, she proceeds to the District Commissioner (DC), a state law official who awards P50 per month as maintenance. Like a typical forum shopper, the woman took her case to the Chief's Court at Kanye when the DC's order was not complied with.

The award made by the chief's court is, however, not in accordance with ideal Ngwaketse procedures, but is typical of statutory awards usually made at the magistrate's court. The passage from the deputy chief's judgement makes it clear that he was making an award for maintenance and not for seduction. This is confirmed by his advice to the girl's parents to pursue the matter of seduction separately. This advice is surprising, in view of the fact that the Kanye chief's court usually deals with both matters simultaneously and makes a single award. His advice appears to encourage the woman and her family to bring another claim against the man, a situation the Affiliation Proceedings Act was specially enacted to prevent. Effectively, the deputy chief encourages the woman and her family to go forum shopping. It also reflects some influence on the chief by state law.

The chief's court appears to be more receptive to forum shoppers than the magistrate's court, which usually sends back people who have already taken their cases to the chief's court. Case four discussed here is an example of this.

Case Four: The Unsuccessful Forum Shopper:[17] This case was brought by a woman who had lived with a man for seven years and by whom she had five children. Following the birth of the fifth child in 1981, the parties had a misunderstanding because the woman complained about the man's relationship with another woman. This flared into a dispute that eventually came before the chief's court two years later, following an assault by the man on the woman. It was decided that her father remove the woman and children from the

man's home and thereafter institute proceedings to recover compensation from the man's family. The latter however pre-empted
this claim by delivering six cattle to the customary court, which
they said were *bogadi* in exchange for the children.

Although the woman's father and two members of the court
objected to the delivery of the cattle, the chief ordered that they
be received and the children be handed over. The woman's father
accepted the cattle under protest and pointed out that he took
them to be damages for seduction and not as *bogadi*. The man's
parents subsequently demanded that the children be handed over
to them, but the woman refused, saying they could have their
cattle back instead. She also challenged them to take the matter
back to the chief's court, which they did not do.

Instead, the woman registered a complaint with the Kanye
magistrate's court, where the case was heard a week later. She
presented the above background and claimed maintenance whilst
the case at the chief's court was still pending. At the magistrate's
court, the man countered that he would not pay maintenance
whilst the case was still pending at the chief's court. He said that
his parents had been trying to encourage her parents to register the
case at the chief's court, but that the latter had failed to do so. At
the end of this evidence, the magistrate made no order, but advised
the parties, especially the plaintiff, to register the case with the
customary court and have it finalised as soon as possible.

Discussion of Case Four: This case illustrates a number of interesting
points. First of all, it shows a combination of the strategies litigants
use to achieve their goals. Following the decision by the chief's
court that the woman be taken back by her father and a compensation claim instituted, the man's family adopted the following
strategy. They effectively pre-empted a seduction claim by offering
cattle as *bogadi* in exchange for the children. They did this because
seduction damages would not entitle them to the children, whereas
bogadi would. The response by the man's father that he took the
cattle as compensation for seduction was his strategy to not only
get the cattle but also keep the children. This strategy has sometimes been described as 'issue bargaining'. When the woman refused
to hand over the children, the case reached an impasse, with each
side taking the position on that the other should revive the case
first.

This is the point at which the woman decided to go forum shopping, by registering a case at the magistrate's court. There, she frames her case in terms of *maintenance* for the children while the case at the chief's court was still pending. She did this because she knew this was the issue over which the magistrate had jurisdiction, not seduction and custody. By sending her back to the chief's court, however, the magistrate effectively dismissed her claim.

The magistrate did not explicitly refer to the Affiliation Proceedings Act, which forbids forum shopping, but he does so implicitly. The assumption behind this dismissal appears to be that the remedy she sought at the magistrate's court was either the same or 'substantially the same' as that she sought at the chief's court. But was it? It is clear that the case at the chief's court was much broader, concerning the general relationship between the parties and their rights to the children. The children's maintenance was only a part of this larger dispute, which encompassed accusations of infidelity and the delivery of *bogadi* cattle in exchange for the children.

Although the woman was engaged in 'forum shopping', she did not try to conceal the fact that her case had been heard at the chief's court. In fact, she herself began by presenting the background, explaining that the case at the chief's court was at an impasse. She was, however, unequivocal about her claim at the magistrate's court: she wanted maintenance in the meantime. It is odd, therefore, that the magistrate was unwilling to deal with the issue of maintenance alone and leave the rest to the chief's court. This leads us to conclude that the magistrate wished to avoid jurisdictional conflict with the chief's court, hence his decision to send the parties back there.

The second point which this case confirms is that the remedies of customary law and state law for extra-marital pregnancy are quite different. At a more general level, it is also a vivid illustration of the fundamental differences in procedure between customary law and state law. In customary courts, related claims, such as those involved in this case, are not usually separated. Thus, matters of infidelity, children's custody and maintenance would have been dealt with in the same proceedings.

The magistrate's court, on the other hand, deals with and has jurisdiction over only one issue: maintenance, and would usually separate this from custody, even though they concerned the same parties and the same children. By claiming only maintenance at the magistrate's court, the woman adopted a strategy which was in line with this practice. But she failed because the magistrate decided that she should allow the whole case to be resolved at the customary court. In effect, he stopped her attempt at forum shopping and compelled her to stick to her initial choice in favour of the customary law, irrespective of whether she made this choice herself.

Implications of the Strategic Use of Law

The strategies described in the foregoing section lead us to an important conclusion about the relationship between customary law and state law. That, irrespective of the type of court, disputes may eventually end up in the indigenous model of negotiation—mediation—adjudication, generally informed the resolution of pregnancy disputes in Kanye. Attempts at resolving most pregnancy disputes almost always began with negotiation, especially where both parties were from Kanye. The ideal sequence of resolution was, however, not always followed. It had been affected by other processes, such as the undermining of kinship cohesion and the mobility of young people. As was stated earlier, traditional settlement patterns have changed and continue to change such that members of the same lineage no longer necessarily live in the same part of the village, or render the same support that was expected traditionally. Thus, support networks have become weakened by socioeconomic change and members of the society have had to find coping strategies.

Because the indigenous model is flexible, litigants have adapted it to socioeconomic change as well as legislative intervention. Figures 10.1 and 10.2 provide sketches of the ideal and adopted models. The indigenous model (Figure 10.1) has been adapted mainly by expanding the number of participants involved in dispute resolution (Figure 10.2). At the level of negotiation today, this may involve the parties alone or their kin, who need not be senior or male; as seen, the relatives of only one side are sometimes involved. Should the first stage fail, the matter may be subjected to mediation, but not necessarily; it may go directly to adjudication. Sometimes, cases which are initially taken to adjudication return to the negotiation stage. The important thing to note here is that mediators and adjudicators can be from either the customary system or from the state law system.

What has happened is that instead of taking entirely to the 'new' procedures provided by the state laws of maintenance, the villagers have retained their basic indigenous model and adapted it, by incorporating into it some aspects of the state law. Whether officials of the customary or state law are recruited, or both, depends on the circumstances of the litigants. Women with a higher education, who already have at least one child, and those who came from female-headed households, were found to be more likely to use the state law than the customary law (Molokomme 1991: 191). But the use of a combination of the two systems was the most common feature observed in pregnancy cases. This is an indication that none of the systems by itself is seen by the residents of Kanye as sufficient for addressing issues of extra-marital pregnancy: hence the adaptation of the indigenous model by the inclusion of selected state law remedies and procedures.

It must be pointed out, however, that such strategic adaptations are not available equally to everyone who wishes to use them; nor are they always successful. Case four shows the limits to which litigants can use the law strategically to suit their interests. This is particularly the case for women, who in many customary systems are under male guardianship for their whole lives (cf. Armstrong and Ncube 1987; Armstrong and Stewart 1990). Although some systems have shown flexibility in this respect, in Kanye, women cannot bring cases to the chief's court without male assistance. Such women have little control once their dispute has been introduced into the arena of the chief's court by their male relatives. In case four, the woman's father was in possession of cattle he insisted were for her seduction, but which the man's family said were for *bogadi*. The woman refused to handover the children, and was willing to handback the cattle instead. But the relevant actors who have bargaining power in the customary system are the male elders, and the woman has little say in the matter. To compound her difficulties even further, her resort to the state law was rejected, apparently on the basis that she was engaged in forum shopping. Thus, hurdles to bargaining and forum shopping exist in both customary and state law and, in extra-marital pregnancy cases, put women in a less favourable bargaining position than the men they sue. We also noted that, economically, women were more marginal than the fathers of their children.

Figure 10.1
*Ideal Model and Sequence of Dispute Settlement and
Participants Involved*

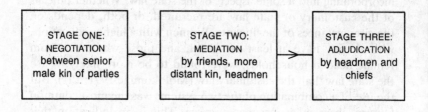

```
┌──────────────────┐   ┌──────────────────┐   ┌──────────────────┐
│ STAGE ONE:       │   │ STAGE TWO:       │   │ STAGE THREE:     │
│ NEGOTIATION      │──▶│ MEDIATION        │──▶│ ADJUDICATION     │
│ between senior   │   │ by friends, more │   │ by headmen and   │
│ male kin of      │   │ distant kin,     │   │ chiefs           │
│ parties          │   │ headmen          │   │                  │
└──────────────────┘   └──────────────────┘   └──────────────────┘
```

Figure 10.2
*Adapted Model of Dispute Settlement with Varied Sequence
and Participants*

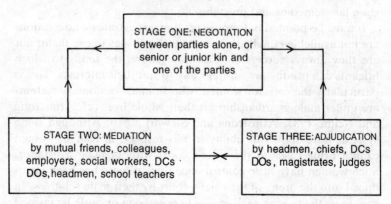

```
                    ┌──────────────────────────┐
                    │ STAGE ONE: NEGOTIATION    │
                    │ between parties alone, or │
                    │ senior or junior kin and  │
                    │ one of the parties        │
                    └──────────────────────────┘

┌────────────────────────────┐        ┌────────────────────────────┐
│ STAGE TWO: MEDIATION        │        │ STAGE THREE: ADJUDICATION   │
│ by mutual friends,          │        │ by headmen, chiefs, DCs     │
│ colleagues, employers,      │──╳──▶  │ DOs, magistrates, judges    │
│ social workers, DCs         │        │                             │
│ DOs, headmen, school        │        │                             │
│ teachers                    │        │                             │
└────────────────────────────┘        └────────────────────────────┘
```

The implications here are that women who have children outside
marriage need strong support networks. They can no longer rely
upon the assistance of their male relatives for support. What some
women do in such a situation is to make arrangements with other
unmarried sisters and perhaps an unmarried or widowed mother
for support (See Ingstad and Saugestad 1987; Molokomme 1991;
van Driel in this volume). Some unmarried sisters stay at home
and work in subsistence activities, looking after all the children,
while some of them are employed in the urban areas and bring in
cash. These and other strategies may be seen as an attempt to
consciously create support networks outside traditionally-based
family arrangements which have been weakened by socioeconomic
change.

Conclusion

This chapter has presented a case-study in state intervention through legislation in the area of compensation for pregnancy and child support. The social changes which contributed to the separation of reproduction from marriage were outlined, as were the procedures of the customary system of the Bangwaketse for dealing with the situation. It was noted that compensation in cattle was available to the father of an unmarried woman for her seduction and he in turn, was responsible for the child's welfare. Although these procedures were still in common use at Kanye, their effectiveness was found to have been undermined by socioeconomic change.

It is on this basis that statutory intervention in this areas was justified, the aim being to provide women with means independent from their male guardians to recover maintenance for their children. It was observed that the statute introduced the new concept of periodic maintenance, paid to the woman herself and not to her father. Certain problems were noted in the implementation of this statute, which included lack of awareness of its provisions, delays in serving summonses, setting hearing dates and enforcing maintenance orders.

While this indicates that the statutory changes have not been an all-round success, it would be an oversimplification to end there. The findings of the research illustrate that the people of Kanye have adopted certain aspects of the statutory innovations. As was pointed out in the model of dispute settlement presented, certain statutory provisions have been absorbed into their strategies. Thus, the statutory innovations have made an impact by providing the people with additional options with which to manipulate the two systems.

Certain policy lessons for state intervention may, therefore, be drawn from our study and recommendations made to improve the situation. The most important policy lesson of all is that, in order to make an impact on the lives of ordinary people, state intervention must take account of the reality of pluralism. Pluralism, here, refers to more than just the coexistence of customary law and common law, the sense in which lawyers and the state often use the term. It is a pluralism based upon a social reality, which is characterised by a variety of relationships and arrangements; a pluralism based on the concrete lives of people who belong to different groups. These are groups of different cultures, religions and classes, with varied laws and practices, something akin to Moore's (1973) semi-autonomous social fields.

In order to succeed therefore, state intervention through law reform must take this pluralism as a starting point and not the abstract individual it normally imposes. State reforms, such as the *Affiliation Proceedings Act*, have tended to assume uniformity. Moreover, they have offered themselves as alternatives to local customary arrangements, which people could use instead of their own. We saw that in practice, this was not the case; people used a combination of customary and state laws and procedures. This means that neither of the two systems by itself is regarded by Kanye residents as sufficient for dealing with issues of extra-marital pregnancy. *The proper policy approach should, therefore, be one which is flexible enough to be accommodated by the consumers of the law into their own realities, not the other way around.*

Once enacted, the basic provisions of welfare-oriented state laws, such as the *Affiliation Proceedings Act*, must be disseminated to the people, so they can exercise informed choices in using the legal system. This is particularly important for women in maintenance cases, who, we saw, often had their complaints dismissed because of inadequate or inaccurate information on state law procedures. More importantly, the state must be willing to invest sufficient resources to ensure the effectiveness of such welfare-oriented law reforms.

Policy lessons are to be learnt at various levels: local institutions, such as customary courts, can be more effective in ensuring the success of legal remedies. This study showed that the chief's court at Kanye was not always willing to be flexible in their application of certain ideal norms and procedures. Their strict application of the rule requiring women to be accompanied by senior male kin and the restriction of compensation of first pregnancies only, were cited as examples. The wide prevalence of extra-marital pregnancy and the erosion of kinship cohesion revealed by this study require that customary courts should be more flexible in their application of ideal norms. That customary law is capable of such adaptation is demonstrated by the successful abandonment of both these norms among the Bakgatla, through the innovative decisions of a chief. Although they are today dependent upon the state for their resources, customary institutions, such as the chief's court at

Kanye, should also be willing to enforce judgements made in cases of extra-marital pregnancy.

Finally, this study has confirmed previous findings showing that the socioeconomic position of unmarried mothers as a group is marginal. It is clear that while they can make a contribution to improving the situation, legal reforms in the areas of extra-marital pregnancy alone are far from sufficient. From a national policy point of view, these must be supplemented by a more comprehensive and effective programme that addresses problems of poverty among unmarried mothers and other disadvantaged social groups.

To conclude therefore, state intervention in the family is sometimes necessary, especially to protect the interests of marginalised groups, such as women and children. Be it through law reform or economic development programmes, such intervention must take sufficient account of the reality of pluralism, if it is to make any positive impact on these groups.

Notes

1. See volume III, Laws of Botswana.
2. One of the major ethnic groups in Botswana today, successor to one of the precolonial Tswana chiefdoms. Although there has been much mobility and intermingling between the various groups, the area described as the Ngwaketse district today is inhabited by roughly 10 per cent of the national population.
3. Men prefer to pay customary court fines in cash, also because the cash equivalent of a cow in the customary courts is much less than its actual market value (See Molokomme 1991: 151).
4. There is a dual court system in Botswana, consisting of customary courts on the one hand and courts of general jurisdiction on the other. The customary courts are the successors to the precolonial traditional courts and although they have less jurisdiction than the general courts, they remain an important sites of dispute settlement for the rural majority. Customary courts range from the family court at the bottom, the court of the ward headman, the court of the village headman, and finally the chief's court at the top of the hierarchy.
5. See the following cases (among others): Sichinga vs Phumetse 1982 (1) Botswana Law Reports; Makwati vs Ramohago Civil Appeal 10/83 (High Court, unreported).
6. See, for example, Judge Hannah in Kgamane vs Diteko Civil Appeal 13/1983 (High Court, unreported).
7. The *pula* is the name of the Botswana currency, and one *pula* is approximately 0.5 US Dollars.
8. Cap. 29:04, Laws of Botswana.

9. This may, in some cases, be just an excuse given to the researcher, since there is evidence to the effect that many brothers are abandoning their obligations towards unmarried sisters and their children (Windhurst 1988).

10. In Zimbabwe, the Legal Age of Majority Act has been used to preclude fathers from claiming damages for the seduction of their unmarried daughters. Although a similar statute exists in Botswana, it has not been used in this way.

11. The cases discussed under the different strategies were selected from a random sample heard at the Kanye magistrate's court during a 10 year period (Molokomme 1991).

12. This is confirmed by the common complaint on the part of magistrate's court officials that too many women register complaints and subsequently fail to follow them through. In actual fact, the Kanye magistrate's court material which shows numerous cases recorded as pending, may have been registered by women who merely intended thereby to pressure men into compensating them.

13. Case 16/84, Kanye magistrate's court.

14. Case number 41/85, Kanye magistrate's court.

15. This level of knowledge about the state law is not common among the public in general and women in particular, so this woman is exceptional.

16. Case number 503/84, Kanye magistrate's court.

17. Case number 94/84, Kanye magistrate's court.

References

Alexander, E., 1991, *Women and Men in Botswana: Facts and figures*. Gaborone: Central Statistics Office, Ministry of Finance.

Allot, A.N., 1980, *The Limits of Law*. London: Butterworth.

Armstrong, A. and W. Ncube (eds.), 1987, *Women and Law in Southern Africa*. Harare: Zimbabwe Publishing House.

Armstrong, A. and J. Stewart (eds.), 1990, *The Legal Situation of Women in Southern Africa*. Harare: University of Zimbabwe Publications.

Botswana Government, 1970, *Official Report of the Proceedings of the National Assembly, Vol. 34*. Gaborone: Government Printer.

———, 1981, *National Population and Housing Census*. Gaborone: Central Statistics Office, Government Printer.

———, 1985, *Country Profile*. Gaborone: Central Statistics Office, Ministry of Finance.

Comaroff, J.L. and S. Roberts, 1977, 'Marriage and extramarital sexuality: The dialectics of legal change among the Kgatla'. *Journal of African Law 21 (1)*: 97–123.

———, 1981, *Rules and Processes: The cultural logic of dispute in an African context*. Chicago: University of Chicago Press.

Griffiths, J., 1990, 'Legal pluralism and the social working of law'. Paper presented to a seminar held at Wageningen, The Netherlands.

Gallanter, M., 1981, 'Justice in many rooms: Courts, private ordering and indigenous law'. *Journal of Legal Pluralism 19*: 1–47.

Gulbrandsen, O., 1986, 'To marry or not to marry? Marital strategies and sexual relations in a Tswana society'. *Ethnos 51*: 7–21.

Ingstad, B. and S. Saugestad, 1987, 'Unmarried mothers in changing Tswana society: Implications for household form and viability'. Oslo: Forum for Utviklingsstudier, Norsk Utenrikspolitisk Institutt No. 4.

Kocken, E.M. and G.C. Uhlenbeck, 1980, 'Tlokweng, a village near town'. *ICA Publication no. 39*. Leiden: Institute of Cultural and Social Studies, Leiden University.

Kuper, A., 1987, 'The transformation of marriage in southern Africa', in A. Kuper, *South Africa and the Anthropologist*. London: Routledge and Kegan Paul.

Molenaar, M., 1980, 'Social change within a traditional pattern: A case study of a Tswana ward'. Leiden : Leiden University, M.A. thesis.

Molokomme, A.L., 1991, *Children of the Fence: The maintenance of extramarital children under law and practice in Botswana*. African Studies Centre Research Report no. 46. Leiden: African Studies Centre, University of Leiden.

Moore, S.F., 1973, 'Law and social change: The semi-autonomous social field as an appropriate field of study'. *Law and Society Review* 7: 719–46.

Roberts, S., 1977, 'The Kgatla marriage: Concepts of validity', in S. Roberts (ed.), *Law and the Family in Africa*. The Hague: Mouton.

Schapera, I., 1933, 'Pre-marital pregnancy and native opinion: A note on social change'. *Africa VI*: 59–89.

van Rouveroy van Nieuwaal, E.A.B., 1977, 'To claim or not to claim? Changing views about the restitution of marriage prestations among the Anufom in northern Togo', in S. Roberts (ed.), *Law and the Family in Africa*. The Hague: Mouton.

von Benda-Beckmann, F., 1989, 'Scapegoat and magic charm: Law in development theory and practice'. *Journal of Legal Pluralism 28*: 129–47.

von Benda-Beckmann, F. and K., 1991, 'Law in society: From blindman's bluff to multilocal law'. *Recht der Werklykheid (Special Issue) 1991*, 119–39.

von Benda-Beckmann, K., 1984, *The Broken Stairways to Consensus: Village justice and courts in Manikabau*. Dordrecht: Foris.

Windhurst, R., 1988, 'The changing position of Tsopye women'. Leiden: University of Leiden, M.A. thesis.

11 Gender Relations in the Family: Law and Public Policy in Post-colonial Sri Lanka

Savitri Goonesekere

Early laws and policies in colonial Sri Lanka distinguished between the legal and the non-legal family on the basis of the formal solemnisation of marriage. Laws and policies discriminated against the non-legal unit, strengthened patriarchal norms and developed new ones. Colonial modifications come to be perceived as 'tradition', as reflected in current middle-class antagonism to changes in the divorce law. While social welfare measures, initiated since the 1930s, contributed to high social indicators for women, new free-market economic policies are creating fresh stresses on poor and non-legal families, further discouraging the assumption of responsibility for non-marital children. Emerging trends in practices such as dowry and virginity tests suggest that an earlier egalitarianism was undermined. Laws and policies on family authority, sexual relations and economic activity for men and women transmit double messages, contradict each other and fall behind social practice at points. Girls are encouraged to utilise equal opportunities, but in an environment imbued with a negative stereotype of femininity. The incidence of domestic violence and the fact of marriage breakdown indicates that even the marital family is under stress today, imposing special burdens on women who are expected to be the care-givers. In this context, individual strategies of poor women and new collective initiatives of organised groups are encouraging.

Sri Lanka's situation as a colonised society in South Asia can be best understood on the basis of a single reality; it is a country that has experienced 443 years of Western colonial rule and 46 years of independence.[1] Family relations have been exposed to the impact of laws and policies derived from colonial economic and social needs, for four and a half centuries. They have had to respond to post-Independence policies that have veered from three decades of social welfarism to new free-market philosophies and economic theories. This chapter will discuss the manner in which family and kinship relations continue to experience the impact of colonial laws and policies, even in the post-Independence period, and the urgent need to review them, if the family unit is to become a source of support and caring for its members. The source materials used are legislation, case law, literary sources and newspaper reports. Information obtained in legal literacy and counselling clinics organised by universities and non-governmental organisations has also been included.

Changing Perceptions of the Family Unit

The Factor of Pluralism

The plural society of Sri Lanka today represents a long existing diversity (Samaraweera 1977; de Silva K.M. 1981), with a majority population of Sinhala Buddhists and minority communities of Tamil Hindus and Muslims. There are, however, converts to Christianity in both the Tamil and the Sinhala communities. These diverse communities are governed by a plurality of laws that impact on the family, even though there are large areas of uniformly applicable law. This chapter will, therefore, focus on the uniform laws as well as Kandyan Sinhala law, Tamil Tesawalamai law, and Muslim personal law. Due to developments in the British colonial period, Kandyan law applies to Sinhala people with a regional link to the central provinces, while Tesawalamai applies to Tamils with a link to the northern provinces.

Certain similarities in the recorded indigenous laws of the Sinhala and Tamil people on marriage and inheritance suggest that the family arrangements among them recognised the concept of female-headed households and that these arrangements preceded the later male focused family arrangements. For instance, indigenous Sinhala law in the central or Kandyan provinces of the country, recognised a woman's property rights and the concept of a *binna* marriage with a female head of household. In the *diga* form of marriage, it was the man who became the head of the household (Hayley 1923: 193–95). With the later shift towards patriarchy, a woman acquired full status as head of the household and family, in this system, only as a widow. A similar impression of the earlier family relations that recognised a woman's independent social and economic status being diluted by an expansion of the rights of the husband is seen in isolated provisions of the Tesawalamai Code (1806: Part IV s.1)—a record of Tamil customary law, from the Jaffna region of the North, compiled by the Dutch in 1706. The laws of the Muk-kuvas, a Tamil speaking people who migrated from the western coast of India and settled in the coastal regions of north, north-west, and east Sri Lanka, reveal a strong focus on the female family member's rights. However, at a later stage of development in this system, a woman's property was placed under the power of her brothers and her own son (Britto 1876: 42–44).

Polygyny and polyandry were practised by both the Sinhala and the Tamil people, as an acceptable basis for family relationships. Tesawalamai law (1806: s.18) refers to polygyny practised by the non-Christian Tamils of Jaffna. However, both Mukkuva and indigenous Sinhala laws recognised a polygynous family, created by a man living with two sisters, and a polyandrous family in which two brothers lived with one woman. Polyandrous and polygynous relationships were perceived by the people as family relationships based on living together or 'keeping house together'. Since sexual relations were an accepted aspect of keeping house together, there was no bar to widow remarriage in the indigenous Sinhala law. Widows could remarry and remarriage with relatives within the family including a former brother-in-law or sister-in-law was acceptable.

Norms and taboos on sexual relations out of caste or between parallel cousins did exist, but social and legal commentaries of the early colonial period indicate that most people entered into cohabitation arrangements or dissolved them without ceremony and formality (Britto 1876: 41; cf. also Knox 1966). The attitude to children born of unions that did not conform with accepted norms on legal marriage was also liberal by the standards of Western legal systems influenced by Christianity and Canon law. Such a child could be 'accepted' as a family member in indigenous Sinhala law (Goonesekere 1987a: 95, 160; Hayley 1923: 170–72).

The perceptions in the Muslim community were dramatically different. The Dutch could not find an accepted core of customs among the local Muslims. The first compilation of marriage and inheritance laws of the Muslim community in Sri Lanka was, therefore, brought from Batavia in Indonesia, by a Dutch governor, and accepted by certain leaders of the community, who were consulted, as consistent with their own customs. This code, enacted as Muslim law by the British in 1806, recognised that a man could practice polygamy and exercise authority over females, as head of the family. The family law of the Muslim community, thus, clearly reflected a patriarchal focus that was different from other communities on the island. There is, however, evidence that Muslim social practices were influenced by local customs. Women contracted marriages in the *diga* and *binna* forms familiar to the Sinhala population, in the early part of the 19th century. This phenomenon has also been noted in recent years (cf. Yalman 1971). The Muslims appear to have accepted the local institution of adoption that is not recognised in Islam and in many Muslim communities.[2]

The Nuclear 'Legal' and 'Non-legal' Family

One striking feature of indigenous Sri Lankan family relations in all communities is that wider family relations did not take the rigid form and structure of a joint family system as in other parts of South Asia. Recorded indigenous laws on family support indicate that obligations of 'assistance and support' to parents, collaterals and others who were in the household were recognised and gave certain rights of inheritance. Adoption for the purpose of perpetuating a lineage and expanding the nuclear family or for affording foster care was recognised. Nevertheless, the main focus was on the immediate relationships between a man and woman, their partners and their children, rather than the joint family (Hayley 1923: 388; Goonesekere 1987a: 406).

Colonial law and policy created a new concept of the nuclear 'legal' and 'non-legal' family, based on a regulatory legal framework. From the middle of the 19th century, the legal family for non-Muslim communities was one created exclusively through a monogamous marriage formally registered according to state specified procedures. There is no evidence of Portuguese efforts to interfere with local custom, while the Dutch are known to have imposed their views of marriage only on Christian converts. However, British policy on marriage, though confined initially in 1846 to the Christian inhabitants, was imposed by legislative intervention in 1859 and 1863, on non-Muslim people throughout the island. Thus, while polygyny was recognised in both private and public law for Muslims in Sri Lanka, according to the tenets of their religious law, only monogamous marriages were recognised in the case of other people.[3]

This emphasis on monogamy and state regulated solemnisation of marriage not merely reflected Christian values, but was colonial policy to help clarify title to land (See Risseeuw in this volume). The difficulties of enforcing the law on formal registration of marriage persuaded the British colonial administration to remove the compulsory requirement of registration for non-Muslim marriages in the maritime regions of Sri Lanka in 1863. However, this policy was not altered in the central provinces, the heartland of the British plantations in Sri Lanka. At the time of Independence, in the central provinces, a legal non-Muslim family could be created *only* within a registered monogamous marriage.

Besides, colonial laws influenced by an English common law tradition perceived a non-Muslim registered monogamous marriage as a patriarchal nuclear unit consisting of a male head of household, his wife and their children. The man was perceived as the 'breadwinner' and major source of family support. The woman surfaces as the source of family authority and support, only when an 'illegal' family was constituted outside lawful marriage or as widow on the death of her husband. English colonial law was superimposed upon the system known as Roman–Dutch law, traced to the Dutch period of colonial rule, and strengthened a legal value system which saw the woman as the person responsible for this 'inferior', 'illegal' family created outside marriage.

These norms on legal marriage have not been altered in the post-Independence period and represent the legal basis for creating family relations. The Constitution (1978) now declares that 'the State shall recognise and protect the family as the basic unit of society' (Article 27 [12]). Sri Lanka's post-Independence laws distinctly continue the colonial legal tradition and regard 'the family' as the 'legal family' created within monogamous, formally solemnised marriages or a potentially polygamous Muslim family.

Legislative interventions and administrative policies in regard to the family, even today, are all derived from the basic premise that the 'legal family' has a male head of household and the 'non-legal family' a female head of household. The traditional Sinhala law concept of a female head of household in the *binna* form of marriage has been retained by the legal system. However, very few Kandyan marriages are solemnised in *binna* today, and a man who settles for that type of marriage is described in local idiom as one who 'lowers himself' into that union. Over the centuries, the patriarchal *diga* form has become the common form of marriage, where Sinhala people from the central regions register marriages under Sinhala law now described by a regional name, as 'Kandyan' law. Besides, no other laws and state policies give recognition to this type of *binna* marriage.

Muslims too must subscribe to these same perceptions of the 'legal' and 'non-legal' family. The approach to illegitimacy in this system conformed with the English common law perceptions, but the distinction is not, as in the case of other communities, an alien imposition of values.

Not surprisingly, the concept of the male head of household and the discrimination against families created outside marriage are endorsed in state policies in key areas such as birth registration, citizenship, tax law, pensions and social security benefits. This has produced striking anomalies. For instance, Sri Lanka's post-Independence citizenship laws confer Sri Lankan citizenship through the paternal line on children born to married parents, but through the maternal line only on non-marital children. Thus, the child of a Sri Lankan woman who marries a foreigner cannot claim Sri Lankan citizenship by descent. On the other hand, a child born out of wedlock to a Sri Lankan woman can do so (Goonesekere 1990).

This focus on 'legal' and 'non-legal' family units operates, even today, to undermine equity in gender relations and denies women the equality guaranteed as a fundamental right to all citizens by Article 12(1) of the 1978 Constitution. The judiciary has no power to review past, discriminatory laws and only state administrative or executive action that involves an infringement can be questioned in the courts of law. The discrimination faced by children and women in a family unit created outside marriage has never been addressed. Concepts of equality before the law and gender equity in the 1978 Constitution have not yet been used by policy makers to re-evaluate basic premises, because the distinction between these two types of families is perceived as a deeply entrenched value that conforms with the indigenous cultural value system on family relations.

The Impact of Law and Policy on Family Relations

The procedures for registration of marriages seem to be fairly well-known on the island, to all classes. However, most men and women in rural, peasant communities and the urban poor are unaware of, or do not use, the complicated court procedures to obtain a divorce, nor even the simpler procedure of divorce by registration before an administrative authority, possible under Kandyan law. Since the rural peasant and urban poor populace constitutes the majority of Sri Lankans, even people who register a first marriage may simply cohabit with someone else at a later stage. If this happens in the Central regions, where marriage registration is compulsory for persons governed by Kandyan (Sinhala) law, neither the cohabiting couple nor the children can claim the status of persons who belong to a 'legal family'. Registration has not been compulsory for other Sri Lankans since 1863, whether Muslim or non-Muslim, and cohabiting couples may claim that their union is a legal 'customary' marriage, because they lived together and were accepted as husband and wife in their community, even when they have not registered. However, if the first marriage has been registered, the second union will be illegal in the absence of a divorce. Besides, Sri Lanka courts have been influenced by the colonial policies and values on cohabitation without formal registration and they require some proof of customary ceremonies of marriage prior to cohabitation. In other words, another system of regulatory procedures has been introduced through judicial intervention, even when statutory policy has dispensed with the requirement of formal registration. The required customary ceremonies of marriage are not always clear and they may not be followed by low income persons. Thus, if the inception of the family unit is disputed, or has to be proved, it will not be easy to claim that cohabiting couples are legally married according to customary formalities. The emphasis on form, placed by the courts in the post-Independence period, thus, denies legal status to some families.

The artificial nature of the legal classification of families as 'legal' and 'non-legal' is illustrated vividly in cases that come before the courts. In one recent case, a cohabiting couple were able to prove that their unregistered union was a marriage because they had solemnised their union in a church. On identical facts, another couple's marriage was not recognised as a lawful union, because they came from the central provinces and the law there required the formality of registration.[4] On the other hand, if persons succeed in establishing a lawful unregistered marriage based on cohabitation and a customary ceremony of marriage, a woman who contracts a later registered marriage will find that her union has no legal effect and her children are illegitimate since monogamy is the legal norm!

The distinction between the 'legal' union and a 'non-legal' union formed in cohabitation has become difficult to sustain, also in middle-class communities familiar with the 'respectable', legal, monogamous marriage. This social and legal norm of monogamy has been undermined in recent years by the legal system itself. Divorce laws in Sri Lanka are strict. Yet, an important judicial decision of 1964 gave a man the right to practice polygamy after a unilateral conversion to Islam. He can now contract a second marriage during the subsistence of an earlier monogamous marriage.[5] Thus, a union that would be considered illegal cohabitation according to middle-class mores is converted into a legal marriage by the simple act of the man's conversion to Islam. The social attitudes to monogamy had become so entrenched that the concept of a Muslim's right to contract polygamous marriage used to evoke snide comments by non-Muslims and some embarrassment on the part of Muslims. However, the convert's polygamous marriage has now acquired social legitimacy among the middle-classes.

The current distinction between 'legal' and 'non-legal' unions has created problems in a context where 17 per cent of households in most districts are said to be female-headed (Women's Bureau of Sri Lanka 1985). If these households have been formed outside what the law refers to as 'lawful marriage' (registered marriage or those solemnised according to custom), both the women and the children suffer various disabilities because of their unrecognised and/or increasingly low status. Since administrators tend to perceive 'legal' families as families, these women and children without a male head of household form an 'odd' category. The laws and policies on 'legal' and 'non-legal' families place women and children who do not belong to marital units at greater risk.

Sri Lanka had developed policies on free health and education that had a broad based impact. In the first decades prior to and after Independence, a substantial allocation of resources for education in the rural areas and community health contributed to impressive social indicators for women, despite rural and urban poverty. Central schools were developed, that attracted low income students from the provinces who could compete with students from the urban schools, academically and in sports and other activities.

Cutbacks on public expenditure, the neglect of provincial schools, structural adjustment policies, as well as the consumerism that has surfaced with new free-market economic policies have changed the earlier scenario and created new stresses on survival for middle and low income families. The incidence of child abandonment, abortion and even infanticide by young women in Sri Lanka today, the situation of unwed mothers picked up for vagrancy or prostitution in institutions, as well as trafficking for foreign adoptions, suggest that there are increasing pressures on women to reject children born out of marriage.

There is evidence that babies have been given in adoption informally from state hospitals or from homes for unwed mothers, for many years, without going through required, regulatory procedures of formal adoption. The recent demand for Sri Lankan babies for foreign adoption and liberal policies on inter-country adoptions has encouraged organised baby trafficking with the complicity of local people.

Inevitably, baby trafficking has led to the exploitation of low income women, especially in a context where they are unwed mothers or single parents, unable to support their children. The government has, from 1977 to 1992, attempted to balance its liberal policy on foreign adoption, with some stricter controls on foreigners adopting local children. Punishments and sanctions have also been imposed for baby trafficking. It has initiated the Foster Parents Scheme, meant to encourage sponsorship of low income children, so that they continue to live with their families. Neither the regulatory controls, the procedures for foreign and local adoption, nor the Foster Parents Scheme appear to have more than touched the problems of child abandonment and trafficking. Adoption has, thus, been transformed from a traditional institution to expand the family to one where low income women are pressurised by economic need or social factors to reject/abandon their children.

A similar transformation of the family unit can take place because of the phenomenon of low income women migrating as domestic workers, due to economic need. Government policy encourages migration, but affords no system of child support. A woman who cannot make suitable arrangements for her children, sometimes, abandons them or places them in a state or non-governmental institution for children. They may have to be cared for by a male family member. While the last, sometimes, results in a sharing of family responsibility, the arrangement can also lead to abuse and neglect. Some efforts have been made to provide administrative supports to these women, but the implications of migration for the family unit have not been addressed.[6]

The above discussion indicates a clear need to review current perceptions on the creation and functioning of the family unit in Sri Lanka. Registration of marriage is a legal procedure that places constraints on the exploitation of women. For instance, there will be an incentive to conform to certain norms, such as those on the age at marriage and the prohibited degrees of marriage in relationships of consanguinity and affinity. Registration encourages conformity with norms on incest. The concept of registration is also important for the purpose of maintaining records of critical domestic events.

Nevertheless, even British colonial policy which introduced formal solemnisation was modified to accept the legality of informal cohabitation, where it did not violate laws on capacity to marry. Sri Lankan law needs to adopt a similar approach and develop concepts which recognise some types of informal cohabitation and the status of child born outside marriage. The procedures and rationale for registration need to be publicised in the community so as to encourage conformity. The law of divorce also needs to be liberalised so that persons are encouraged to form relations within a duly solemnised and registered marriage. A family policy, formulated to encourage conformity with norms on capacity, such as age at marriage or incest, must logically concede that cohabitation in such situations will not have any legal consequences. However, if children are born of such unions, the status of the children should be recognised and both parents must be encouraged to assume legal responsibility for support.

Property and Economic Relations

The area of economic relations reflects an official unwillingness to introduce fundamental changes in law and policy. However, while the linkage to colonial laws and policies is apparent, new economic conditions have led to some shifts on the ground (Goonesekere 1989).

Colonial legislation and recent judicial decisions on Tesawalamai have combined to strengthen the concept of the husband's marital power over economic rights of women, so that the trend has even impacted on commercial policy in the banking sector. A Tamil woman governed by Tesawalamai may not transact with immoveable property, litigate or obtain a loan from a bank without her husband's consent. The need for change has been discussed in research as well as in public forums but, to date, no changes have been introduced. Though the policy interventions are a product of both legislative and judicial policy, particularly in the British colonial period, these laws are now perceived as indigenous ethnic laws which should not be interfered with.

This is also the attitude to Muslim personal law which discriminated between the inheritance rights of male and female heirs. A recent decision of the Supreme Court imposes Islamic rights of inheritance on Muslim children adopted according to a secular adoption statute.[7] Ironically, as Islamic law does not recognise adoption, Sri Lankan Muslims utilise the statutory law of adoption. A Supreme Court, sensitive to the dimension of cultural and religious rights of minorities, has diluted the rights of Muslim adopted children by grafting Islamic law on to the non-Islamic concept of adoption.

The reluctance to interfere with what are perceived as ethnic laws may also account for the failure to review the content of indigenous Sinhala law as it is applied today. A woman had separate property rights in Sinhala law, but a local élite influenced by

Victorian values and trends in Roman–Dutch law substantially modified the indigenous law on marital property, inheritance and illegitimacy, by statutory reforms introduced even prior to Independence.[8] These reforms diluted a woman's rights in the area of matrimonial property and inheritance and the rights of non-marital children. In a classic irony, women governed by Sinhala (Kandyan) law today do not have the equal property rights enjoyed by men and women in the 'General law' which applies to most non-Muslims in Sri Lanka. This 'General law' gives men and women equal rights of inheritance if a family member dies intestate, i.e., without leaving a will.

The right of any person to dispose of property by will, however, can operate so as to discriminate against females, since they can be given less or even be excluded by a parent or family member who chooses to leave a will. The law does not provide for restriction on testation or the concept of fixed shares in family property which cannot be disposed of by will. This represents a departure from indigenous legal values in both Sinhala and Tamil laws, which recognised the concept of a family member's claim on the estate for support or assistance in times of need and the right of children to support from property inherited by a surviving parent. Islamic law, too, restricts the right of testation to disposal of only one-third of the estate by will (Goonesekere 1987a: 456, 463).

The concept of separate property of husband and wife after marriage, as well as the freedom to dispose of property by will, can operate to the disadvantage of females. Even the matrimonial home may be the separate asset of her husband. A woman may also be pressurised to dispose of her separate property after marriage. Indeed, counsellors at legal literacy clinics find that there is popular belief among low income women that the husband has a legal right to do so.

Traditional Tesawalamai Tamil customary law provided for a system of community, or pooling of properties acquired during marriage, while Roman–Dutch law provided for community of property, so that even a non-contributing spouse could acquire half the other's property on a dissolution of marriage. These concepts were, however, replaced in the British colonial period by the theory of separate property. This theory continues to represent the basic foundation of matrimonial property law in the post-Independence period.

There is evidence that women of low income urban families in the city of Colombo have developed their own insurance against the risk of a husband pressurising them into transacting with property, by making pre-marriage settlements so that a man will be required to account for any property acquired by a woman after marriage.[9] These women often travel overseas as migrant workers and remit their savings. Besides, male alcoholism contributes to a woman's savings being dissipated by a husband or male relative. The 'marriage settlement' or marriage deed appears to have developed out of women's desire to protect themselves against this exploitation and the social reality of male power over a woman's property and assets. The marriage 'deed' is a strategy for delimiting the man's control over property or cash belonging to the woman, which she owned during the marriage.

Dowry gifts which were treated in both traditional Sinhala and Tamil laws as the woman's own property (Goonesekere 1987b; Hayley 1923; Tesawalamai Code 1806) are being increasingly perceived as gifts made 'in consideration' of marriage to a bridegroom, fostering the dimension of trade and barter in the marriage relationship. The Sri Lanka courts have intervened in some judicial decisions, to hold that property given to a daughter on marriage as dowry is either given to her as a wedding gift or held in trust for her, even if it is actually transferred to the man.[10] However, there is at the moment no law that prohibits a bride's family from transferring property to a bridegroom on marriage. This has increasingly become the form in which dowry property is gifted on marriage. In fact, the law on transfer of land in Sri Lanka encourages this kind of financial barter in marriage by describing a dowry gift as a transaction for 'valuable consideration'—the 'consideration' for the gift being the marriage. It is ironic that courts which have struck down marriage brokerage contracts have not perceived dowry gifts in this form as transactions contrary to public policy and a woman's interests and personal dignity.

Women of all communities have raised their objection to dowry in public forums, but have not lobbied actively for legislative intervention to prohibit it. The transformation of dowry, over the years, seems to reflect the increasing consumerism and negative impact of new 'open' and free-market economic policies on family values. Money is seen as the sole rationale for even personal relationships and parents of male children use the marriage transaction to obtain financial support for their own family. In the

Tamil community, dowry brought by a bride is sometimes recycled and used to dower the bridegroom's sisters.

The modern phenomenon of dowry represents a type of social preference and value for males that in general is not typical of the traditional egalitarianism found in economic transactions within the family. It harmonises, however, with changing trends that seem to focus on female virginity, the slur of illegitimacy and the inferior status for widows. All these aspects conflict with the human development trends on female literacy in Sri Lanka and the rhetoric of gender equity used in policy approaches on women in development. It would appear that the commercialisation of market forces and the absorption of women into new sectors of low paid employment are undermining society's perception of their right to equity. There is some evidence of gender stereotyping in schools which contributes to low self-esteem among girls (CENWOR 1993).

The emphasis on males in inheritance to state lands distributed in land settlement schemes or under land legislation entered the legal system through a colonial Land Development Ordinance in 1935. A statutory scheme of inheritance, based on the English law concept of primogeniture (preference for the eldest male in any category of heirs), was enacted in this statute and found its way into *all* the key land legislations in the post-Independence period. It has now been removed from all areas, except the distribution of state lands in agricultural settlement schemes. Policy makers give the fear of fragmentation as the reason for their reluctance to introduce a change. In fact, the law has created a culture in which there is a reluctance to allocate state lands in settlement schemes to females in the family. The Land Commission queried the anomalous nature of this land settlement inheritance scheme, in its report submitted after Independence. The issue has also been raised by women's groups. Yet, changes in the law have not so far been enacted. Nevertheless, the fact that women have raised the issue, has led to more women obtaining land. The Commission on Human Rights, which is authorised to inquire into complaints of violation of fundamental rights, has also mediated to ensure that women who complain of discrimination are allotted land.[11]

Family Authority and Responsibility

The regulatory provisions on the aspect of family authority in non-Muslim law are derived from Roman–Dutch law as well as English law, and reveal the impact of local judicial attitudes. They show a lack of consistency, reflecting both liberal and egalitarian trends. The concept of the husband's marital power was eliminated through British colonial reform on matrimonial property, while this concept was never introduced by statute into Sinhala (Kandyan law) or Muslim law. However, colonial legislative reform at the beginning of this century, based on a Commission report, introduced a Roman–Dutch law derived concept of the husband's marital power over his wife's immoveable property into the Tesawalamai Code. A judiciary that was very egalitarian in its approach to the matrimonial property rights of other women, adopted a very conservative attitude to marital power over Tamil women in the north. This has helped to expand the rights and authority of a husband over Tamil women, in property and business transactions.

The ambivalence in regard to marital rights of women has not, however, found its way into either legislation or judicial decisions in the area of marriage and personal freedom. Thus, the Penal Code punishes restraint of the personal freedom of a woman as an offence. Judicial decisions prior to and after Independence have followed early English cases and decided that 'a girl of 16 is free to go where she pleases', reflecting the perception that she has reached the legal age of discretion. These judicial decisions also accept a lower age of discretion of 14 years for boys, without providing a rationale for the difference, in the Sri Lankan context.

The concept of an age of discretion of 16 years, before the current age of majority (18 years), is in clear conflict with the policies on sexual maturity that we refer to later, since the age of capacity for marriage as well as the age of statutory rape is as low as 12 years. The egalitarianism in regard to personal freedom within the family has, however, been carried through in legislation and court cases on parental authority over marriage.[12] A girl's consent to marry is required by law and the courts do not approve of agreements to give a girl in marriage or marriage brokerage contracts, perceiving them as contrary to public policy and in conflict with the concept of free consent to marry (Goonesekere 1987a: 309–10).

Muslim law in Sri Lanka in the post-Independence period moved away from the colonial code and is now based on principles of Islamic law recognising a wide marital and guardianship power of the males of the family. There are several significant areas, however, in which constraints have been placed on male authority. For instance, the mother is the preferred custodian for very young children and a woman has complete legal authority to transact in respect of her separate property. Both aspects are recognised in litigated disputes that have surfaced in the courts. Muslim law does not recognise a minimum age at marriage and child marriages among Muslims are known to take place. Yet, this law is subject to the Penal Code so that even a Muslim husband may be charged by the police with statutory rape if there is a complaint that he had sexual intercourse with a child under 12 years of age.

This egalitarianism in regard to the personal freedom of girls is in conflict with the basic legal concept derived from Roman–Dutch law that the father of a legitimate child is the natural guardian of his children, with a preferential right to decision-making and their custody. This concept is basic to parental authority in non-Muslim law and has entered various important laws. Correspondingly, the mother is the natural guardian of non-marital children and the father is excluded from any legal relationship to the child, with the exception of a limited obligation of support.

Administrators, be they educational authorities or immigration officers, generally impose constraints on a woman's right to act for her children, because of the notion that the father is the 'natural' and legal guardian in his lifetime.[13] This concept is a serious constraint on a woman retaining custody when a marriage has broken down. Women come for legal aid claiming that a father has forcibly abducted a child or refused visitation rights and access. Courts and the community perceive the father as asserting his legal rights in refusing access. In this situation, the woman has to use a range of legal procedures to establish that he is 'unfit' for custody. She must obtain medical or other evidence to show that the child's best interests require that she should retain custody. In custody disputes, the courts can interpret their duty to act in the child's best interests, so as to confer custodial and parental rights on the mother. Nevertheless, since the father has preferential legal rights, courts are known to give this greater weightage, sometimes, even ignoring the dimension of the child's interests.

The preferential status of the father as natural guardian also connects with the legal system's perception that he is the 'breadwinner'. Thus, the law of Sri Lanka places the obligation of support on a man. He must support his wife and family.[14] The woman's obligation of support is not clearly stated in non-Muslim law and it is uncertain whether she has a duty to contribute to support. Many cases that come to legal aid clinics involve claims by women for maintenance on behalf of themselves (if they are married) or of marital or non-marital children who are in their care. Though an employed man's salary may be attached on a court order for the purpose of enforcing an order on family support, women find it very difficult to enforce support orders, even when they use legal procedures. Inadequacy in the law and legal procedures and a failure to review them for the last two decades has made maintenance action an unrealistic remedy for many women. However, if they obtain a divorce in adversarial proceedings, there is a better chance of obtaining a financial or property settlement. Women's ignorance of the divorce law and the inadequate coverage of free legal services result in their often bearing the exclusive burden of family support.

Sri Lankan law, based on Roman–Dutch law as well as indigenous values, generally recognises the status of the widow as head of the family after the death of the husband, though an isolated statutory provision may place a constraint on her status. Nevertheless, the notion of a male as breadwinner and head of the house has so permeated social perceptions, that there is a strong sense of diminution of social status when a middle-class woman is widowed or divorced. This perception is more typical of urban areas in the maritime regions where the attitude to widowhood contrasts with those of low-income communities and even middle-class families in the central (Kandyan) regions of the country.[15]

The laws on parental authority and sexual maturity of children do not conform with social realities today. Education and health policies, child growth and development have improved social indicators. Even low income communities perceive a 12-year old as a child rather than as a young girl who has acquired sexual maturity. Loss of males, through years of ethnic conflict and political violence, has probably increased the number of widows, altering the statistics from the average of 17 per cent recorded in 1981. Women are contributing increasingly to family survival and development and to the care and nurturing of children as a sole breadwinner and guardian. Though unemployment rates for Sri Lankan women are high, the phenomenon of Middle East migration, as well as the needs of family survival place women in a situation where they are the major or only care-givers and breadwinners. Women who have become single parents, in particular, due to desertion by or the absence of a male, must operate in an environment where the legal culture continues to focus on male authority over minor children born within a legal marriage.

Sexual Relations

Post-colonial Sri Lanka is striking for its commitment to colonial legal values in the area of sexual relations within the family. Non-Muslim Sri Lankan laws on marriage reflect, even today, the perceptions of the old Roman law that were received into English common law and articulated in British colonial statutes. The legal age at marriage for a girl continues to be as low as 12 years, but child marriage is not an issue, and the average age at marriage for women in Sri Lanka today is 24 years. Policies on free education in particular, have helped to bring girls into the school system (Jayaweera 1991; Kazi 1989; Women's Bureau of Sri Lanka 1985). However, the concept of sexual maturity at the age of 12 years for a marriage, remains unchanged and has impacted on the definition of rape. Thus, the age of statutory rape or the age at which sexual intercourse is considered rape, irrespective of whether the girl consented, is as low as 12 years. The consent of a girl above that age is, thus, a complete defence to an allegation of rape. As in most countries, the law emphasises that the victim's evidence alone is adequate, only in exceptional situations. Rape convictions are, therefore, difficult to sustain, particularly in the case of a child victim.

Statements by colonial observers indicate a society which did not adopt a strict and puritanical attitude to sexual relations, divorce and remarriage (Knox 1966: 175). However, doctors today record growing parental concern with a woman's virginity and the custom of a virginity test after the wedding, particularly in urban communities and in southern Sri Lanka. Similarly, some doctors are known to be inhibited in making medical reports in cases of sexual violence because of family concern with protecting a girl's reputation as a virgin.

These practices pertaining to virginity which violate a woman's dignity and self-respect are fostered rather than undermined by the legal system. The civil law of Sri Lanka, derived from Roman–Dutch law, recognises that financial compensation can be claimed by a woman for seduction, the award being computed in terms of a sum for loss of virginity and marriage prospects. When a rape case does come before the courts, social values on virginity and legal norms on seduction combine to influence judicial decision-making. Judges fail to see rape as a crime of violence and focus on compensating a woman for loss of virginity. This is why prison sentences for rape and sexual molestation of even young children are very low or suspended and the offence does not attract sanctions as a grave crime. Though the law contemplates a maximum sentence of 20 years' imprisonment, rape is invariably perceived by judges as a private 'injury' for which a couple of years' imprisonment or a suspended sentence may be awarded, with a modest sum as financial compensation for the rape victim. The law on civil injuries and rape, thus, ignores the reality of the violence against the woman and reflects the perception of English common law on male supremacy in sexual relations with the family. The Attorney General's department, sometimes, does take steps to have these low or suspended sentences set aside, by application to the superior appeal courts.[16]

This same perception of a woman's sexuality is carried through into family support laws where affiliation between a man and his illegitimate child has to be established according to strict legal norms and within a very limited period after the child's birth. These regulatory provisions are derived from Victorian British bastardy laws, introduced in the colonial period into many countries in Asia and Africa. They have not been modified in the post-Independence period. Though the quantum of maintenance has been increased through later legislation, no effort has been made to amend the provisions relevant to proof of paternity and applications by unmarried women. Yet, family support and maintenance represent an important area in which low income women in particular, want to come to court and obtain financial support for children born out of marriage.

There is evidence that in traditional Sinhala law, a man had the right to kill his wife and her lover if they were caught in adultery. However, other statements indicate that adultery was not taken seriously, unless the man was of a lower caste (Knox 1966: 173). Adultery was not recognised as a criminal offence in the colonial period. Since courts are required to determine whether or not the defence of provocation can be raised in circumstances where the reasonableness of the conduct is in issue, the criminal law does not recognise a husband's right to kill his wife caught in the act of adultery. Early Sri Lankan court cases have also rejected the concept of a man's right to claim restitution of conjugal rights.

Adultery was a ground for divorce for both a husband and a wife, but under colonial legislation, only the husband could sue for damages against the third party. The Marriage and Divorce Commission criticised this discrimination in 1959. Today, either spouse can sue for compensation from the third party responsible for committing adultery or for enticing a spouse. Such actions can be brought in Sri Lanka by both men and women.[17] Yet, these legal actions for 'interference' with marital rights, combined with the focus on virginity, encourage the perception that male violence by a spouse, father or brothers is a legitimate effort to protect family honour.

Divorce and Marriage Breakdown

It is in the area of divorce and marriage breakdown and that of domestic violence that Sri Lankan law and policy retains greatest commitment to a scale of values based on colonial perceptions of gender relations.

Indigenous Sinhala law recognised mutual consent and breakdown of marriage as a basis for divorce. Robert Knox, writing of this 'novel' phenomenon for a 17th century Western readership, records with surprise that 'if they disagree, and dislike one the other they part with no disgrace' (1966: 176). Yet, from the year 1859, the English attitudes to divorce permeated the Sri Lanka legal system. The marriage statute of 1859 introduced limitations on divorce under indigenous Sinhala law, which were loosened somewhat, in the latter part of the century. Thus, mutual consent and separation were later recognised as grounds for divorce. However, the concept that a husband could obtain a divorce on the ground of a wife's adultery alone, while she could divorce him for adultery only coupled with incest or gross cruelty, was a policy derived from marriage legislation in England enacted in 1857. These limitations were retained and have found their way even into post-Independence Sri Lankan legislation.[18] Besides, the General Law of divorce applicable to all other non-Muslim persons has been derived from a statute of 1863 and subsequent colonial legislation which recognised only the matrimonial faults of adultery and malicious desertion as grounds for divorce.[19] Cruelty is not a ground for divorce, unless it can be established that it amounts to desertion with an intention to terminate cohabitation. Cruelty is only a ground for the lesser relief of legal (judicial) separation, unless an intention to desert can be proved. While the indigenous concept of non-adversarial dispute settlement in divorce, accepted in colonial legislation for persons governed by indigenous Sinhala law, has been retained, others must obtain a divorce in adversarial court proceedings. The Marriage and Divorce Commission, which studied the law on divorce in 1959 after Independence, could not arrive at a consensus on either liberalisation of the grounds or the procedures for divorce.

In 1991, certain proposals for reform of divorce laws, formulated by an unofficial women's committee, recommended recognition of marriage breakdown as the exclusive basis for divorce. The committee also suggested a change in the adversarial nature of divorce litigation whilst strengthening the legal controls on distribution of assets, so that women and children would not suffer economically after a divorce. However, divorce reform has become controversial today. There are many professionals including women lawyers, who believe that a liberalisation of the law will weaken the institution of marriage and operate as a 'Casanova's charter', to the disadvantage of both women and children. Women's groups are divided because a cross-section of women themselves have come to value the status a marriage gives them, even if it is an empty shell of a relationship. Over the centuries, divorce has acquired a social stigma, and marriage and a male head of household a special status of respectability. Women who come for legal counselling, request relief as a last resort and, even then, seek family support on the basis of desertion rather than a dissolution of the marriage. The earlier indigenous social values of marriage as a contract and divorce as a response to marriage breakdown are rejected by the middle-classes, who invariably are the policy and decision-makers.

The high point of resistance to the reform of the divorce law is reflected in a decision of the Supreme Court of Sri Lanka in 1988 and the response to divorce law reform in 1991. This court interpreted a legislative effort to introduce the concept of divorce on seven years' separation into the General Law of Sri Lanka in 1977 so restrictively, as to permit divorce only on seven years' separation *combined* with matrimonial fault. In justifying his decision, the judge perceived the concept of matrimonial fault as a 'deep-rooted' feature of the Sri Lankan jurisprudential and social values on divorce. His lordship stated that recognition of the marriage breakdown principle was 'revolting to the mind of any reasonable man' and 'undermines the moral and social foundation of our society'.[20]

The resistance of policy planners and middle-class lobbies to divorce reform in the post-Independence period and the commitment to limitations on providing this relief, is in sharp contrast to social realities on marriage breakdown. Men who want a divorce have found various methods of bypassing the divorce laws. We have already observed that a man may convert to Islam and contract a polygamous second marriage. The uncontested divorce action is another strategy and a woman may be pressurised not to contest the divorce, but receive no property settlement or alimony. In a more recent aberration, a man bribes officials to falsify the serving of summons, so that a divorce decree is obtained in a false proceeding. Since there is a social stigma on divorce, a man who wishes to remarry may want to be the 'innocent' party to a divorce action, free of matrimonial fault. It is such a man, who conspires with a lawyer to falsify divorce proceedings. Some women have moved court to have these illegal proceedings declared void.[21] Nevertheless, others feel disinclined to go through these public legal procedures and, therefore, accept the 'false' decree for divorce.

Domestic Violence

As indicated earlier, the law on illegitimacy and virginity encourages social practices such as male violence, in the form of pressures for abortion, physical violence by family members to protect 'family honour' and unilateral repudiation by the husband, if he finds that a woman is not a virgin on the wedding night.[22] The incidence of abortion and rape among workers in the new investment promotion zones is indicative of these pressures. Traditional abortifacients have been known to women for centuries, and they have been used, despite the strict criminal norms on abortion introduced by a colonial penal code based on early English common law.[23] A recent report suggests that 20 per cent of the hospital beds in gynaecological units in state hospitals are occupied by women suffering from septic abortions performed illegally (Perera 1993). Since the abortion law is very strict, women who cannot afford abortions in discreet clinics, opt for traditional methods and use state hospitals when complications set in. Yet, reform of the abortion law remains an emotional and controversial subject for legislators and professionals.

Marital rape is also not an offence under Sri Lankan law, while incest is not punishable as a crime under the penal code. Incest is only a minor offence under the marriage laws of Sri Lanka. The attitude to marital rape and the location of incest laws in the marriage statutes reveal the influence of the English common law. This system did not recognise marital rape and viewed incest as an offence, but considered it a matter subject to the ecclesiastical courts. This legal position has never been changed in Sri Lanka, even though domestic violence and the incidence of incest is becoming more visible in the community. Cases of incest are known to have surfaced, particularly in situations where children are left with a male relative or the father, when the mother has had to travel overseas as a migrant worker.[24]

Restrictions in the law of divorce encourage women to bear the trauma of domestic violence and abuse against themselves as well as their children and contributes to police and community insensitivity to such abuse. If abuse takes place, the practice in Sri Lanka so far has been for parties to report this conduct to the police. There is a special Women and Children's Bureau in Colombo, but most cases are reported to ordinary police stations. Sri Lankan law does not recognise a male's right of 'reasonable chastisement' as a defence to assault or hurt. Nevertheless, police officers admit that they attempt to reconcile the parties and this invariably means that a woman is encouraged or sometimes intimidated to go back to the husband and put up with the continuing hazard of his violence. Sri Lankan law has never recognised a husband's right to have conjugal rights restored. Yet, police officers think that their duty is to prevent the break up of the family. There are no legal procedures for obtaining restraining injunctions to prevent molestation, or orders for excluding the man from the marital residence, unless the woman takes the step of filing an action for divorce in court. The police cannot easily be persuaded to take the husband before a magistrate for assaulting or causing hurt. Sri Lanka courts have recognised that a woman and her children have a right to stay on in the marital residence as deserted family members. However, if violence is used against them, the law is ineffective to afford protection.

Domestic violence in Sri Lanka reflects, as in other countries of South Asia, power relations between females as also between men and women in the family. Violence against women may, therefore, be perpetrated by both sexes. Often, domestic servants are abused by female members of the family. This is also a special area where post-Independence laws have *diluted* the protection afforded to child domestic servants in early colonial legislation. Not surprisingly, law enforcement has been ineffective to prevent gross cruelty to domestic servants in general, and girl child domestics in particular. The permissive attitude to this type of domestic violence is also seen in legal proceedings where cases of violence are compounded. The child receives minimal compensation and the adult offender goes unpunished for violation of the child labour laws and the perpetration of physical violence.[25]

Both divorce reform and violence against women have been raised as issues of public concern by women. The division amongst middle-class women and NGOs, on the 'risks' of liberalising divorce law, has prevented the government studying these reforms seriously. However, there have been recent initiatives which recognise that violence in the family and a family under stress because of dysfunctioning adult relationships are not merely 'private' problems, but national issues that can impact on the wellbeing of the whole community. In 1993 a dialogue was initiated with the police and a commitment obtained from them, to address the issue of violence against women by establishing special units within police stations. A special unit manned by a senior police officer has been created in 1993 at Police Headquarter in Colombo. A battered women's centre, established by a non-governmental organisation, 'Women in Need', and legal aid organisations have intervened since 1992–93, to offer legal assistance as well as shelter and other support in court cases of women victims and victims of child abuse whose situations received publicity in the media. Coverage, however, is limited.

Since the issue of violence has received media attention, this problem and the connected issue of child abuse, prostitution and violence against child servants has evoked a response from the government. In 1993, the cabinet approved far-reaching changes in the law on sexual abuse of children and exploitation of children in domestic service. The proposals also call for connected policies, such as allocation of resources for compulsory education, monitoring violations and law enforcement. Proposals for reform of the rape law, which complements the proposals on child abuse, have just been submitted to government. The focus on child abuse and violence against women, appears to have captured the public mind. A recent public campaign to reopen a case of rape of a young child was successful because the media, professional organisations of lawyers and women's groups combined to question the withdrawal of the prosecution.

Conclusion

Early laws and policies in Sri Lanka in the colonial period distinguished between the legal and the non-legal family, redefining the nature of family relations in terms of formal solemnisation. This, combined with laws and policies which discriminated against the non-legal unit, strengthened existing patriarchal norms and developed new ones. These official policies conformed with the perceptions of the élites and the middle-classes, but contributed to changes in, and attitudes to, family units in the country (See Risseeuw in this volume).

Social welfare policies initiated from the 1930s onwards, however, reached into communities across the country and contributed to high social indicators for women, as well as access to opportunities. Nevertheless, the continued transmission of double messages in laws and policies on family authority, sexual relations and economic activity for men and women has impacted on the social environment in which girls must function both within the family and the community. Girls are encouraged to utilise equal opportunities, but find themselves trapped in an unsympathetic environment with a stereotyped vision of femininity. Emerging trends in practices such as dowry, virginity tests and gender stereotyping in schools suggest that an earlier and traditional egalitarianism is being undermined. The entrenchment of discriminatory values on illegitimacy and the economic pressures discourage the assumption of responsibility for non-marital children. Meanwhile, consumerism and economic stress seem to be affecting even the marital family and imposing special burdens on women, who continue to be expected to be the care-givers. The incidence of domestic violence and the fact of marriage breakdown, which have become more visible in recent years, also suggest that families are in crisis today.

Sri Lanka does not have an activist, community-lobbying and NGO tradition. Community organisations are more service than issues oriented and it is only very recently that we see the sign of such activism emerging. Consequently, the state plays an important role in policy formulation and implementation. The recent enactment of a charter on women's rights in 1993, has set a comprehensive policy agenda for the state on women's issues. It was drafted in a participatory process involving women's groups of all communities, the official agencies concerned with women's issues and academics. Though cautious on the subject of introducing uniform laws on family relations, it articulates a consensus on policies relating to economic rights, health, education and violence. The charter may help to develop a common agenda that will impact on some of the problems discussed in regard to gender relations in the family.

New initiatives on a women's agenda, law reform and enforcement are encouraging and must be followed through, if families are to be supported in caring for their own members. Since the constitutional guarantees on fundamental rights affect only state actors, it is important to reflect constitutional norms and international standards that Sri Lanka has accepted by local uniform legislation applicable to all communities. Areas of uniform law must be strengthened and developed and pluralism modified by a concept of the citizen's right to opt out of personal or customary law. Reforms within systems such as Muslim family law, in line with the basic norms of state policy in core areas such as health and education, must be encouraged. Rationalisation of divorce laws to account for marriage breakdown, strengthening the laws and procedures—for family support and against domestic violence—must be basic aspects of a new state family policy.

Despite the impact of colonial élites on policy formulation, patriarchal values on gender relations in the family did not prevent the development of egalitarian social welfare measures that impacted on the lives of men and women. Awareness of new dimensions of discrimination that are emerging in the family must be used to carry the debate on equity in family relations and allocation of resources to support stable family relations, to the grass roots level. This is one way of ensuring that the state will allocate resources for these measures, as well as for law enforcement and monitoring. A new family policy reflecting these perceptions is necessary if the state is to fulfill its responsibility under the Directive Principles of State Policy in the constitution to 'recognise and protect the family as the basic unit of society.'

Notes

1. 1505 to 1948, Portuguese, Dutch and British periods of colonial rule, successively.
2. See Hayley (1923: 26, 170–72) and Yalman (1971: 282, 284), discussing Muslim communities in Wellassa; Goonesekere (1987a: Ch. IX) and Ghouse v. Ghouse (1988) 1 Sri Lanka Law Reports (Sri L.R.) 25.
3. The relevant laws are the Mohomeddan Code 1806, the Penal Code 1883, Marriage Registration Ordinances 1863 and 1907; and the Kandyan Marriage Ordinances 1859 and 1870.
4. Gracia Catherine v. Wijegoonewardene (1986) 2 Sri L.R. 190; Podinona v. Herathhamy (1985) 2 Sri L.R. 237.
5. Attorney General v. Reid (1964) 67 New Law Reports (NLR) 25.
6. On the issues discussed in the above paragraphs, see Kotelawela (1991); de Silva (1991); Goonesekere (1991); Kodagoda and Senanayaka (1982); Cumaranatung (1989); Wijetunga (1991); Trafficking, Talpitiya Baby Farm Case, Panadura magistrate's court (1985) reported in Weekend (17 November 1985, 10 September 1989); in *Island* (12 November 1992); and in *Daily News* (25 July 1993); Perera (1993); Middle East migrant workers, *Daily News* (19 December 1992); and the Adoption Amendment Act 1992.
7. Ghouse v. Ghouse (1988) 1 Sri L.R. 25.
8. Kandyan Law Ordinance 1938, based on the report of the Kandyan Law Commission 1935.
9. Based on participant observation in legal literacy clinics, conducted by Open University Legal Aid and Mediation Project 1992.
10. Samarasinghe v. Samarasinghe (1989) 2 Sri L.R. 180; Somawathie v. Perera (1984) 1 Sri L.R. 78; Ranaweera Menike v. Rohini Senanayaka (1992) 2 Sri L.R. 180.
11. See the Land Commission Report 1958 and the Report of the Commission on Elimination of Discrimination in Sri Lanka (Human Rights Commission) 1992.
12. For example, Vythialingam v. Gnanapathipillai (1944) 46 NLR 235; Re Evelyn Warnakulasuriya (1956) 56 NLR 525; Re Shamila Begum (1989) 2 Sri L.R. 239 restraining parental authority over marriage supports this judicial view; See also Goonesekere (1987a: Ch. VII, and 1990: 166–67).
13. Marriage Registration Ordinance 1907; Education Ordinance 1939; Civil Procedure Code 1889. The constraint on representation was applied recently in Ratnayaka v. Chandrathileke (1987), 2 Sri S.R. 299.
14. Maintenance Ordinance 1889 as amended in 1972; See Goonesekere (1987a: Ch. X).
15. This comment is based on participant observation, especially in clinical legal aid counselling. A recent film, Sagara Jalaya, directed by Sumitra Pieris, is based on this theme.

16. See Goonesekere (1991: 16, 20); *Island* (11 February 1993); *Daily News* (6 June 1989, 15 September 1992, 15 October 1992); Sirisena (1992); Basnayake (1989).
17. Civil Procedure Code 1889 as amended in 1977, Marriage and Divorce Commission Report 1959.
18. Kandyan Law Ordinances 1859 and 1870; Kandyan Marriage and Divorce Act 1952.
19. Marriage Registration Ordinance 1907, Civil Procedure Code 1889 as compared with Kandyan Marriage and Divorce Act 1952.
20. Tennekoon v. Tennekoon (1986) 1 Sri L.R. 90: 100.
21. Ittapana v. Hemawathie (1991) 1 Sri L.R. 476.
22. Basnayaka (1989). A recent case of repudiation after the wedding night is Wijesundera v. Wijeykoon (1990) 2 Sri L.R. 1.
23. Knox (1966: 173) states 'they very exquisitely can prevent being with child'. See also, note 6 supra; Daily News (28 January 1993, 15 October 1992, 2 January 1993, 23 November 1990); On incest, see de Silva (1991).
24. This is based on cases referred to me confidentially by lawyers and counsellors in legal aid and counselling work at Women in Need, Colombo and Sumitrayo. Also probation officer, Colombo and confidential records of the Juvenile Court, Colombo.
25. The Children and Young Persons Ordinance 1939 and the Adoption Ordinance 1941, Part II, introduced stricter controls than the Employment of Women Young Persons and Children Act 1956. See also, Open University, Legal Aid and Mediation Project (1993).

References

Basnayake, S., 1989, 'The virginity test', Paper presented at the National Convention on Women's Studies. Colombo: Centre for Women's Research.
Britto, C., 1876, *The Mukkuva Law*. Colombo: H.D. Gabriel.
CENWOR (Centre for Women's Research), 1993, *Shadows and Vistas: On being a girl child in Sri Lanka*. Colombo: Centre for Women's Research.
Cumaranatung, L.K., 1989, 'Coping with the unknown', in V. Kanesalingam (ed.), *Women in Development in South Asia*. New Delhi: Macmillan.
de Silva, K.M., 1981, *A history of Sri Lanka*. New Delhi: Oxford University Press.
de Silva, W., 1991, 'Child abuse with special reference to girls', in Sri Lanka Federation of University Women, *Half our Future*. Colombo: Sri Lanka Federation of University Women.
Goonesekere, S., 1991, 'The girl child in the Sri Lanka legal system', in Sri Lanka Federation of University Women, *Half our Future*. Colombo: Sri Lanka Federation of University Women.
———, 1990, 'Status of women in the family law of Sri Lanka', in S. Kiribamune and V. Samarasinghe (eds.), *Women at the Crossroads*. New Delhi: Vikas.
———, 1989, 'Legislative support for improving the economic condition of Sri Lankan Women: The experience of the last decade', in V. Kanesalingam (ed.), *Women in Development in South Asia*. New Delhi: Macmillan.
———, 1987a, *Sri Lanka Law of Parent and Child*. Colombo: M.D. Gunasena.
———, 1987b, 'Dowry, law and social policy', Unpublished lecture. Colombo: Royal Asiatic Society.

Hayley, F.A., 1923, *A Treatise on the Laws and Customs of the Sinhalese*. Colombo: H.W. Cave & Co.

Jayaweera, S., 1991, 'Education of girls in Sri Lanka', in Sri Lanka Federation of University Women, *Half our Future*. Colombo: Sri Lanka Federation of University Women.

Kandyan Law Commission, 1935, *Report: Sessional Paper XXIV*. Colombo: National Archives.

Kazi, S., 1989, 'Some measures of the status of women in the course of development in South Asia', in V. Kanesalingam (ed.), *Women in Development in South Asia*. New Delhi: Macmillan.

Knox, R., 1966, *An Historical Relation of Ceylon*. Colombo: Tisara.

Kodagoda, N. and P. Senanayaka, 1982, 'Some aspects of abortion in Sri Lanka', Paper presented at the International Planned Parenthood Foundation Conference. Hawaii. October 1982.

Kotelawala, E., 1991, 'Prostitution, destitution, drugs and adolescents', in Sri Lanka Federation of University Women, *Half our Future*. Colombo: Sri Lanka Federation of University Women.

Land Commission, 1958, *Report: Sessional Paper X*. Colombo: Hansard.

Marriage and Divorce Commission, 1959, *Report: Sessional Paper XVI*. Colombo: Hansard.

Open University Legal Aid and Mediation Project, 1993, *Report*. Colombo: Open University.

Perera, W., 1993, 'Changing trends in maternal care', *Daily News*, 4 February 1993. Colombo.

Samaraweera, V., 1977, 'The evolution of a plural society', in K.M. de Silva (ed.), *Sri Lanka: A survey*. London: C. Hurst and Co.

Sirisena, J., 1992, 'The virginity inspection custom', *Island*, 2 December 1992, Colombo.

Wijetunga, S.A., 1991, *A Study of Children's Homes*. Colombo: Redd Barna.

Women's Bureau of Sri Lanka, 1985, *Women of Sri Lanka in Statistics*. Colombo: Women's Bureau of Sri Lanka.

Yalman, N., 1971, *Under the Bo Tree*. Berkeley: University of California Press.

Notes on Contributors

Leela Dube was National Fellow of the Indian Council of Social Science Research during 1992–94 and Senior Fellow at the Nehru Memorial Museum and Library, New Delhi, between 1986 and 91. During a distinguished teaching career, she held the Sree Krishnaraj Wadeyar Chair at the University of Mysore. She was the Chairperson of the Commission for Women, International Union of Anthropological and Ethnological Sciences, from 1976 to 1993 and is on the committees of or works in close collaboration with various other international professional bodies. Besides having contributed to a number of books and journals, she has edited and authored several books in the areas of kinship and gender, including *Matriliny and Islam: Religion and society in Laccadives* and *Sociology of kinship: An analytical survey of literature*. Her new book, *Kinship and gender in south and south-east Asia: A comparative view*, is soon to be published.

Savitri Goonesekere is professor of law at the Open University of Sri Lanka and a former Dean of the University. She initiated and developed the undergraduate and legal literacy programmes of the University, which focus on gender issues in the context of the family and the community. She has authored several books and articles in the areas of comparative family law and human rights, including *Sri Lanka law on Parent and Child*. She is a member of the National Committee on Women (Sri Lanka) and Chairperson of the International Law Association (U.K.) Committee on Feminism and International Law.

Kivutha Kibwana is associate professor in the Department of Private Law, University of Nairobi, and has for many years written on the themes regarding law addressed in this volume. In 1992, he was requested by the National Committee on the Status of Women to review the position of women in the family governed by Kenyan laws, in order to provide a base and framework for initiatives in legal reform. He has published extensively on the issue of constitutional law and its reform.

Athaliah Molokomme is a senior lecturer in the Department of Law, University of Botswana, and has been an attorney at the High Court of Botswana since 1981. Her Ph.D. (Leiden) was entitled *Children of the fence: The maintenance of extramarital children under law and practice in Botswana*. She has written extensively in the fields of family law, customary law and the status of women, including the widely used *The women's guide to law: An outline of how the law affects every woman and her family in Botswana*. She is a member of various community-based organisations in her country, as well as of international professional bodies.

Parveen Walji Moloo is a senior lecturer at the Department of Sociology, University of Nairobi, with a specialisation in demography. She has been teaching at this department since 1973, particularly in the area of family and demography. Her doctoral research was on fertility behaviour of some Asian communities in Nairobi. Among her various publications are two co-authored books, *A demographic analysis of East Africa* and *Children at work in Kenya*.

Rajni Palriwala is a lecturer at the Department of Sociology, Delhi School of Economics, University of Delhi. Her doctoral dissertation was entitled *Production, reproduction and the position of women in a Rajasthan village*. Her work has focused on agrarian relations and women's work, kinship and gender relations, and the women's movement and politics. Other than articles in books and journals, Dr. Palriwala has authored a book on *Changing kinship, family and gender-relations in South Asia: Processes, trends and issues*. She is actively involved with the women's movement in India, particularly in New Delhi.

Carla Risseeuw is currently professor of women's studies at the Department of Anthropology, University of Leiden. She has worked in Ireland, Kenya and Sri Lanka, both as an anthropologist and a film maker over extended periods of time, engagements which continue. She continues to be associated with Siyath—of which she was a founding member—a Sri Lankan organisation which aims at supporting the women coir workers' organisation. She has authored various articles and books on the position of women in Sri Lanka, including *Gender Transformation, Power and Resistance among Women in Sri Lanka: The Fish Don't Talk about the Water*. Her films include *The Wrong End of the Rope* (on Sri Lankan coir workers) and *It Is My Ancestors Who Make You Ask Me All these Questions* (on indigenous healing in Kenya).

K. Saradamoni is currently Senior Fellow of the Indian Council of Social Science Research, working on *Matriliny in Travancore* (Kerala, India). She was trained as an economist and for much of her professional life was associated with the Indian Statistical Institute, New Delhi. She worked briefly with the Government of Kerala. She has written extensively in both English and Malayalam, including the books, *Emergence of a slave caste: Pulayas of Kerala* and *Changing Land Relations and Women: A Case Study of Palghat*.

Dzodzi Tsikata trained as a lawyer and sociologist. She is currently a Researcher at the Institute of Statistical, Social and Economic Research (ISSER) at the University of Ghana. Her research interests include gender issues in development and state policy, kinship and social relations, environmental change and political processes.

Francien van Driel is a lecturer on women, gender and development at the Third World Centre of the Catholic University of Nijmegen, the Netherlands. Since 1987, she has been an editor of a Dutch social science journal, *Derde Wereld*. She has authored the book *Poor and Powerful: Female-headed households and unmarried motherhood in Botswana*.

Index

abortion, 258, 310, 323–24
abstract individual, notion of, 35, 38, 41–42, 298
abuse of children, 34, 264, 325–26
access to land, exclusion of women from, 94, 95, 117, 122
access to resources, unequal, 37, 41, 80, 81, 93–96, 103, 111, 117, 122
Acquired Immune Deficiency Syndrome (AIDS), 257, 258, 264
administration, male control over, 176
adoption, 102, 263, 305, 310–11, 312
Adoption Act, 263
adultery, 320–21
Affiliation Proceedings Act, 270, 272, 279–98 passim
affinal prestations, 201–2, 207, 209, 210, 215, 216–17
African Charter on Human and Peoples' Rights, 255–56
African Christian Marriage and Divorce Act, 268
African customary law systems, 251–68 passim
Aga Khan, 223
Aga Khan Development Network, 238

Aga Khan Social Welfare Board, 244
Age of Majority Act, 262
agency, 30, 32, 40
age-set system, 60
agrarian structures, development of, 20
agricultural products, male control over the sale of, 199
Aiya, Nagam, 138, 139, 140
Akan, 112
alimony, 89, 256, 259
altruism, 19, 31, 214
Anglo-Boer War, 61
aoni-jaoni, 197
arable cultivation, as a decreasing source of income, 67–68, socio-cultural importance of, 68
arranged marriages, for male minors, 257; trend away from, 229
Asafo Companies, 116, 119
Asante, 115–17
Asian-African marriages, 227
Asians in Kenya, as a minority, 224, 225–26, 239, 240, 241, 242; birth rate of, 222; caste concepts of, 226; indicators of women's status among, 228–35, 239; insecurity due to Africanisation among, 242; urban concentration of Indians, 225